The Rainbow People

BY THE SAME AUTHOR

Non-Fiction

Captain of the Queens
(with Capt. Harry Grattidge)

Ten Thousand Eyes

The City That Wouldn't Die

The Sands of Dunkirk

A House Called Memory

The Great Indian Mutiny

The General Next To God

Eagle Day

The River That God Forgot

Duce!

The Plague of the Spanish Lady

The War In The Desert
(*Time-Life* World War II Series)

Bridge Across The Sky

1940: The World in Flames
(U.S. title: 1940: The Avalanche)

Four From Buenos Aires
(*Reader's Digest*, Great Cases of Interpol)

1941: Armageddon
(U.S. title: The Road to Pearl Harbor: 1941)

The War That Stalin Won
(U.S. title: The Freedom Road: 1944–1945)

Fiction

Beautiful Friend

Pay-Off In Calcutta

The Lovely and The Damned

The RAINBOW PEOPLE

*A Gaudy World of the Very Rich
and Those Who Served Them*
BY

RICHARD COLLIER

DODD, MEAD & COMPANY New York

Copyright © 1984 by Richard Collier
All rights reserved
No part of this book may be reproduced in any form
without permission in writing from the publisher.
Published by Dodd, Mead & Company, Inc.
79 Madison Avenue, New York, N.Y. 10016
Distributed in Canada by
McClelland and Stewart Limited, Toronto
Manufactured in the United States of America
Designed by G. G. Laurens
First Edition

Library of Congress Cataloging in Publication Data

Collier, Richard, 1924–
The rainbow people.

Bibliography: p.
Includes index.
1. Upper classes. 2. Millionaires. 3. Upper classes
—United States. 4. Upper classes—England.
5. Millionaires—United States. 6. Millionaires—
England. I. Title.
GT3430.C65 1984   305.5'234   84-10199
ISBN 0-396-08389-7

FOR PAT
my wife
with love as always
and

for Anne　　*for Emilie*
in London　　*in New York*

They believed

The whole object of luxurious living is the delight it takes in irregular ways . . . notoriety is the aim of all these people who live, so to speak, back to front.

SENECA, Letters From A Stoic (ca. A.D. 65)

The moralist cannot deny that, generally speaking, well-bred people addicted to a vice are much more likeable than the virtuous are.

HONORÉ DE BALZAC, Cousin Bette (1846)

If a man is wise, he gets rich, an' if he gets rich, he gets foolish, or his wife does. That's what keeps the money moving around.

FINLEY PETER DUNNE, Observations by Mr. Dooley (1902)

CONTENTS

List of Illustrations

1 La Belle Epoque: *The World of "Edward the Caresser"* 1

2 La Belle Epoque: *The World of "The 400"* 40

3 Portrait of a Tribe: *The Rainbow People* 76

4 The World of Little David: *"All Wars Fought, All Faiths Shaken"* 95

5 The World of Little David: *"A Bender as Big as the Ritz"* 134

6 The World of Babs and "Queen Wally": *"Your Life's a Wild Typhoon"* 168

7 The World of Babs and "Queen Wally": *"Don't Abdicate, You Fool!"* 194

8 "Show Me a Millionaire . . .": *The World of Daddy-O* 215

Acknowledgments 243

Bibliography 245

Index 267

ILLUSTRATIONS

(Between pages 82 and 83)

Betty and Ena Wertheimer by John Singer Sargent *(BBC Hulton Picture Library)*
Monte Carlo casino in 1902 *(BBC Hulton Picture Library)*
A shooting party c. 1900 with King Edward VII and Alice Keppel *(West Dean)*
Edward VII at a Scottish house party *(BBC Hulton Picture Library)*
Lillie Langtry by Downey *(BBC Hulton Picture Library)*
Mr. and Mrs. Willie James in fancy dress, 1910 *(West Dean)*
Cowes Regatta, July 1909 *(BBC Hulton Picture Library)*
Black Ascot, 1910 *(BBC Hulton Picture Library)*
Hotelier César Ritz *(BBC Hulton Picture Library)*
Maître d'hôtel Oscar Tschirky *(Hilton Hotels)*
Peacock Alley in the Waldorf-Astoria, New York *(Hilton Hotels)*
Diamond Jim Brady in 1913 *(The Bettmann Archive)*
Harry Lehr *(UPI/The Bettmann Archive)*
Mamie Stuyvesant Fish with Janet in 1914 *(UPI/The Bettmann Archive)*
Mrs. Cornelius Vanderbilt, 1939 *(UPI/The Bettmann Archive)*
Edward and Letitia Stotesbury, 1937 *(UPI/The Bettmann Archive)*
The Breakers *(The Bettmann Archive)*
Kate Meyrick home from Holloway *(Weidenfeld Archive)*

ix

Santos Casani and partner dancing on a taxi *(Weidenfeld Archive)*

(Between pages 146 and 147)
Doris Delavigne with Viscount Castleroose *(London Express)*
The Prince of Wales in drag aboard Repulse *(L'Illustration)*
Texas Guinan, 1929 *(The Bettmann Archive)*
Mrs. Rosemary Sandars' Baby Party in London *(Weidenfeld Archive)*
Emerald Cunard *(Cecil Beaton photograph/Sotheby's Belgravia)*
Nancy Cunard *(Cecil Beaton photograph/Sotheby's Belgravia)*
Gertie Lawrence and Noël Coward in Private Lives *(Theatre Museum)*
Tallulah Bankhead in sultry mood *(Kobal Collection)*
Douglas Byng as a tree in Charlot's Revue of 1933 *(Weidenfeld Archive)*
Coco Chanel at a Forest Ball, 1938 *(Roger Schall)*
Chanel with her models in 1938 *(Roger Schall)*
The Prince of Wales and Wallis Simpson, 1935 *(BBC Hulton Picture Library)*
Barbara Hutton with Count Kurt Haugwitz-Reventlow in St. Moritz *(Weidenfeld Archive)*
The Ile de France about to sail *(Popperfoto)*
The Palm Court of the Ritz, London *(Popperfoto)*
Michael Arlen in the Ritz barber's shop *(Popperfoto)*
Beatrice Lillie and Sherman Billingsley in the Stork Club *(UPI/The Bettmann Archive)*
Walter Winchell on the air *(The Bettmann Archive)*
Maria Callas and Aristotle Onassis on Christina *(Associated Press)*

1 / LA BELLE EPOQUE:
The World of "Edward the Caresser"

Only the British could have invented—and later invested—a prince called "Tum-Tum." But on August 9, 1902, after a seven-week delay following an emergency appendectomy, this became accomplished fact. In the somber sunlight filtering down into the great nave of Westminster Abbey, the sixty-one-year-old Albert Edward, Prince of Wales, was at length crowned King Edward VII.

It was a coronation with a difference. Sixty-four years had now passed since Edward's mother, Queen Victoria, had ascended the throne; the Permanent Secretary of the Office of Works, Lord Esher, could find only one man, the eighty-five-year-old Duke of Cambridge, who recalled the precedents both for this coronation and the 1830 coronation of William IV. But there were other changes of style. No other coronation had called for the collaboration of a Wall Street tycoon, J. Pierpont Morgan, who one year earlier had created the giant United States Steel Trust, and Joseph Duveen, that cheerful buccaneer of the art salons: above the altar hung the magnificent gold thread tapestry, once owned by Cardinal Mazarin, which Duveen had sold to Morgan for $500,000, and which the financier had munificently loaned to his friend the King. No other coronation had called for a special King's box, irreverently dubbed "The Loose Box," within the Abbey to accommodate a selection of the King's mistresses, past and present: the actress Sarah Bernhardt, Mrs. Hartmann,

I

Mrs. Arthur Paget, Lady Kilmorey, and the current favorite of the hour, Mrs. George Keppel.

No coronation banquet at Buckingham Palace had ever featured as centerpiece such a triumph of gourmet one-upmanship as 250 Côtelettes de Bécassines à La Souvaroff: snipe, boned, stuffed with forcemeat and foie gras, grilled in a pig's caul, and served on a bed of truffles and Madeira sauce. And never in history had the monarch's effigy adorned the black-and-gold necklabel of a Moët and Chandon special cuvée, served by footmen in full state livery, royal-blue Quaker coats, and purple knee-breeches.

For palace-watchers, the implications were plain. "The Marlborough House Set," so called from the mansion on London's Pall Mall where Edward and his Danish Queen, Alexandra, had lived for thirty-nine years, was now "The King's Set." A brisk wind of change would now swirl through the gloomy 600-room Palace, where Victoria, for forty twilight years, had mourned her beloved consort, Prince Albert of Saxe-Coburg-Gotha.

It was an ambiance that Edward had all his life found stifling. Denied his mother's confidence, shorn of all real authority, he had increasingly sought distraction in the social round; the gulf between him and Victoria grew wider with the years. "Your son must be a great comfort to you, ma'am," Lady Beaconsfield remarked on one occasion, to which the old Queen replied, "Comfort! Why, I caught him *smoking* a fortnight after his dear father died!" For Edward, his long years as Prince of Wales often proved tantamount to martyrdom. Deputizing for the Queen all through the Diamond Jubilee celebrations of 1897, he soon had more than his fill of "Eternal Father, strong to save." "It's all very well," he grumbled, "about the Eternal Father. But what about my eternal mother?"

Now, abetted by "The Marlborough House Set," Edward would see the country dance to a different tune.

"If you ever become King," Victoria had once warned him, "you will find all these friends *most* inconvenient, and you will have to break with them *all*." No prediction could have fallen wider of the mark. If time had robbed Edward of some cronies, like Count Miecislas Jaraczewski, known to the Turf Club as "Sherry and Whiskers," who swallowed prussic acid when faced with a gambling debt, others came forward to swell the ranks: men like the Duke of Merigliano, a Neapolitan womanizer who pursued his conquests escorted, as prudence dictated, by his doctor and solicitor, Lord Hartington, "Harty Tarty," almost a caricature of the Edwardian swell with his "haw-haw" voice, and the first Lord Alington, of Crichel, near Wimborne, Dorset, once so bored on a rainy afternoon that he bet £3,000 on which drop of water would first reach the bottom of the windowpane.

By no means all were aristocrats. The London *Times* might deplore what it called "American cattle men and prizefighters" in the royal entourage, but the truth was the King admired self-made men: furniture manufacturers like Sir John Blundell Maple, newspaper proprietors like Sir Edward Lawson, the diamond king Cecil Rhodes, with an assured income of £600,000 a year, multimillionaire grocers like Sir Thomas Lipton—"Sir Tea," he liked to call himself—who had once slept under the counter of his father's shop and whose stunt cartoons depicting a tearful orphan pig (the rest of the family had "gone to Lipton's") drew customers from all over Britain. Famed for his five vain attempts to wrest the America's Cup with his yacht, *Shamrock*, Lipton reveled in the royal patronage like the cheerful vulgarian that he was. "Fancy me, Tommy Lipton, going downstairs to dinner with a princess on each arm," he would marvel.

Unprecedentedly, since the King, even as Prince of Wales, had sought out their company, Jews were now acceptable in London Society. They were, for the most part, financiers, like Nathan de Rothschild, the Sassoons, Baron Maurice von Hirsch auf Gereuth, and Sir Ernest Cassel.

Most especially Sir Ernest Cassel, who appropriately was knighted in this coronation year. A melancholy, bearded man, who confessed to having been happy twice in his life, riding to hounds with the Pytchley, Cassel, to Mrs. Keppel's daughter, Sonia, was "vaguely reminiscent of the genie in 'Aladdin' . . . inscrutably puffing at his cigar." The comparison was apt: the son of a Cologne banker, Cassel, a wizard of railway finance and founder of the National Bank of Egypt, had, as Edward put it, "the cleverest head in England." In 1897, when Edward found he could not make do even on £530,000 a year, Cassel had stepped in. In an unique partnership with Lord Farquhar, a banker in his own right and conveniently appointed Master of the King's Household, Cassel now used his financial acumen to assure Edward the life of a regal Riley from that time on.

It was a role that Edward had rehearsed assiduously for forty adult years. In the Palace Hotel at Biarritz, the Bristol in Paris, the bar of the Cercle Nautique at Cannes, where bartender Charles Forrester knew his favorite tipple to be Dewar's Black Ball whisky, he had long been a familiar figure, often traveling incognito in the guise of Baron Renfrew, the Earl of Chester, or the Duke of Lancaster: a bearded, portly man, turning the scales at sixteen stone, as his nickname attested, clad almost always in dove-gray, marked by his gold-knobbed malacca and yellow-suede gloves with black stitching, rolling his r's Germanically, redolent of eau du Portugal and Henry Clay "Tsar" brand cigars. A man who, noted an equerry, Frederick Ponsonby, "preferred men to books and women to either," his credo was epitomized by one of his mistresses, the Countess of Warwick: "Our occupations are the pursuit of pleasure, our duties the pursuit of pleasure, and our ideals the pursuit of pleasure."

Another mistress, Offenbach operetta star Hortense Schneider, was pithier still: "Frivolity is the secret of happiness. Take care to remain frivolous all your life."

Edward needed no second bidding. Though Christmas and the New Year were always spent at Sandringham, the 7,000-acre Norfolk estate that he had bought for £220,000 in 1863 and spent £80,000 on refurbishing, London beckoned him all through January: an unremitting round of dinners, theaters, and supper parties. Not that he relinquished his role as monarch—"he had a very strong sense of the duties which his position entailed," Sir Charles Hardinge, permanent head of the Foreign Office, was to testify, "and he never shirked them." Thus the end of January always saw him at Buckingham Palace for the State opening of Parliament, but he drove himself like a man possessed; the red dispatch boxes would not be neglected, but the social round did not slacken. But by March, Europe was calling; a week in Paris, sauntering the boulevards, then three weeks in the sunshine of his beloved Biarritz. But after three weeks, even Biarritz could pall; it was time to seek blue water, cruising the Mediterranean in his 5,500-ton steam yacht, *Victoria and Albert III*.

By May, the London Season had claimed him; in the private room behind his box at the Royal Opera House, Covent Garden, apprentice chef Gabriel Tschumi recalled twelve-course supper parties for up to thirty people as the norm. Midway through June, Ascot Races entailed a switch to Windsor Castle; come July, it was time to move on once again, to Goodwood Races, as the house guest of the Duke of Richmond. August saw new headquarters, once more *Victoria and Albert III*, for this was Cowes Regatta Week, on the Isle of Wight.

September was devoted to Marienbad, the small Bohemian spa that Edward had done so much to make fashionable—an ideal place, noted the New York *Tribune*, for "corpulence, gout, anaemia, chronic appendicitis, and constipation." Here, at the Hotel Weimar, his suite redecorated annually, Edward came as close to vegetating as for him was humanly possible: a whole month's sojourn before the October move to his Highland palace at Balmoral. Even here, he was prey to the fidgets: the royal train would shuttle him 430 miles southeast for the autumn race meetings at Newmarket.

It was a pattern of mobility that others would emulate to the letter. Long after his death, the survivors, and then the successors, of the Marlborough House set would follow the same annual round, gravitating like migratory birds to the same resorts in the same seasons, sometimes chancing on new venues, at times pursuing fresh novelties: an eternal treadmill of travel, shopping, and party-going and dancing and long weekends, spotlit increasingly, as the years rolled on, by the popping flashbulbs of photographers.

Other ages would tag them with other labels: Café Society, the Bright Young Things, the Swingers, the Jet Setters, the Trendsetters, the BPs (Beautiful People), the B and Bs (Bored and Beautiful), the Glitterati, and, more obscurely, by *Women's Wear Daily* of New York, as "the Juicy People" (cutting to the heart of a porterhouse steak rather than nibbling round it). But the labels mattered less than the palpable panache they shared, their aura of razzmatazz, their willingness to cross class barriers, transgress accepted codes, and create their own canons, all with an inevitable undertone of "Laugh, Clown, Laugh."

To this writer, though, fascinated by the evanescence of their reign, the shimmering iridescence of their life-style, this unique mix—royalty and railroad kings, steel barons and debutantes, international financiers, heiresses and con men, supertarts and vulgarians, all of them in search of faster yachts and faster roulette-wheels—is and always will be the Rainbow People.

* * *

In his lifetime, King Edward was the man who set the keynote, who forced the Rainbow pace. A man impatient for change, forever seeking out new sensations, he greeted the dawn of the Motor Age as a long-sought liberation. Thus, in April 1905, C. W. Stamper, manager of the testing and repairs department of the Lacre Motor Company, the London agent for Wolseley cars, received an urgent royal summons: a technician was needed to instruct the Palace chauffeurs, all of them London bobbies, in the mysteries of the cars they would control. By July, Stamper found himself seconded to the Royal Mews as the King's "motor expert and engineer."

The king was no quiescent passenger. For official business, he used a Daimler, for private journeys, a forty-h.p. Mercedes—the Queen preferred Wolseleys—but whatever the car, speed was of the essence. It was mandatory to cover the seventy miles between London and Newmarket in two-and-a-quarter hours, and Stamper, perched beside the chauffeur, tool kit at the ready, was well aware of the royal wrath if things went awry. Early motorists came to quail at the sight of the bearded, imperious figure, crouched forward on the blue morocco seat, his fox terrier, Caesar, beside him, urging the chauffeur on to a perilous sixty m.p.h., then three times the legal limit. Determined to overtake every car on the road, the King soon installed a fearsome horn like a four-key bugle, all the time keeping up a flow of exhortation: "Go *on. Go on.* What are you stopping for? Pass him. We don't want his dust."

Success would be rewarded by, "A very good r-r-r-r-un, Stamper; a very good r-r-r-r-un, indeed." Failure, such as a rare breakdown, saw the blue eyes flashing royal fire, a chilling and final "This should not be."

In essence a kindly man, Edward was often childishly impulsive. Once, at a ceremonial dinner, spilling some spinach on his shirt, he crimsoned with fury, plunging his hands into the dish and smearing spinach across the starched white front. In a moment, the mood had passed; to Prince Christopher of Greece he chuckled, "Well, I had to change anyway, hadn't I? I might as well make a complete mess of it." On another occasion, angry that Queen Alexandra was fifteen minutes late for a shooting party luncheon at Windsor, he wolfed through course after course, so peremptorily ringing a hand-bell for plates to be cleared that many guests never got past the salmon cutlets.

These royal rages were something to fear; at Sandringham, when the Prime Minister, Arthur James Balfour, whom Edward disliked intensely, lost all three rubbers at the bridge table, the King's wrath was so palpable that Balfour volunteered, "Sir, there remains one thing to be done. Please send me to bed." Yet he would go out of his way to spare the feelings of the maladroit. Faced with a guest who ate his peas with a knife, Edward promptly followed suit. At one Buckingham Palace luncheon, an Indian prince, a stranger to asparagus, nibbled the green tip and then tossed the white stalk over his shoulder; Edward did the same. Other diners at once followed the royal example; soon, to the consternation of the servants, small white mounds of buttery stalks were littering the fine Turkish carpets.

Like most Rainbow males, the King was a trendsetter. An early patron of Henry Poole, the Savile Row tailor, from whose steam launch he always viewed the Oxford and Cambridge Boat Race, he had launched the new-style dinner jacket as early as 1875: a short, dark-blue cloth jacket worn with black trousers and a black bow tie. Spending up to £300 a year on clothes as early as the 1860s, he made fashionable the Norfolk jacket and the Tyrolean hat; four years after setting his seal on the gray top hat, in 1905, he popularized the soft felt hat. Tweeds, cut, of course, from upmarket Huddersfield worsteds, became the fashion at Goodwood Races; his corpulence decreed the mode of leaving the bottom waistcoat button undone.

Sartorially impeccable himself, he was a perfectionist to the point of pernicketiness. A violinist at Covent Garden Opera House, sporting a black tie, was pounced on by an equerry with a command to change it before the performance began. "He could not endure even a button being an inch out of place," the Duke of Manchester reported, and ministers and ambassadors who wore their decorations incorrectly were taken quietly but severely to task. Even women were not immune; as Prince of Wales, he had observed acidly to the Duchess of Marlborough, who was wearing a diamond crescent, "The Princess has taken the trouble to wear a tiara. Why have you not done so?" The Duchess's excuse—that the bank in which she kept her tiara had closed for the night—entirely failed to mollify him.

His boredom threshold was perilously low, and many a hostess came to dread the impatient "Yes-yes-yes" that signaled the pent-up irritation, followed by the steady drumming of fingers on the dinner table and the warning clatter of cutlery. Sometimes a shaft of wit would dispel the choler, as when Julian Osgood-Field, an American man about town, described a titled fortune hunter's wedding of an heiress as "a black-pudding marriage—he brought the blood, she brought the sack of oatmeal." One hostess, Lady Brougham, even sought to penetrate the king's black mood by enquiring in desperation, "Did you notice, sir, the soap in Your Majesty's bathroom?"

"No!" came the barked response.

"I thought you might, sir. . . . It has such an *amorous* lather!"

"Tum-Tum" was convulsed, and the situation was saved.

The essential tonic, all were agreed, was to keep him on the move. In London, this was relatively easy; he was the first royalty to visit the Empire Music Hall, and after 1903, when the new Gaiety Theatre opened in the Strand, he hummed his way four times through Lehar's *The Merry Widow*. To him, music was the trills and roulades of the diva Nellie Melba at Covent Garden, the sobs and high C's of Enrico Caruso; he relished the brittle banter of Oscar Wilde, but Shakespeare was anathema to him. Reportedly he finished only one book in his entire life, Mrs. Henry Wood's lush *East Lynne*.

At the races, too, whether at Epsom, Newmarket, or Doncaster, he came into his own; it was the sport of kings that brought him closest to the nation at large. In 1896, his Sandringham-bred horse, Persimmon, won not only the Derby, at odds of five to one, but the St. Leger and the Jockey Club Stakes besides. One of the few men to make racing pay, Edward's wins and stud fees over twenty years were to top £250,000.

Cowes, too, saw him in his element, for as commodore of the Royal Yacht Squadron he could indulge unashamedly in all the panoply of royalty, the glitter and the pantomime that he loved. This was the golden age of the great steam yachts, with Lloyd's Register alone listing 1,558 in 1905; among them were A. J. Drexel of Philadelphia's *Margarita*, a £100,000 craft with a crew of ninety-three, J. Pierpont Morgan's black-hulled *Corsair III*, King Alfonso of Spain's *Giralda*. It was an era when rich owners vied greedily with one another for ostentatious trappings: if the *Victoria and Albert III*'s state dining room featured silk curtains and blue morocco chairs and settees, Tsar Nicholas II's *Standart* went one better, with a private chapel. For these saltwater palaces, velvet pile carpets and cheval glasses were now de rigeur; the twenty staterooms of William Kissam Vanderbilt's *Valiant* outdid the teakwood fittings of the Earl of Rosebery's *Zaida* with carved walnut ceilings, Spanish mahogany paneling, and Steinway pianos. Aboard *Ethleen*, in 1903, the first owners had installed coal fires.

"By day," one observer of the scene recalled, "the sails of the racing yachts spread across the blue waters of the Solent like the wings of giant butterflies, by night the riding-lights and lanterns gleamed and shone against the onyx waters, and fireworks burst and spent themselves against the night sky. And over this splendid scene presided the King, a genial, portly, yet always majestic figure."

It was a time of rich pickings for designers like St. Clare Byrne (*Valiant*, the press baron James Gordon Bennett's *Namouna*) and James Beavor-Webb (Pierpont Morgan's *Corsair II*); equally for brokers such as Herbert E. Julyan, whose clients included the Duc d'Orléans, Archduke Stephan of Austria, and Baron Henri de Rothschild. On a £35,000 sale (and fifty deals a year were not uncommon), Julyan's fee from the vendor would total £1,750, or 5 percent; a £100,000 yacht like Drexel's *Margarita* could net £5,000 for its designer, G. L. Watson, who usually had sixteen annual commissions. It was not surprising that Pierpont Morgan warned a colleague, "Anyone who asks how much it costs to run a yacht cannot afford to keep one."

There were other ways of frittering away money; all through Edward's reign, the weekend house party had become a way of life. No monarch since Elizabeth I had journeyed so indefatigably to the great houses set in parklands, polka-dotted with oak and elm, girdled by walls ten miles in circumference: Knowsley, the ancestral home of the Derbys; Rufford Abbey, the home of the Saviles; Chatsworth, where the Devonshires held sway; Welbeck Abbey, seat of the Duke of Portland, the Master of the King's Horse. Edward's hosts viewed these sudden descents with mixed feelings: pride at forming part of the chosen elite, dismay at the crippling costs often involved. For the King's standards of housekeeping were as punctilious as his dictates on dress: all state livery must be as new, gardens, stables, kennels, and outhouses must be overhauled as for a parade-ground inspection. Typical was the plight of Lord Hartington, who, before entertaining the monarch to one dinner, had his eighty house footmen outfitted in liveries of gold cloth.

Even by the standards of the age, the outlays were formidable. At Knowsley, the household expenses were rarely less than £50,000 a year. At Chatsworth, the Devonshires hailed the King with blazing fireworks and an avenue lined with 300 torch-bearers. The sporting fifth Earl of Lonsdale had eleven automobiles for his Saturday-to-Monday guests at Lowther and greeted them with a squadron of yeomanry, blue-coated outriders, nine carriages drawn by chestnuts with footmen up behind, and a private orchestra of twenty-four musicians.

But this was only the tip of the iceberg. Each January, when Edward and Alexandra descended on Chatsworth, an orchestra had to be imported from London to titillate the Queen with Strauss waltzes during meals. The King was a glutton for ortolans, small garden buntings trapped in nets then gorged on millet in darkened rooms; they were imported at prohibitive cost from the south of France, then eaten by hand, in servings of three, from the feet upward. After dinner, the King demanded a cathedral hush for his game of bridge, so the grandest room had to be stripped of all furniture save a single table. His gambling mirrored his life-style: a £225 loss on cards in one evening.

Whether at Chatsworth, Knowsley, where the fifteenth Earl of Derby maintained 727 servants, or Welbeck (lower down the league with a mere 307), the Sunday routine rarely varied. There was the descent to breakfast, promptly at 9:30 A.M.; only decadent Parisians breakfasted in their rooms. The Queen, like the other ladies, wore their "best dresses," usually of velvet; Edward and the gentlemen wore black clothes, with gray silk ties and white, frilled shirts. In the dining room, rows of small spirit lamps twinkled like votive lights, warming lidded silver chafing dishes of crisp bacon, poached or boiled or fried eggs, salmon kedgeree, sausages, and plump, pink kidneys. For the peckish, there would be porridge, topped with clotted yellow cream; at a later stage, the sideboards offered cold York ham, tongues, and cold grouse, partridge, and ptarmigan in season.

Over all these great houses, there hung at times three distinctive aromas: the sharp tang of spirits of wine that heated the chafing dishes; Mr. Penhaligon's Hammam Bouquet, when a gentleman took his bath; and the fragrance of Guerlain's new perfume, Jicky, in the ladies' boudoirs.

On Sundays, after church service and before lunch, there was a ritual change into tweeds. For the ladies, afternoon tea called for another change still, this time into a tea-gown, perhaps a Delphos, a pleated silk robe hanging loosely from the shoulders, designed by the rising young Venetian-based Spaniard, Mariano Fortuny. By the dinner hour, 8:30 P.M., all had changed again: the men into white tie and tails, the ladies into long dresses with trains and sporting ostrich-feather fans. And since no lady wore a dress more than once on a weekend, a four-day visit entailed sixteen dresses (with Jean-Philippe Worth's ball gowns priced at £100), all of them folded in tissue paper, packed in vast Saratoga trunks. One firm alone, Asprey, of 166 New Bond Street, had found fortune overnight through their superb crocodile weekend dressing cases; priced between £125 and £145, they housed such vital Edwardian necessities as ivory hairbrushes, eight-day clocks, blotting books, pincushions, jewel cases, and a plated railway lantern.

Weekend traffic was now so heavy that royalty's hosts must house not only their guests but their chauffeurs, valets, and lady's maids besides. Lady Iveagh rightly complained when Lord and Lady Howe invaded Elveden, "I do think it is too much when *two* people bring five servants." But this had become a two-way trade, for the guests, in turn, must tip the house staff, and a regular tariff prevailed: a sovereign to the butler, half a sovereign to the chauffeur, five shillings to the room maid, half a crown (12½p) to the footman who carried down the luggage. A ten-day visit might have involved disbursing £5 in tips.

A world apart, the guests spoke a language apart, a private shorthand of childish diminutives. Anything disgusting was "diskie"; to borrow money with little hope of repayment was "lootin'." "Ratin'" was finding fault; a tea gown was a "teagie," which might also be "expie" (expensive), "deevie" (divine), and "fittums" (an excellent fit). A royal personage, such as Edward, was a "man-man." It was fashionable, too, to add Italian terminations to English words: "After dinn-are, we might have a little dans-are." To which the accepted replies would be, "What a deevie idea," or "Who will Sebastian bring as his partner-ina?"

No household was better equipped to cater to the Royal whims than Alfred de Rothschild's Halton Manor, near Wendover, where an elaborate program of the day's events was drawn up for the King's prior approval and a copy placed in each guest's bedroom. Time had long effaced the memory of the tiny house with the red shield in the ghetto of Frankfurt-am-Main, from whence Rothschild fortunes had stemmed in the eighteenth century; opulence was now the order of the day, for Alfred was a Rainbow financier par excellence, like his nephew, Lionel Walter, who regularly bowled down Piccadilly in a four-in-hand drawn by zebras.

A wealthy and eccentric dilettante, all Alfred's weekends began as a ritual: Each Friday, an employee from the bank's offices at New Court, in the City of London, arrived at his town house, 1 Seamore Place, with Mr. Alfred's "spending money," £1,000 in cash. Thus bankrolled, Alfred would board his private train at Baker Street, equipped in winter with mink foot-warmers, its carriages decked out in the blue and yellow family racing colors, en route to another Halton weekend.

It was a house renowned for its ghastly good taste—"a cross between a French château and a gambling house," where even the ivy festooning the summer houses was fashioned from painted metal. "Oh, but the hideousness of everything, the showiness!" one aesthete lamented. "The sense of lavish wealth thrust up your nose! The coarse mouldings, the heavy gildings always in the wrong place . . ." Since Sandringham, where a large stuffed baboon in the main hall held a salver for visitors' cards, was furnished on similar lines, Edward could feel instantly at home.

The service was gracious, almost good-gracious. Breakfast at Halton was served in the rooms, and bemused guests might find a £100 note tucked in the folds of their napkin. The house specialty was *gigot Rothschild,* lamb baked for twelve hours until it literally fell apart in the mouth. An often-told story, which yet bears retelling, happened in fact at Waddesdon, a "French château" owned by Ferdy de Rothschild, but it perfectly sets the Halton mood. A footman, followed by a lackey with a trolley, would enter the bedroom and enquire politely: "Tea, coffee, or a peach off the wall, sir?"

"Tea, please."

"China tea, Indian tea, or Ceylon tea, sir?"

"China, if you please."

"Lemon, milk, or cream, sir?"

"Milk, please."

"Jersey, Hereford, or Shorthorn, sir?"

No host to leave his guests to their own devices, Alfred would stage a series of diversions as the weekend wore on. A slim, blond hypochondriac, who kept a resident doctor (to guard his health), a full-time detective (to guard his treasures), and a lawyer (to tinker with codicils if he felt ill), he also maintained a private philharmonic, conducting it himself with an ivory baton banded with a circlet of diamonds. On fine afternoons, attired as a circus ringmaster with a blue frock coat, whip, and lavender kid gloves, he would set a team of trained King Charles spaniels, painted blue-and-white, jumping through tiny hoops.

The main raison d'être of these long weekends, which might see forty guests under one roof, was the shooting party: "Tum-Tum" was now too stout for the hunting field. Though he never shot at a tricky bird, preferring "masses of pheasants driven over his head about the height of an ordinary tree so that he never seemed to miss," he was a familiar figure at all the Norfolk shoots, clad in an Inverness cape, aiming from a low-slung pony carriage, his favorite retriever, Diver, at his side. For shooting was now a veritable industry; at Sandringham alone, where 12,000 pheasants were reared annually, the game larder could hold 3,000 brace. Whole hecatombs of birds fell to the guns of men like the Marquis of Ripon, who stayed up in his library into the small hours with two loaders to practice the art of changing guns. His ultimate bag was 500,256 birds of all varieties, and every all-time game record dates from this era: 6,943 rabbits to six guns at Blenheim in 1898, 2,319 pheasants at Gorhambury in 1906. But no rabbits were ever shot at Halton; for fear that he stumble and break his neck, Alfred de Rothschild had blocked up their holes.

The waning morals of the age now posed a problem for ambitious hostesses: that of *placement*. At the dinner table, accepted protocol could be followed, but what of the matter of bedrooms? "In my day," complained Lady de Grey, "we used to hide the portraits of our lovers and put our husbands' on the mantelpiece. Now it is the other way round." For Edward was notorious for his *ménages à trois,* and no house party that he graced would dare omit Alice Keppel, wife of the younger son of the Earl of Albemarle, from the guest list, or fail to site the King's suite conveniently close to hers.

Edward's errant sex life had long been common knowledge; *The Queen,* known as *The Lady's Newspaper and Court Chronicle,* freely printed photos of him in Alice's company. Some of his subjects resented it bitterly; to the novelist Henry James, he was and always would be "Edward the Caresser," while Rudyard Kipling, who had worshipped Victoria, "the Widow at Windsor," scorned him as "a corpulent voluptuary." For years, Society had buzzed with names; there had been hostesses like the Princesse de Sagan, Mrs. Willy James, and Lady Susan Vane Tempest, who bore him a child, but equally there had been Parisian demimondaines like Giulia Barucci, who proclaimed herself "the greatest whore in the world."

For thirteen years there had been the notorious Emilie Charlotte Langtry, known as "Lillie," who was, in the phrase of a later age, "famous for being famous"; launching herself into London Society with a complaisant, alcoholic husband and one black dress, her face became the "pinup" of the day, the darling of the picture postcard vendors everywhere. Her liaison with Edward was the subject of early press comment; the scurrilous rag *Town Topics* assured its readers one week, "There is nothing whatever between the Prince of Wales and Mrs. Langtry." A week later, they noted, in a sentence that was an apparent non sequitur, "Not even a sheet." Like the Rainbow beauties of years to come, Lillie set the styles that other women copied: if she was seen in public with a muff or a pink dress, all London followed suit. "The Langtry Hat," a scrap of black velvet twisted into a toque, pierced by a quill and worn at Sandown Park Races, was an overnight best-seller.

Reportedly, the affair split up after Lillie clinched a heated argument at a fancy dress ball by thrusting a lump of ice from a champagne cooler down Edward's Pierrot collar. That ended her spell as reigning favorite, but Lillie, the black dress long discarded, and equipped with the Worth wardrobe that Edward had bought her, embarked on a second career as a world-famous actress.

There had been many, many more women, especially in his time as Prince of Wales—so many that the tolerant Alexandra referred to him ruefully as "My naughty little man" and to his women as "Bertie's little toys." During one Parisian visit, the prefecture could justifiably wonder if he suffered from satyriasis. Despite his attempts to give detectives the slip, he was clocked in as calling on twelve identifiable women in the space of days. At the Moulin Rouge he was greeted as " 'Ullo, Wales" by La Goulue (literally Greedy Gal), a cabdriver's daughter named Louise Weber, and tolerantly bought her champagne. At Maxim's, on the rue Royale, he was known to all the great *cocottes* whose haunt this was: Gaby Deslys, who took London by storm as a danseuse at the Gaiety in 1906 and reputedly charged 1,000 francs for fifteen minutes, Caroline Otero (La Belle Otero), Cléo de Mérode, and Liane de Pougy. For the benefit of clients like Edward, Hugo, the maître d', kept a cryptic notebook on each girl's current status: R.A.F. meant *rien à faire* (nothing doing, already protected), YMCA meant *Y a moyen de coucher avec* (available).

If women were the besetting passion, gluttony ran a close second. At the outset of his reign, the Buckingham Palace staff of 350 was pared down to 300, but the kitchen staff of forty-five, under M. Ménager, was sacrosanct. How else could they prepare a fourteen-course luncheon to be served at 1 P.M. when the King, like Winnie-the-Pooh, demanded "a little something" at 11 A.M.—normally a trifle like a lobster salad? Then there were always some staff at work on sustaining snacks to garnish the occasional tables in the main living quarters—perhaps York cakes (circular biscuits joined with a filling of sardine and anchovy) or Biscuits Parmesan (the same piped with whipped cream and cheese).

The richer the dish, the more he relished it: pheasant stuffed with woodcock, which was in turn stuffed with truffles, grilled oysters, crayfish cooked in chablis, deer pudding, or quails stuffed with foie gras, served cold in a sherry-flavored jelly. Henri Charpentier, a young *commis de rang* at the Café de Paris, Monte Carlo, always recalled the disastrous moment when a pancake garnish, a bubbling blend of maraschino, curaçao, and kirschwasser, he was preparing for Edward, when Prince, caught fire in the chafing dish. Miraculously it worked, and Edward, demolishing every pancake, called for a spoon to scoop up the remaining liquor. (It was christened Crêpes Suzette, after his anonymous table companion.) But that had been in the 1880s, and now twenty years later, in his sixties, he was still eating five gargantuan meals a day. The twenty-course dinner that he shared with Lord Rosebery in 1903 was exceptional, but fourteen-course dinners were commonplace.

That was almost, but not quite, all. A solicitous hostess like the Duchess of Devonshire, always ensuring that he suffered no hunger pangs in the night, would dispatch a plate of sandwiches and, to be on the safe side, a cutlet or a quail, to the sanctity of the Royal apartments.

* * *

None of this highest-of-high living, these larger-than-life styles would have been possible without a near-invisible army dwelling below stairs behind the green baize door; in the terminology of the time, the servants' hall.

Theirs was a hierarchy now almost impossible to conceive: a pullulating hive in which every worker-bee knew his or her place to the letter. (The drones, of course, were above stairs, tugging for service on velvet bell-ropes.)

It was virtually a world of apartheid, far more confining than any distinctions prevailing in the cretonned drawing rooms. "There were greater snobs among the servants than the nobility," Frederick John Gorst, a footman with the Duke of Portland, was to recall, "because we had more to lose." At Blenheim, ancestral home of the Dukes of Marlborough, one guest was even obliged to lend his valet a discarded dinner jacket; his blue serge suit had been quite unacceptable to the other valets in residence.

In all the great houses, a rigid caste system divided the hired help into two distinct groups: the Upper Ten and the Lower Five, though there were neither ten in one nor five in the other. Normally numbering eight or nine, the Upper Ten would comprise the butler or house steward, the housekeeper, the wine butler, the under butler, the groom of the chambers, the valet, the head housemaid, the lady's maid, and the cook. In some houses, like Welbeck, all their meals were taken in the seclusion of the steward's room, waited on by the steward's footman. But at Longleat, ancestral home of the Marquis of Bath, thirteen-year-old Gordon Grimmett, a lamp boy, witnessed a variation that seemed only to emphasize the gulf: at lunchtime, as a bell was rung, the Upper Ten filed into the servants' hall, arm in arm, in order of precedence, the butler, Mr. Brazier, leading in the housekeeper, Mrs. Parker, followed by the lady's maids, the valet, Mr. Pilgrim, and the groom of the chambers.

Only when Mr. Brazier gave the command could the lower servants, standing at attention round the long table, take their seats. This done, Mr. Brazier carved the roast, with a hall boy bidden to pass the plates, serving all in order of precedence. This main course, Grimmett recalled, was eaten in funereal silence; the Upper Ten took claret or white wine, the Lower Five made do with home-brewed beer. Then the Upper Ten rose solemnly, departing—still in order of precedence—to the Steward's Room, or "Pug's Parlour," where the sweet course was taken. Finally—in order of precedence to the bitter end—they repaired to Mrs. Parker's room for tea or coffee.

The Lower Five, who might consist of three times that number, included footmen, chambermaids, housemaids, laundry-maids, dairymaids, maids of all work, lamp boys, hall boys, and "odd men." Living and eating in the basement, they at length retired to rest in the attics, sometimes ascending, by a separate stairway, 150 steps. Aside from the annual Christmas ball for domestic staff, no social mix with the Upper Ten was permissible.

Most of their tasks were more tedious than arduous, though sixteen-hour work days were not unknown. As Longleat's lamp boy, in the days before electricity, Gordon Grimmett's daily chore was to clean, trim, and fill 400 lamps: paraffin for the corridor and staff lamps, and colsa oil, which gave a kinder, mellower light, for the house. This done, he polished the funnels and the glass globes and cleaned the stands. "The sheer monotony," he was to recall, "took some beating." At Blenheim, in the winter months, the "odd men"—servants who had never quite made the grade—had to haul logs and coal scuttles to fifty-eight grates; the rest of their year was devoted to washing the windows.

It was the scullery maids, at this time paid £6 a year, who traveled the rockiest road, thought Alfred Lee, butler to Waldorf Astor at Cliveden. Their task was to clean the kitchen ranges, prepare staff breakfasts, scour pots, and scrub the kitchen, often until 1 A.M. "Poor little devils," Lee was to reminisce, "washing up and scrubbing away . . . their hands red-raw with soda. I've seen them crying with exhaustion and pain. . . ."

Veterans of this era still recall a definite sense of servitude. "There's no question," says Gordon Grimmett, "but that servants were owned body and soul." "You lived totally with the family," agrees Arthur Elvin, who began his service as a second footman at a slightly later date. "It was your life." Rachel Morran Teggin, who began as a "tweenie," or between-maid, confirms, "You were totally absorbed with the family—you belonged to them."

"It was like working for the reigning prince of a state within a kingdom," was how Frederick John Gorst summed up his time with the Duke of Portland, for one of Gorst's more bizarre duties was to sit for hours at a time behind a twelve-foot screen, within earshot of the Duke, who disliked ringing bells, in the event that he might want something. Yet life for some was undeniably brisker; Arthur Inch, a footman at Londonderry House, donned a pedometer for one day at the height of the London season and found that he had clocked up eighteen miles without ever leaving the house.

Yet there was a rugged pride, too, in the assimilation of the strange skills that kept such households turning over in the days before detergents and vacuum cleaners. Ernest King, who joined the Chichester family as a junior footman two years after King

Edward's coronation, found that he first had to acquire "plate hands." Cleaning the family silver with a paste of jeweler's rouge and ammonia, his hands developed blisters, which burst time and again, but ultimately became as calloused as a karate champion's. He learned other wrinkles, too: boots were best cleaned with Day and Martin's blacking mixed with vinegar, worked into the leather with a deer's shinbone. For hunting pink, soiled with mud and perspiration from the field, the solution was unpalatable but effective: a drenching from a chamber pot of urine, followed by a swift brush with rainwater.

At Longleat, all dustpans were numbered and equipped with a thumbhole, so that each housemaid had her own; brushing with one hand, she could hold the pan and a candle with the other. Old polish was washed off furniture with vinegar, replaced with beeswax and turpentine, then rubbed again until the wood glowed gently in the lamplight. Blacking for grates and ranges was brewed from ivory black, treacle, oil, small beer, and sulphuric acid. Often carpets were treated with damp tea leaves.

Living conditions varied enormously. At Floors Castle, the seat of the Duke of Roxburgh, Arthur Elvin, engaged for a trial month, left after one week—"The servants' quarters were awful, bare—just benches, mean." Yet at Knowsley, the Derby's staff "were treated like lords"; Ditchley Park saw "the greatest luxury ever laid on." Food, culled from the great estates, was almost uniformly good. At Longleat, Gordon Grimmett recalled an echo of Halton Manor: three sheep of different breeds—a Southdown, a Westmoreland, and a Brittany—were butchered each week to supplement a diet of goose, game, and venison.

The duties varied little from household to household. Butlers like Alfred Lee of Cliveden and Charles Cooper, who served the Broughams, literally knew their place, which at mealtimes was behind the master of the household's chair—unless they were serving cold dishes from the sideboard—wearing tails with a black tie to denote their status. Versed in wine and skilled at carving, "The Skipper," who had charge of the plate chest and the cellars, must also know how to read a French menu and understand the timing of a dish well enough to know when to ring for the next course.

For men who as early as the 1890s could command $75 a month in the United States and sometimes £260 a year in England, butlers had a lively sense of their own importance. At Blenheim, no butler would put a match even to a laid fire; he would pass on the request to a footman.

For footmen, it was a life, in more ways than one, of waiting in the wings. Most great families like the Portlands promoted "from within," so that even a junior footman like Frederick Gorst, earning an unprecedented £100 a year, might ultimately aspire to dining in the Steward's Room and having his own silver napkin ring. But much of a footman's prospects depended on his stature. Even in the 1890s, a footman topping six feet in height could command £40 a year as against the £30 of a footman of 5' 6"; "calves come before character," was the saying of the time. A first footman's place, at meals, was behind the mistress's chair, though it was forbidden ever to serve her breakfast in bed; the tray must be left outside the door for her maid. Arthur Elvin, who held this position with the Queensboroughs, recalls another "perk": the most generous house party guest was his by right.

At Buckingham Palace, Welbeck, and Longleat, all footmen were required to "powder," a hangover from the eighteenth century; this brought an automatic entitlement of £2 a year. Many great houses had their special powder rooms, equipped with long mirrors and wash basins, where the footmen first shampooed their hair, then instead of rinsing away the lather let it dry before dousing their heads with violet powder (or even flour), which congealed to a firm paste. "The purpose," Gorst summed up, "was to have all the staff look as much alike as possible and to create a picture of uniformity when we served together."

If footmen were seldom off parade, parlormaids and housemaids fared no better; the subtle distinction was that the former were addressed by their surnames, the latter by their Christian names, emphasizing their lowlier status. Three sets of clothes, packed in their little tin trunks, met their basic needs: cotton print dresses for the mornings, black dresses with frilled mob caps and frilled white muslin aprons for the afternoon, plus their own town clothes for their weekly half-day off. In an age of naked male chauvinism, it was not surprising that a girl paid for her own uniforms, including stockings at 4½d (2p) a pair, whereas employers outfitted the menservants for free. But Rachel Morran Teggin, once promoted from "tweenie" to parlormaid, still recalls the excitement of "the on-show duties . . . seeing all the ladies' dresses . . . helping the guests into coats as they left."

To these domestics, over-staffing often proved a boon: at Ashridge, where the Duke of Bridgwater's payroll never dropped below 500, housemaids could divide into two groups, with the seniors preempting lighter jobs like bed-making, dusting, and keeping the rooms in good shape. Even so, their days began, like those of the wretched scullery maids at Cliveden, at 6 A.M. It was small wonder that William Lanceley, house steward to the Duke of Connaught, always plumped for the children of farmers and servants: both were attuned to early rising.

Among the menservants, the real powers of make-or-break were vested in these house stewards. Men like Mr. Spedding, the Duke of Portland's steward, were the true behind-the-scenes arbiters, keeping the household accounts, paying the bills and wages, engaging all male staff, save for the Duke's valet, from established agencies like Massey's of Baker Street (who charged a shilling on the pound commission on a year's wages), firing those who failed to please, and ordering most of the household supplies—with an average rake-off of 10 percent from the tradesmen favored. On the distaff side, dragons in black bombazine, like Longleat's Mrs. Parker—all housekeepers were "Mrs.," whether married or single—reigned supreme, with the power to hire or fire all female staff except the nanny, the lady's maid, or the cook. A housekeeper's kingdoms were the store room, the still-room, and the china closet; it was she who doled out the china daily, bought and oversaw the household linen, supervised all sewing and the bottling and preserving of fruit. Always announced by her jangling keys, she kept the entire household, including the present Marquis of Bath, in quaking terror.

Valets, although housed, clothed and fed, and inhabiting a private kingdom of their own, were not overpaid; twenty years after the Edwardian era, Arthur Elvin received only £100 a year from the royal trainer, Captain Cecil Boyd-Rochfort. Again, it was a question of "perks"; as a valet in the 1920s, Ernest King's tips never went below £16 a week.

For ladies' personal maids, who were often French, the pace could be more exacting. True, they had their private quarters, and a lower maid to clean both their room and their shoes, but their hours were erratic; if a lady had lingered at a ball her maid might be up until past midnight, to brush her hair for twenty minutes before retiring, even to squeeze the paste onto her toothbrush. As maid to Nancy Langhorne Astor, of Cliveden and St James's Square, Rosina "Rose" Harrison worked an eighteen-hour day seven days a week for £75 a year. Dressed in what was virtually a uniform for a lady's maid—navy serge skirt, white silk blouse, and black silk stockings—Rose's day always began at 7:30 A.M., collecting the clothes that Nancy had worn the night before for pressing later.

At 8:30 A.M., she delivered Nancy's breakfast tray; at 9 A.M. she ran her bath. The rest of her day was a nonstop round of pressing, cleaning, and repairing, since Nancy got through five sets of clothes a day and several sets of underwear, which was always packed into a blue and pink silk pouch, Waldorf Astor's racing colors, before dispatch to the laundry. Then there was the regular restringing of Nancy's pearls by Hopton Jones, the jewelers, and the cleaning and repair of Nancy's twelve fur pieces, including a sable cape, a black broadtail, and a chinchilla cape, by Bradley's of Bayswater. "She didn't let me forget a hairpin," was a current saying among lady's maids, and Rose has assured us that Nancy never did.

Nannies, then as now, were in a class all their own. Neither Upper Ten nor Lower Five, they lived in a world apart; they demanded and got room service, including morning tea, brought by nursemaids, who were forbidden to mix with the other maids, to their own private quarters. Formerly, on a haphazard basis, nurses had trained other nurses, but from 1892, when Mrs. Emilie Ward, an early disciple of Froebel, established the Norland Nursing School (later the Norland Nursery Training College) at Notting Hill Gate, West London, the status of the Norland

Nurse, with her distinctive fawn and brown cape, had grown apace. Not for nothing had Mrs. Ward exhorted each graduation class, "Girls, take your silver-backed hairbrushes to impress the servants."

Thus, by 1908, nannies, although paid no more than £35 a year, were an integral part of the great London houses and the country seats. Wheeling their five-guinea Sociable Vis-à-Vis prams, they were seen daily in the Daisy Walk, at the east end of the Serpentine, in London's Hyde Park, by the Albert Memorial, where benches were reserved for "titled Mummy's nannies," and even in Central Park, New York, at the west end of East 77th Street, where sat what Tom Wolfe later called "The Nanny Mafia." Such latter-day Rainbowites as Cornelius Vanderbilt IV, the oil tycoon Nubar Gulbenkian, and superdeb Margaret Whigham were already in their youth imbibing such classic nannyisms as "Waste not, want not," "I want to see a clean plate," "Don't-care was made to care," and "There'll be tears before evening."

Some strangely anachronistic functionaries still loomed large in this Edwardian upperworld. Through Chatsworth and Knowsley and Rufford, a ghostly figure named the groom of the chambers glided silently four times a day, checking the refueling of the fires, the supply of paper, quill pens, and ink in the reception rooms, noiselessly opening and closing doors. Directly beneath him was the underbutler, who laid the dinner table and was deft at folding napkins into whimsical semblances of miters and water lilies. The high point of their day was when the *Times* arrived from London; the groom's job was to iron it, stitch the center pages, and sometimes perfume it before it was deemed fit for the family to read.

A new phenomenon on the scene, capable of turning many feminine hearts, was the chauffeur, resplendent in his maroon or bottle green uniform, peaked cap, and brown leather gloves and boots. He, too, provided he wore uniform and not livery, the badge of servitude, was entitled to take his pudding in "The Pug's Parlour". Of course, the sweeteners for men like Sidney Letzer, King Edward's first chauffeur, and Oliver Bush, who drove King Alfonso XIII of Spain, were considerable—all car showrooms set aside sums for the chauffeur—although as supply exceeded demand they had taken a drop in earnings. In 1905, a chauffeur had boasted £6 a week against a butler's £5, yet two years later the going rate was only £2 10s.

Yet such was the mystery of their calling, they rated high in the pecking order. They gloried in keeping their cars spotless, and no matter how late the hour the car must be cleaned before turning in. And "cleaning," given the mud and dust of Edwardian roads, meant removing each wheel in turn, washing it with sponge and spoke-brush, black-leading the front axle and brake-drums—the kitchen range principle again—then burnishing the bodywork with buckets, sponges, and soft chamois leathers. For the windows, a moistened copy of the *Times* was the best cleansing agent.

This accomplished, there were other niceties to attend to before the next run: a racoon-skin foot warmer, tartan rugs to tuck round the knees, or musquash lined with blue cloth to match the carpet. The tapered silver vase should always hold fresh flowers, scented if possible. In this rarefied atmosphere, it sometimes seemed that the chauffeurs were becoming as Rainbow-oriented as their employers.

One chauffeur, F. R. Ashment, always recalled the withering scorn of Lord Lonsdale's chauffeur at Lowther Castle. A young guest, making an inspection round of Lonsdale's fleet of yellow cars one Sunday morning, chanced on the chauffeur beside an open bonnet, tinkering with the engine. Merely to make conversation, he ventured, "What a huge engine! It must use a lot of petrol. Terribly expensive to run."

The chauffeur stared at him with ill-concealed loathing. He gestured dismissively. "To his lordship," he remarked icily, "the cost of petrol is *nothing*."

* * *

To the French, the golden nine and a half years of Edward's reign—for he had, in fact, become king on January 22, 1901—would always be *La Belle Epoque* (The Beautiful Era). But others were less enchanted. To the writer and diplomat Harold Nicolson, who came of age in 1907, "the Edwardians were vulgar to a degree. They lacked style . . . they lacked simplicity, and their intricacies were expensive but futile." The up-and-coming young photographer Cecil Beaton thought "the age of opulence proved to be a short-lived wedding party."

Contemporary critics were not lacking. Max Beerbohm could find no sympathy for "those tall, cool, ornate people." Edith Wharton, on a visit from Lenox, Massachusetts, found them "so exhausted by their social labors of the past weeks . . . that beyond benevolent smiles they had little to give." Another commentator deplored "how the craving for publicity has involved all classes, including the highest . . . they are smitten with the universal mania for notoriety." Lady St. Helier was equally indignant: "Society now runs after anyone who can get himself talked of . . . to have a good cook, to be the smartest dressed woman, to give the most magnificent entertainments where a fortune is spent on flowers and decorations, to be the most favored guest of Royalty . . . are . . . features which characterise some of the smartest people in London society. . . ."

In short, the coming of the Rainbow People was now an inescapable fact of life.

It was a cosmopolitan age, such as had never been known, as if the English Channel had shrunk to the dimensions of a ditch. With truth, Edward was known as "The Uncle of Europe," for indeed he was: the uncle of Kaiser Wilhelm of Germany, whom he distrusted profoundly, of the Tsarina Alexandra, of Queen Ena of Spain, and of Marie, soon to become queen of Romania. Yet he was equally king of the Côte d'Azur, as at home in Biarritz, Monte Carlo, or Cannes as ever he was at Sandringham. His "set" had never felt so intensely European.

But the North Atlantic, too, had contracted its shores; if wealthy Britons felt European, more and more affluent Americans were finding a kinship with the British. Many of them now felt as relaxed on Piccadilly as on New York's Fifth Avenue; fashionable Bond Street shops, as well as London's Berkeley Hotel, took full-page space in the New York dailies. Thanks to the King's example, Americans were liked, not patronized, and their wealth was now the passport to English high life. In August 1905, *Punch* reported with awe: "Five American millionaires were staying at Claridge's Hotel last week"—among them a tycoon typical of the new-rich, John Warne "Bet-a-Million" Gates, the barbed wire king.

A onetime $25-a-month hardware store clerk from San Antonio, Texas, Gates in 1871 had convinced a consortium of skeptical cattlemen that barbed wire would prevent their herds from straying, by staging a noisy demonstration with thirty steers in a wired-in San Antonio plaza. By 1901, as head of the powerful American Steel and Wire Company, he was constantly at loggerheads with Pierpont Morgan, whose United States Steel Trust wanted no part of him and bought him out.

A rowdy, mustached barbarian, worth $50 million when he died in 1911, Gates's wealth broke down all barriers. In 1900, after his horse, Royal Flush, had won the Steward's Cup at Goodwood Races, Gates had scandalized Society by war-whooping deliriously as he waltzed his wife, Dellora, across the clubhouse lawns, but with time Society had grown more tolerant. No complaints were heard when Gates, hosting a £20 dinner at London's Savoy Hotel, paid out £200 in five-pound notes and happily waived the change.

Typical of the ostentation of the age was a party thrown by Gates's crony, George A. Kessler, a Wall Street financier, champagne millionaire, and chief representative of Moët and Chandon. A tall, dark-bearded, imperious man, Kessler was already famous in New York as the man who had tried to buy the champagne country for Pierpont Morgan, giving up only when he found that 16,000 separate estates were involved; he was the man who nightly toured the New York lobster palaces like Rector's and Delmonico's, tipping the wine waiters fifty cents for each quart cork they could produce, a dollar for a magnum. But to celebrate his birthday in July 1905, Kessler staged a party that gave London a hint of the revels to come.

His Gondola Dinner involved first flooding the forecourt of the Savoy Hotel with four feet of water. In the courtyard, where

400 Venetian lamps shone on ceiling-high murals of St. Mark's and the Doge's Palazzo, a vast silk-lined gondola bobbed gently, seating Kessler's two dozen dinner guests, among them the famous American actress, Edna May, "the Belle of New York." A hundred white doves fluttered overhead among canopies of 12,000 white carnations and roses; waiters togged out as gondoliers served a twelve-course banquet. Finally, a baby elephant, bearing a candle-lit birthday cake five feet high, ambled across a gangplank and on to the gondola, where Kessler and a bevy of chorus girls from the Gaiety Theatre raised brimming glasses of Moët and Chandon 1898. The super-salesman's angle was never far from Kessler's mind.

The crowning highlight was almost an anticlimax: a series of arias from Enrico Caruso, who was paid £450 for the evening, a bagatelle for a shindig that had cost Kessler £3,000, with a further £1,000 in tips for the staff.

As such, the age has attracted many labels: the Age of Optimism, the Age of Extravagance, the Age of Excess. Yet, paradoxically, all these tags, undeniably true, had ushered in a concomitant age: the Age of Caring.

In their different ways, five men epitomized that spirit, as if a tacit conspiracy now existed to give those who, in Joseph Hergesheimer's words, "knew more than what to expect—what to demand," the very best that their worlds could offer.

All were quiet, modest, even taciturn men, of relatively humble origins, yet all of them were to give new meaning to that vexed word, "quality."

At 24 Morskaya, St. Petersburg (now Leningrad), Peter Carl Fabergé, a Huguenot expatriate, an elegant man in black well-cut tweeds, who never used two words where one would do, was rarely seen without a magnifying glass to his eye, scrutinizing the latest creations of his 700 Swedish craftsmen. As far back as 1883, Fabergé, the greatest goldsmith ever to serve two Tsars, had hit on the idea of constructing an Imperial Easter Egg as a surprise present from Tsar Alexander III to his wife. What Alexander had received was much like an ordinary hen's egg made of gold, enameled in opaque white. Once opened, it revealed a yolk of pure gold, and this, when opened in turn, revealed a minuscule golden chicken. Inside the chicken was a dazzling miniature of the imperial crown, and inside *this* was a tiny ruby egg.

Thereafter it became an annual guessing game, with first Alexander and then his successor, Nicholas II, probing delicately as to what form the new egg would take—with Fabergé venturing nothing more than, "Your Majesty will be content."

He was always as good as his word. One egg was fashioned from pink enamel, with sprays of lily of the valley; another from rock crystal, enclosing a jeweled peacock; a third from lime-green enamel with a model of the Imperial Coronation coach. There were more than fifty eggs in all. But from 1906 on, when Fabergé opened a London branch on the first floor of 48 Dover Street, Mayfair, all the King's circle became privy to this exquisite work; one of Edward's gaming partners, being short of a sovereign when settling up, later sent it mounted in the lid of a Fabergé box.

There was no standing on ceremony; Fabergé's Rainbow customers just dropped in. "May we open the drawers?" Queen Alexandra once asked timidly, though she had arrived with a retinue that included the King and Queen of Norway, the King of Greece, and the King of Denmark. Alice Keppel, too, was a loyal patron; for Edward's Royal Derbies and Laurens cigarettes she bought him a royal blue translucent case of enamel on guilloché gold, with an encircling snake in diamonds and a diamond thumb-piece. Others who returned time and again were Mrs. Leopold de Rothschild, Mrs. Florence Hwfa Williams, and Mrs. Willy James, for Fabergé, a steely perfectionist, never rested on his laurels. Though some wares like his Karelian birchwood cigarette cases were priced at only a few pounds, he was constantly experimenting with new and rare stones to whet the hungers of the satiated—chalcedony rhodonite, lapis lazuli—and with enameling colors so rare that many collectors have never chanced on them—raspberry red, opalescent pink, "lovebird" green, and varying shades of steel-blue.

One block east of Fabergé's London branch, at 30 Duke Street,

St. James's, thirty-four-year-old Alfred Dunhill, who had started in life manufacturing leather accessories for the Motor Age, had found himself saddled with six dozen tobacco pipes in settlement of a bad debt and resourcefully switched into the pipe and tobacco business. From the first, Dunhill thought Rainbow—"Price is immaterial for unbeatable quality"—and Mary, his daughter, still recalls how he knelt for hours at a time on the drawing-room floor of the family house at Harrow-on-the-Hill, experimenting with blends of No. 1 leaf, perique, and latakia to woo the palates of individual customers.

This was the inception of Dunhill's astonishing "My Mixture" books, which listed the preferences, in old-fashioned cursive script, of such dedicated smokers as the film star Douglas Fairbanks, Sr., the novelist and playwright W. Somerset Maugham, and the youthful Prince of Wales (later Edward VIII and later still the Duke of Windsor), who favored Mixture 26, 276 (a secret blend including perique, a choice dark Louisiana tobacco), a record that ultimately grew to number 36, with 460 separate blends.* From these beginnings, Dunhill progressed to an impressive mahogany showroom fitted with green Turkish carpets and Venetian glass lights, where the shop manager, Malcolm Somerset-Johnston, himself impressive in morning dress with silk hat and monocle, supervised a sales staff of twenty.

Always an innovator, Dunhill pioneered other features: a Royal Pipe Drawer, whose shell briars were priced at an equally impressive twenty-five shillings apiece, and a miniature factory for hand-made cigarettes, where an early employee, Dora Watkin, turned out 2,000 cigarettes per day, to retail at five shillings per hundred. Cabbies who deposited Alfred at 30 Duke Street always knew their tip in advance: ten Dunhill cigarettes, doled out by Jeffrey, the commissionaire.

Cuban cigars—Flor del Punto, Don Candido, Por Larranaga—were imported in cedar-wood cases holding 1,000 at a time, and soon Alfred was providing the customer service of free storage space at an even temperature of 65°. ("If a man buys 3,000

---

*As of August 1983.

cigars at a time," explains S. F. Gomershall, an old Dunhill hand, "it isn't always convenient to store them at home.") New lines in cigar cutters, tobacco pouches, and cigarette cases ultimately brought him world-wide renown; a Paris branch on the rue de la Paix, in 1920, was followed, in 1923, by a branch on New York's Fifth Avenue. At least some of his fame was spread by two eccentric Maharajahs who knew very well "what to demand": the haughty Maharajah of Alwar, noted for his £252,000-a-year income and for using live babies as tiger-bait, for whom Alfred manufactured hookahs, and the Maharajah of Patiala, who as a matter of course took thirty-five fifth-floor suites at the Savoy Hotel, a dandy who spent £31,000 a year on underwear.

Once, when a Dunhill salesman tried to dissuade Patiala from an ornate jeweled table-lighter—he thought it a shade effeminate—the Maharajah, eyes flashing dangerously, demanded, "Am I any less a man because I wear diamond earrings?" Since the 6′ 6″ Maharajah had a harem 350 strong—he was known as "His Exhausted Highness"—the salesman gave in.

Ten years before the Dunhill era, two men from highly improbable backgrounds had set their seals on the nascent world of the luxury hotel, a world they were to revolutionize. As the twentieth century dawned, a French gastronome, Humbert de Gallier, noted, "Great palaces are rising in place of the ugly ill-conditioned hostelries of old"; plainly the men he had in mind were César Ritz, the thirteenth son of an Alpine shepherd, and Georges Auguste Escoffier, a blacksmith's son from the Alpes Maritimes.

Both men had learned their trade the hard way: Ritz as a waiter in a workman's bistro, which fired him for breaking plates, later as a floor waiter at Paris's fashionable Hôtel Splendide; Escoffier as a kitchen apprentice from the age of thirteen, and then, from 1870, as a sauce chef at the Restaurant Le Petit Moulin Rouge. From 1883, at the Grand Hotel, Monaco, he and Ritz entered on their long and fruitful partnership.

The two were a perfect complement. Escoffier was a dedicated dreamer, the archetypal absent-minded professor, a man who would work all night to perfect a dish, relying solely on his sense of smell, himself subsisting mainly on rice, fruit, and barley water. Ritz, ably backed by his wife, Marie-Louise, was a lean, ambitious visionary, the nineteenth-century equivalent of a workaholic. As far back as the Hôtel Splendide, Ritz had made his first contacts with the great American merchant princes—the Goulds, the Pierpont Morgans, the Vanderbilts—and later at the Grand Hotel, Monte Carlo, with Edward, Prince of Wales. Now at last he knew what he wanted: the custom of the wealthy Americans and "the Marlborough House set." As Marie-Louise Ritz put it, "His years of wandering in the wake of a migratory society had begun."

It was Lillie Langtry who tipped the scales. In August 1889, Richard D'Oyly Carte, impresario of the Gilbert and Sullivan light operas, had at last realized a dream: the brand-new Savoy Hotel, abutting on his own Savoy Theatre, on London's Strand, modeled on the lines of the Palace in San Francisco, famous for its red African marble bar, its thirty-four elevators, and its oyster-omelette breakfasts. D'Oyly Carte's intent was that his own luxury palace, unique for its seventy bathrooms and its "ascending rooms" (elevators), which ran all night, should be managed by Alfonso Nicolino Romano, whose raffish restaurant nearby was haunted by racing "swells" and Gaiety Girls.

Lillie Langtry, an old friend of D'Oyly Carte's, disagreed; she recalled the *Poularde Derby* she and Edward had sampled at the Grand Hotel, Monte Carlo. "Romano is a man's man," she said with truth. "Ritz will attract the ladies."

Ritz, when approached, was unenthused. He had recently opened the Hôtel de Provence, in Cannes, which demanded all his personal attention. Above all, he doubted that any English gentleman would leave his club to dine out in public with his wife. Pressed by D'Oyly Carte, he came grudgingly to London—and stayed to marvel at the splendid marble bathrooms, the dazzling electricity, the Canaletto vistas of the Thames. Without hesitation, he agreed to take over as manager—with six months' annual leave of absence to superintend his other hotels. But a permanent fixture at the Savoy would be little Escoffier, who needed built-up heels to scan the huge open ranges.

For the Rainbow People, hotel history was in the making. From the first, Ritz insisted on full evening dress and table reservations. Early on, he persuaded Lady de Grey, leading patron of the Royal Opera House, to invite her friends to a banquet—enclosed by screens—in the main restaurant. When Mrs. Langtry and Alice Keppel followed suit, it became at once respectable and in the height of fashion to dine in public at the Savoy—to the music of Johann Strauss and his orchestra, no less.

Soon Edward, as Prince of Wales, had bestowed the royal imprimatur by sampling a dish Escoffier had created for him: *cuisses de nymphes à l'Aurore* (frog's legs served in a cream jelly with Moselle, spiked with paprika). Next day came an urgent note from Marlborough House: Could they please have the recipe?

With peasant shrewdness, Escoffier understood the uses of flattery: single-handed he made this, above all, the Age of the Dedicated Dish. No greater culinary cliché exists than the *Pêches Melba* he created for his favorite diva: fresh peaches on a bed of vanilla ice cream, served in a swan carved in ice, with raspberry puree. But, equally, there was wafer-thin toast Melba, though this, in fact, was dreamed up for Marie-Louise Ritz, who found most toast too thick for her liking, and many other long-forgotten dishes that Escoffier created to delight Rainbow palates and inflate Rainbow egos: *Poularde Tosca* (chicken stuffed with rice and served with fried bread and braised fennel roots) again for Melba; *zéphyr du Poularde Belle Hélène* (chicken breasts on pâté de foie gras, served with asparagus salad) for his beloved Sarah Bernhardt; *Supreme de Volaille Adelina Patti* (with gnocchi and creamed artichokes) for Melba's hated rival; *Mousselines de Volaille Alexandra* (with béchamel sauce and asparagus) and *Fraises Romanov* (strawberries laced with orange juice and Curaçao) for the Russian Imperial Family.

Pressed as to the secret of his art, Escoffier would reply coyly, "It is simply that most of my dishes were created for ladies"—and Ritz might have echoed this as the secret of his hotels.

For Ritz, being Ritz, could not relax one instant. By 1898, a new "great palace" had risen, on a site he had chosen two years earlier, at 15, place Vendôme, Paris. Here his passion for detail had run riot, after time and again touring the former royal residences of Versailles and Fontainebleu. Ritz and Marie-Louise set cabinetmakers to work duplicating the sofas, chairs, and tables that had been created for royalty alone. For 300 hand-drawn lace counterpanes for the beds, Marie-Louise journeyed to Venice; the down for the pillows, César ordered from County Cork.

One day, while experimenting on the placing of lights, Ritz hit upon the concept of indirect lighting—and his Hotel Ritz, in Paris, was to feature this for the first time. As patient as an artist's model, which in a sense she was, Marie-Louise sat motionless for hours, while César and an electrician studied the effects of different lampshades on her complexion, her clothing, even her jewelry. Finally they hit upon the shade that has flattered Rainbow ladies from that time: a delicate apricot pink.

In June 1898, the 210-room hotel, with every room having its own bathroom (then an unheard-of luxury) and its Service Privé buttons to summon one's own servants, had its grand opening. As always at such moments of crisis, Ritz was on the verge of collapse. "Will they come?" he tortured both himself and Marie-Louise. "Are they still my friends? Will they come?"

But come they did: Rothschilds and Vanderbilts, Grand Duke Michael of Russia, Melba, Bernhardt, and, most welcome of all, Lady de Grey from London with a personal message from Edward: "Tell Ritz that wherever he goes we shall follow."

Thus heartened, Ritz dared to dream an impossible dream: to build a London hotel exclusively for Edward's delectation.

This was the Carlton Hotel, in the Haymarket, now the site of the indescribably hideous New Zealand House, whose Palm Court, Dining Room, and Grill Room were all designed by Charles Mewès, creator of the Paris Ritz. At vast expense, the floor of the Palm Court was made lower than that of the Dining Room, with a fine open staircase connecting the two, so that ladies entering or leaving the Dining Room could do so "dramatically." Then, despite his backers' protests, Ritz moved the Dining Room wall back two yards, to give the glass-roofed Palm Court a balcony. The Prince of Wales, he said, would appreciate a private corner.

"How often," the backers scoffed, "do you think the Prince of Wales will dine here?" "Very frequently," Ritz replied.

Once again, it was Lady de Grey who saw Ritz through the launching in 1899, transporting the entire company of Messager's light opera *Véronique* from Paris for a one-night stand at the Lyric Theatre, with an inaugural supper at the Carlton to follow. A young *commis-de-rang*, Filippo Ferraro, later restaurant manager at the Berkeley Hotel on Piccadilly, never forgot the splendor of that June evening, when Lillie Langtry wore deep blue velvet and Lady de Grey wore pearls to match her complexion: "It seemed as if all the wealth and beauty and youth of the world was concentrated in that human stream which poured through the stately doors."

Edward was indeed to dine "very frequently" at the Carlton, but Ritz was rarely there to receive him; his race was almost run. By 1902, coronation year, he had suffered a total mental collapse; though he lingered on in a Swiss clinic until 1918, he gradually, as Marie-Louise phrased it, "sank out of life, as helpless and docile as a child," his questing brain eroded by years of overwork. Yet his triumph was greater than he knew; the £345,000 London Ritz that opened on Piccadilly in May 1906 was in essence his creation. The architects, Charles Mewès, a Frenchman from Alsace, and his British partner, Arthur J. Davis, knew what Ritz—and Edward VII—would have wanted, as precisely as if he had drawn up the blueprints.

A bath to every room, of course, for this was now the Ritz criterion, but this time Doulton baths, six feet long and solid to the floor—no longer on feet. Dust-hoarding fabrics like plush velvet and even wallpaper were out, and equally to minimize the dust, wardrobes were replaced by fitted closets. In every detail it was a hotel that César would have approved, a caravanserai of solid Edwardian comfort, with its Louis XVI chimneypieces, armchairs, and sofas and panelled Petit Trianon salons.

Just as Ritz's name became an eternal synonym for luxury catering, another's, in this same era, came to symbolize flawless precision engineering: a onetime newsboy for the W. H. Smith bookstall at London's Clapham Junction Railway Station, who for much of his life signed his name as "H. Royce, Mechanic."

A miller's son, whose father died when he was nine years old, in 1872, Henry Royce at first seemed fated for no more than dead-end jobs—newsboy, telegraph messenger boy—barely holding his own on a poverty-line diet of bread and jam. Only the kindness of an aunt, who came up with £20 for Henry to be bound apprentice to the Great Northern Railway Works at Peterborough, in the Midlands, changed both his luck and his life. At Peterborough, Henry roomed with a Mr. and Mrs. Yarrow, whose son was also an apprentice; their backyard held a workshop equipped with a lathe and hand tools. Each evening Royce and young Yarrow practiced turning, fitting, and the correct handling of tools. The bedrock of Royce's consummate craftsmanship was being laid.

By 1880, a callow, introspective seventeen-year-old, Royce had moved on, seeking new skills, this time to a job with the Electric Light and Power Company, London, to probe the primitive mysteries of generating electricity. Slowly his talents were emerging from the shriveled chrysalis of his youth; four years later, with a friend, A. E. Claremont, and £70 worth of capital, he had set up a workshop at Cooke Street, Manchester. They were on to a winner, and both of them knew it: electric door bells, a "must" for respectable bourgeois households, retailing at eighteen pence (18p) each.

Seven years later, after long hours at the work bench, living mostly on sausages and sandwiches, Royce and Claremont broke into the dynamo market with a "sparkless" drum-wound dynamo; by 1894, Royce Ltd. were marketing some of the first electric cranes to quarries, mills, and factories. As 1900 dawned, they were a £30,000 public company. Royce, like Alfred Dunhill, was now thinking Rainbow: "The quality remains after the price is forgotten."

Thus, early in 1903, Royce was tinkering absorbedly with a second-hand motor car, a two-cylinder, ten-h.p. Decauville. Soon after, the decision was taken: he would build a batch of three light cars to his own design.

One director, Henry Edmunds, a committee member of the

newly formed Automobile Club of Great Britain, was already looking far beyond Cooke Street—to the Brook Street, Mayfair, showrooms of the Hon. Charles Steward Rolls, a blue-blooded motoring enthusiast who had set up an early dealership with another buff, Claude Johnson. Promptly, Edmunds went south: would Rolls and Johnson consider adding the new two-cylinder Royce to their list?

It was a partnership very nearly unconsummated. Royce, morose and ill at ease in society at large, stubbornly resisted journeying to London to meet a jumped-up "swell." Instead, the urbane and worldly Rolls pocketed his pride and went north to Manchester, for lunch at the Grand Central Hotel followed by a trial run, in the city's back streets, of a car that was plainly in a class of its own. Within the hour, Rolls was persuaded. If a two-cylinder Royce was this refined, what motorist could resist the six-cylinder version, which Royce was willing to produce, if an outlet could be found?

And an outlet would be found, Rolls was determined; for every car that came from the Cooke Street workshop, the Hon. C. S. Rolls would act as dealer. On December 23, 1904, the brand-name "Rolls-Royce" was born; by 1906, a new twelve-acre factory site at Derby, in the Midlands, was ensuring that the first of the legendary Silver Ghosts, their radiator lines slightly bowed to give a rectilinear effect, the principle used by Kallikrates when building the Parthenon, became an international phenomenon. Among the earliest American customers were Pierpont Morgan, the showman Florenz Ziegfeld, and the department store chief Samuel Bloomingdale; another was Henry Ford, who was dumbfounded when two Rolls-Royce engineers journeyed from Derby to Detroit in 1913, one year after he had bought his Silver Ghost, to check that it was still running well. With refreshing candor, he cabled Royce: "When I have sold one of my cars, I don't ever want to see it again."

They were then far from the most expensive cars on the road. In 1905, a two-cylinder, ten-h.p. chassis (currently valued at £250,000) was priced at £395, a six-cylinder, thirty-h.p. at £890. Bodywork, lamps, and tools, supplied by Hooper, of St. James's, or H. J. Mulliner—until 1950, Rolls-Royce made the chassis only—might run to an extra £500. But Panhard and Daimler four-cylinder chassis were already priced at £750 apiece.

What made the Rolls-Royce, as they themselves claimed, "The Best Car In The World," was the same relentless perfectionism that motivated Fabergé, Dunhill, and Ritz, an assumption that even the very best was barely good enough. Royce tested all the early Silver Ghosts by dragging granite curbstones up and down steep hills; from the first, he and Rolls issued three-year guarantees with every chassis sold, as against the ninety-day guarantee still common fifty years later. Their engines were so silent that extraneous noises were detected only by testers using doctors' stethoscopes and so vibration-free that a penny balanced on end on the edge of a radiator cap in 1910 remained obstinately upright.

Fiercely jealous of their reputation, Royce and Rolls took infinite pains to preserve it. To impress on an owner or a chauffeur how a fine car should be handled, they started a twelve-day driving course—with four days devoted to gear-changing—rewarding the graduates with a silver pin. Though Rolls was killed in a flying crash in 1910, and Royce's health, like Ritz's, cracked a year later, Royce still ran the company by mail from the French Riviera for twenty-two years thereafter, keeping a permanent staff on tap. Once, after discovering minor imperfections, he smashed twelve cylinder blocks in succession with a sledgehammer. In 1911, outraged that frivolous motorists were decorating their bonnets with golliwogs, miniature policemen, even Scotties cocking their legs, he commissioned the artist Charles Sykes to produce the four-inch Spirit of Ecstasy mascot, cast in copper, nickel, or tin. To achieve the gleaming sterling silver effect, technicians labored until, in time, they came up with the answer: to polish each mascot with powdered cherry stones.

From the earliest days, Rainbow motorists flooded the coachbuilders with requests for bizarre installations. The dilettante composer, Lord Berners, insisted on a clavichord, which he could carry into his hotel at night; others outfitted their Silver Ghosts or Phantom Is with such quirks of fancy as pianolas, espresso coffee machines, hot and cold running water, a $3,000 makeup case, a dashboard with all the operational switches labeled in Olde Englysshe, an interior roof depicting the heavens, and a commode. (A cocktail cabinet with cutglass decanter was always standard equipment in the Phantom.) And as with Alfred Dunhill, the Maharajahs helped to keep Rolls-Royce in the spotlight—in particular Patiala, who bought thirty-five Rolls-Royces at one swoop, equipping them all with gold-plated dashboards, fur floor-coverings, and built-in medicine chests. Another, the Maharajah of Mysore, so revered his Rolls-Royce he had it blessed annually with a shower of rose petals.

Thus Royce had been proven right; with six out of ten of all Rolls-Royces built still on the road today, the quality *had* remained—long after the price was forgotten. It was Royce himself who summed up his contribution to the Age of Caring: "It's impossible for us to make a bad car. The doorman wouldn't let it go out!"

2 / LA BELLE EPOQUE:
The World of "The 400"

Across the North Atlantic, there was none of the freewheeling social mobility that marked out King Edward's court. Ever since the Civil War ended in 1865, Society had been engulfed in a permanent identity crisis. Ironically, the caste lines of the Great Democracy were as stratified as in the servants' halls of Longleat and Welbeck Abbey.

The distinction was essentially between the Old Guard and the New, which translated as Old Money versus new-rich. Old Money, as Cornelius Vanderbilt IV defined it, was "aged-in-the-wood" money, fortunes accumulated from railroads, banking, tobacco, and cotton long before the 1863 Battle of Gettysburg. In New York, the Fifth Avenue "set" were a class apart; some resided in the East Sixties and the East Seventies, others had gravitated to London or to their estates on Long Island, but all had been born or had at some time lived on the broad boulevard connecting Washington Square with the 110th Street plaza.

They shrank from gambling on margin as they shrank from the French Riviera; their money was salted away in government bonds and cash, and they shrank even more fastidiously from the Park Avenue "set," who were still painfully acquiring their first pearls, their first yachts, and their first chinchilla wraps.

The crucial date in this class war had been 1876, when the Old Guard grew alarmed at the onslaught of the "climbers" and the nouveaux-riches on the citadels of society—men and women who had found their wealth in the mines of California, the mountains of Montana, and the forges of Pittsburgh. Since the Civil War, New York had become not only the largest commercial center but also the nation's social metropolis—and now the new-rich, exchanging their two-button gloves for arm-length gloves, their ginghams and calicos for Jean Philippe Worth's French silks, were clamoring for admission. It was time to close the ranks, and thus Mrs. William Backhouse Astor, Jr., the former Caroline Webster Schermerhorn, abetted by her social arbiter, Ward McAllister, coined a mysterious phrase to divide the sheep from the goats: "The 400."

The origins of this talismanic number are hazy. Some thought it signified the exact number that would fit into Mrs. Astor's ballroom at 350 Fifth Avenue—which, in fact, could hold 800. Years later, McAllister did attempt to define the phrase to a New York *Tribune* reporter. "If you go outside that number," he explained, "you strike people who are either not at ease in a ballroom or else make other people not at ease."

A plain, markedly homely girl with a large nose, a small mouth, and a heavy jaw, Mrs. Astor, who styled herself *the* Mrs. Astor, to dissociate herself from William Waldorf Astor's wife, Mary, was a triumph of mind over unpromising matter. From the 1870s, determined to dominate New York Society, she demonstrated that nothing would succeed like excess. Her servants were attired in exact replicas of the blue livery worn at Windsor Castle. Her nine-course dinners, served on heavy gold plates costing $400 apiece, lasted as long as three hours; her table was massed with Gloire de Paris roses costing one dollar per bloom. In Box No. Seven of the Diamond Horseshoe, as the Metropolitan Opera's circle of boxes was known, she wore at one and the same time a triple necklace of diamonds, a diamond stomacher, a twelve-row fall of diamonds over her bosom, a diamond tiara, and diamond stars in her hair. Such was her power that the most signal honor accorded was an invitation to join her on "The Throne"—a divan covered with red silk cushions—in the ballroom of her home. To be passed over was a slight so devastating that Mrs. John Drexel once hastened the entire length of the dance floor, exiting with noisy sobs to the strains of "The Blue Danube."

Of course, Mrs. Astor's list was flexible—in a nation of *arrivistes*, it could hardly have been otherwise. John Jacob Astor I, the stout, guttural son of a drunken German butcher, who had netted $20 million from fur trading and New York real estate, would scarcely have been eligible, but he had died in 1848, posing Caroline no problem. Jay Gould, the bearded, tubercular robber baron, whose fortune stemmed from 8,500 miles of railroad track and the Western Union Cable Company, never gained admission—he died in 1892—but room could be found for his son, George. "Commodore" Cornelius Vanderbilt, an illiterate, profane roughneck who chewed—and spat—tobacco, would not have passed muster, despite the $95 million he had piled up from steamships and railroads, but he, too, had died, in 1877. No barriers were raised to exclude his son, William H., or his grandsons, Cornelius II, William Kissam, Frederick, and George Washington.

On the surface, at least, Society, as pictured by Edith Wharton, differed little from King Edward's world: "a little 'set' with its private catchwords, observances and amusements, and its indifference to anything outside its charmed circle." Yet under Mrs. Astor and McAllister there existed a near-Napoleonic code, relentless in its declaration of who was in, who was out.

A southerner, who never lost his lazy Georgia drawl, Ward McAllister—"Mr. Make-a-list-er" to his many detractors—devoted his entire life to Society. A connoisseur of fine Madeira, a fusspot who always served roast turkey with the tail feathers reassembled, he claimed the Court of the Grand Duke of Tuscany as his inspiration for "The 400." For him, eligible Society was divided into two distinct groups: the "nobs," or old families with more position than money, and the "swells," the more newly rich, who had to entertain to keep their ends up. Thus a Van Rensselaer was a "nob," a Vanderbilt a "swell." Those who had prudently switched to real estate were, of course, socially secure; the Rhinelanders had begun as bankers, the Goelets as ironmongers, the Schermerhorns as ship's chandlers, and the Drexels, from the Austrian Tyrol, as gold rush bankers.

From 1887 on, McAllister had further sterling support from *The Social Register,* a snob's bible drawn up by Louis Keller, a patent lawyer's son from Summit, New Jersey; like McAllister, Keller's mind "never went beyond Society." Inclusion called for at least five letters of recommendation from those already listed; Jews and Catholics were virtually excluded, and social solecisms such as going on the stage, marrying somebody not in the Register, or divorcing somebody who was, called for instant ejection.

Aside from their yachts, the true status symbols of "The 400" were their private trains, ninety tons of welded steel, stayed with throughbolts and braced with angle irons, boasting Axminster carpets, crystal chandeliers, and rosewood salons, always attached to the rear of the great "name trains." Most were built for the first families by Webster Wagner's Palace Car Company, which merged in 1899 with George Mortimer Pullman's company; as early as 1900, they cost $50,000, though every Vanderbilt had one as a matter of course. Ostentation, condemned in others, was of course permissible to the charmed circle of "The 400." Thus, aboard George Gould's private train of five palace cars, the servants were dressed in black satin knee breeches and crimson tailcoats with gold frogs and loops, and guests were thus expected to dine in full evening dress. As the Rothschilds' New York representative, it was proper for August Belmont to have the staff of his train, *Mineola,* outfitted by Charles Wetzel of Fifth Avenue, the most expensive tailor in the United States. As a matter of course, Mrs. Hamilton K. Twombley, the granddaughter of "Commodore" Cornelius, traveled with a small army of domestics in maroon Vanderbilt livery, including her $25,000-a-year chef de cuisine, M. Josef Donon, who rarely ordered less than fifty pounds of lobster a day.

Just as at London's Savoy, it was now acceptable for ladies to dine in public—and even, from January 1907, to dine unescorted—and from 1897 *the* place for hostesses like *the* Mrs. Astor to be seen was the Palm Garden of the newly opened $13 million Waldorf-Astoria Hotel, a 1,000-room palace on Fifth Avenue, stretching from Thirty-third to Thirty-fourth streets. There were accepted nuances; every member of "The 400" expected the maître d'hôtel, the dignified, heavy-set Oscar Tschirky, to greet them by name, and, if possible, to suggest appropriate food and wine. Often six weeks' advance notice was needed to secure a table in the Palm Garden, which featured its own artificial trout stream, the hotel speciality, chicken à la king, cooked in the newly fashionable chafing dishes, rose-shaded candles, in the Ritz tradition, and the new Waldorf salad—chopped celery, apples, and walnuts bathed in mayonnaise.

The desire to view "The 400" at table was now so great that Oscar, as great a snob as McAllister, had to think up the hitherto unthinkable: the purple velvet rope, barring the entrance to lesser breeds, who must make do in the Empire or the Rose rooms. Thus Oscar, and the hotel's lessor, George Boldt, tacitly conspired with "The 400" to sit in judgment on who was who. Each lady guest who rated approval had flowers sent to her room. Families roosting at the Waldorf en route to Europe had champagne and a basket of fruit sent to their liner with Boldt's compliments. When one tightwad objected that his bill was too steep, Boldt tore it in half, telling the complainant that he need not pay it, nor need he return. The Waldorf was for those who could afford the best; the Waldorf was for "The 400."

Strangely, two areas of the Waldorf—the Men's Café and Peacock Alley, a wide, 300-foot-long corridor of amber marble on the Thirty-fourth Street side of the hotel—were the stamping grounds of men quite beyond the pale of "The 400": John Warne "Bet-a-Million" Gates, who maintained a $20,000-a-year Waldorf suite, and "Smiling Charlie" Schwab, president of the Bethlehem Steel Corporation, whose Riverside Drive mansion had a refrigerator holding twenty tons of meat and three French chefs on duty to cook it. Armed with an introduction from Sir Tommy Lipton, Schwab had been a welcome guest of King Edward's at Buckingham Palace, but neither he nor his crony, James Buchanan "Diamond Jim" Brady, whom Edward would likewise have welcomed, could penetrate "The 400."

"Diamond Jim" was a man as infatuated with precious stones as *the* Mrs. Astor. A super-salesman for the railroad supply house of Manning, Maxwell and Moore, he had a genius, in this age of burgeoning railroads, for luring out-of-town customers to Charles Rector's opulent Broadway restaurant, between Fifty-third and Fifty-fourth Streets, to gorge them on Lobster Newburg and Moët and Chandon before clinching substantial deals for brake rigging and patent couplings. All told, his collection of diamonds was valued at $2 million—thirty complete sets, one for each day of the month—and he was as uninhibited as Mrs. Astor in his display of them: "Them as has 'em, wears 'em." But Jim, an Irish saloon-keeper's son, had been born, in August 1856, on the wrong side of the tracks, on the city's Lower West Side. Even diamonds could not get him past Ward McAllister.

Not that "The 400" was really Brady's scene; a gourmand topping the scales at more than eighteen stone, he made Edward VII look like a health farm patient in the last stages of a fast. At Rector's, a twelve-course dinner was merely a preliminary skirmish before he settled down to the serious consumption of six dozen oysters, a saddle of mutton, half a dozen venison chops, a brace of mallard, and a twelve-egg soufflé, all of it washed down, since he was a teetotaler, with a gallon of chilled orange juice. (Not surprisingly, a final surfeit finished him off in 1919.) If Jim cared at all, it was because his girlfriend, Edna McAuley, envied "The 400" their life, but even McAllister's successor, Harry Lehr, wanted no part of "that dreadful Brady person."

The more "The 400" changed, the more they hewed to the same pattern. In 1905, *the* Mrs. Astor, resplendent in a Marie Antoinette gown of purple velvet trimmed in pale blue satin, received her guests in her ballroom for the last time, standing as she had always stood under the portrait that Carolus Duran had painted of her. The next year she stumbled and fell; the ball could not be held. At last, her mind affected, she could no longer give dinners and balls. She wandered like a wraith through the white-and-gilt halls of her new home, at 842 Fifth Avenue, in imagination greeting old friends like McAllister, who had died in 1895, and whispering nuggets of gossip into nonexistent ears. Standing by the portrait of her father, she asked who he was.

When heart stimulants and oxygen could no longer help, *the* Mrs. Astor died, aged 77, on October 30, 1908.

The leadership of the pack was now equally divided among a trio of the most formidable matrons the United States has ever known: Mrs. Mamie Stuyvesant Fish, wife of the longtime president of the Illinois Central Railroad; Mrs. Tessie Fair Oelrichs, wealthy in her own right as a Comstock Lode heiress; and Mrs. Oliver Hazard Perry Belmont, daughter-in-law of the Rothschild representative, formerly Mrs. William Kissam Vanderbilt, earlier still, Alva Smith, a cotton planter's daughter from Mobile, Alabama. Not only did they reign supreme in New York but in the fashionable watering-place and bastion of privilege that they had made their own: Newport, Rhode Island.

None of the trinity was a woman to be crossed lightly. At Rosecliff, her $3 million Newport "cottage"—all Newport's palaces were "cottages"—Tessie Fair Oelrichs, who could swear like a tugboat skipper if need be, could also, if need be, betray her plebeian origins by getting on her hands and knees with a pail of water and a brush to show the hired help exactly how a floor *should* be scrubbed. A woman used to having her own way, Tessie was irked that Rosecliff's white marble balustrade overlooked the sea but not Newport Harbor. Daunted by nothing, she ordered a shipyard to construct a dozen full-sized skeleton ships with white hulls, anchored them on the water, and floodlit them at night, achieving her concept of a fleet under full sail.

At Belcourt Castle, another $3 million, fifty-room cottage, Alva Belmont's pleasure was to throw parties for 500 guests at a time, many of them foreign nobility like the Grand Duke Boris of Russia. "I know of no profession, art, or trade that women are working in today," she once proclaimed, "as taxing on mental resource as being a leader of Society." She it was who introduced the first French motor car, a DeDion Bouton, to Newport Society; at once the Drexels and the Vanderbilts, forsaking their polo ponies, followed suit.

Her husband, Oliver Hazard Perry Belmont, was unimpressed. His idea of bliss was to live under the same roof as his beautifully groomed and beloved horses, so that the ground floor of Belcourt accommodated the horses, the upper story the Belmont family. Thus thirty horses bedded down in their stalls each night, wrapped in white initialed Irish linen sheets, which were changed daily, covered by blankets embroidered with the Belmont coat of arms.

At "Crossways," her handsome white colonial cottage, Mamie Stuyvesant Fish, whom one Newporter recalled as having "the impatient strut and the mannerisms of a cockatoo," was a law unto herself. She was the first hostess, though by no means the last, to set out to make bad manners fashionable. She was rude, she was witty, she was adept at "flip" remarks, and her criterion, like many a hostess after her, was that things must be consistently "amusing." Impatient at *the* Mrs. Astor's three-hour dinner parties, Mamie set her English butler, Morton, to serving an eight-course dinner at a brisk clip of thirty minutes flat. Smoking with the soup was encouraged, champagne was the only wine served, and Strauss waltzes gave place to early ragtime combos.

She was a past mistress of the snappy comeback. One young scion, offended by exclusion from a party, enquired languidly, "I never can remember the name of your house, Mrs. Fish. Isn't it the Cross Patch?" "It's a patch you'll never cross, young man," was Mamie's tart reply. When a guest apologized for leaving early, Mamie cut in, "Don't apologize—no guest ever left too soon for me." "Make yourselves at home," she greeted new arrivals, "and believe me, there is no one who wishes you were there more than I do." When a dancing partner begged for one more two-step, Mamie retorted, "There are just two steps more for you—one upstairs to get your coat and the other out to your carriage."

How large was "Crossways"? one guest wanted to know. Mamie didn't know for sure, "because it swells at night." "Here you all are again," was her opening sally, as another Newport Season began, "older faces and younger clothes."

On the face of it, Newport was hardly the most stimulating resort on earth; originally a watering place where southern planters had migrated for the summer, the novelist Joseph Hergesheimer found it a place of "old women and old men with thin futile voices." All through the season, precisely from July 4 to the first Saturday in September, two days before Labor Day, it was virtually a seaside replica of Fifth Avenue, for New York and Newport society were virtually interchangeable; Trinity Church pewholders of the summer months were the Metropolitan boxholders of the fall. It was an environment totally hostile to outsiders, as Sir Tommy Lipton found to his cost. Nobody but reporters and autograph-hunters would even speak to him.

Every weekday afternoon, from 3 P.M. onward, the coaching parade in Bellevue Avenue, lush with its blue hydrangeas, roses of Sharon, and thirty-foot-high rhododendrons, was the high spot of the day: the silent whirring of the coaches' rubber wheels, the staccato clatter of horses' hooves, the coachmen rigidly immobile on the boxes, in Vanderbilt maroon or Astor blue, black boots gleaming in contrast with breeches as white as a holystoned stoop. The etiquette could be overwhelming; it was the greatest of gaffes to overtake a coach socially superior to one's own. The object of this daily round was to drop calling cards at other people's houses, but since everybody was abroad, dropping his own, the exercise was in vain. Since the coaches passed and repassed several times, there was an agreed etiquette for these moments, too: the first time warranted a ceremonial bow, the second time merited a smile, the third time faces were rigidly averted.

Aside from each other's houses, the other main venue was Bailey's Beach, a small, cramped cove guarded from the hoi-polloi by watchmen in gold-laced uniforms. Only a letter of introduction secured a newcomer a small, green-painted cabana, barely large enough to turn around in, on Bailey's; even so, new-rich aspirants made "Bailey's Beach Or Bust!" the rallying cry of the day. But even Bailey's closed ritually down at 6 P.M., when a small army of beach attendants arrived to dispose of deck chairs and sun umbrellas.

To enliven this soporific round, the Newport Triumvirate now turned to a new Court Jester to organize their fun-fests: Harry Lehr.

Of all those linked with the Rainbow People, then or later, Harry Symes Lehr somehow emerges as the most despicable. The son of a Baltimore snuff-importer who had fallen on hard times, he was tall, blond, with vivid blue eyes, a high-pitched voice, and a braying laugh. In 1886, aged seventeen and penniless, he had known the torments of poverty as a bank clerk in Cologne. "I must have beauty, light, music around me," he confided in his diary. "I am like Ludwig of Bavaria, I cannot bear the cold greyness of everyday life." His solution was simple: "Most human beings are fools . . . they want to be entertained and be made to laugh. They will overlook most anything so long as you amuse them."

Starting with Baltimore Society, Lehr found a chance encounter with *the* Mrs. Astor, following McAllister's death, that opened all doors. Lehr now became The Compleat Sponger. In New York, George Boldt gave him free Waldorf board and lodging during the off-season; Lehr would bring the right crowd to the Palm Garden. For the same quid pro quos, Charles Wetzel tailored him for free; Black, Starr and Frost lent him jewels. From George Kessler, too, came a $6,000 annual stipend; the cellars of the rich must always be well stocked with Moët and Chandon. Through Mrs. Stuyvesant Fish came free railroad passes, and even postal charges were circumvented. By courtesy of Mrs. Clarence Mackay, wife of the Atlantic cable king, Lehr communicated solely by wire and cable.

If Lehr could gull "The 400" into picking up his checks, well and good, but in 1901 he practiced a far baser deceit on the widowed Mrs. John Dahlgren, the former Elizabeth Drexel, of Philadelphia. On their wedding night, Lehr and his bride dined in separate rooms; the epicene Lehr, an unashamed transvestite, had confessed that he had courted her solely for her money. "If I am never your lover when we are alone, at least I will not neglect or humiliate you in public," was the only cold comfort he could offer her, but since the Newport Triumvirate had agreed to "take her up," at least she would have "a wonderful position in Society." The abject Elizabeth's response to this was to guarantee him $25,000 a year pocket money. The marriage was to remain in name only, unconsummated, for twenty-eight years.

To live the life of Ludwig of Bavaria, Lehr sang for his supper unremittingly. He was an accomplished party pianist, a witty raconteur, a first-rate mimic. It was he who devised most of the frolics for which Mamie Fish became famous; to spite Mrs. Ogden Goelet, wife of the New York real-estate king, who was hosting a dinner for the Grand Duke Boris, Mamie countered with an invitation to dinner with Tsar Nicholas II. At the eleventh hour, most guests offered lame excuses, threw over the Goelets, and descended on "Crossways"—to find that the "Tsar," seated on Mrs. Fish's right, ablaze with jewels and decorations, was a heavily disguised Harry Lehr. Inwardly fuming, the guests could only simulate hearty and bonhomous laughter.

It was likewise Lehr who dreamed up Mamie's immortal Dogs' Dinner, a Newport function at which only the dogs of the colony's ladies were guests—a field-day for the press, who were ready to depict the privileged pooches as seated at a silver-laden table, while Morton and the other domestics doled out pâté de foie gras. This time the laugh was on the press; the dogs were fed an innocuous meal of stewed liver, rice, and dog biscuits on Mamie's verandah—one dachshund so overdoing it that it fell in a coma beside its plate and had to be carried home.

The Monkey Dinner was another of Harry's japes. Elizabeth Lehr, persuaded to give a dinner for a visiting Corsican prince, spent much of the evening smiling wanly as she played hostess to an outsize monkey in full evening dress. On another occasion, James de Wolfe Cutting, an eligible bachelor, was cajoled into hosting a dinner for eight at his Rhode Island farmhouse. In due time the baffled Cutting found his dinner table filling up with Mamie Fish, the Harry Lehrs, a life-sized mannequin modeled on a girlfriend of Cutting's, two dogs, a parrot, and a framed portrait of a Spanish Infanta.

Such were the pranks and pratfalls with which Lehr enlivened Newport Society in the years after *the* Mrs. Astor held sway.

An even more engrossing topic in the years leading up to the turn of the century had been: how would "The Commodore's" heirs handle his colossal wealth? To this question, the heirs returned one unanimous answer: they would spend it, and what was more they would spend it on houses. The race was on for the Vanderbilts to become the greatest house-building family in American history.

The first of the big spenders were William Kissam Vanderbilt and his wife Alva (later Alva Belmont). Cutting loose from New York tradition, they opted not for the local brownstone for their Fifth Avenue palace but for gray limestone, with an entrance hall modeled on Milan Cathedral. "It is not sufficient merely to possess wealth," noted Thorstein Veblen, a social economist of the time. "The wealth must be put in evidence. . . ." And both on Fifth Avenue and at Newport, in their "cottage," Marble House, based in part on Louis XIV's Grand Trianon, in part on the Temple of the Sun at Baalbek, William and Alva saw to it that much *was* in evidence; in the dining room, solid bronze chairs weighed seventy pounds apiece, threatening with an incipient hernia any footman who tried to lift them. A nice touch was the front doors, innocent of outside handles; the assumption was that a hovering servant would be there to open them in the nick of time.

Evidence of sibling rivalry was early apparent. Cornelius Vanderbilt II was a hard-working, conscientious man, but his wife was the socially ambitious Alice Claypoole Gwynne. Thus Alice was not content with the $5 million palace that Cornelius had raised on Fifth Avenue; she wanted to shine in Newport, too. To outdo his brother, Cornelius embarked on an even greater white elephant—the phrase is Henry James's—the seventy-room mausoleum known as "The Breakers."

In the end, Cornelius II triumphed; even today "The Breakers" ranks as one of the greatest examples of conspicuous consumption in American architectural history. Although it was occupied for barely two months of each year, its ornamental fence alone cost an annual $5,000 to paint. The house itself, completed in 1895, was entered through a seventy-ton front door, which gave on to a baronial hall rising forty-five feet through two floors. All its statistics were purposefully mind-boggling: a billiard room done from top to bottom in twenty varieties of pale-green marble; its thirty bathrooms; its fifty-eight-foot-long dining room, where shafts of red alabaster supported a gold cornice decorated with garlands and masks. In the library, the motto inscribed above the sixteenth-century French fireplace seemed strangely inapposite: "Little do I care for riches, since only cleverness prevails in the end."

This was a throwaway line typical of "Alice-of-the-Breakers," as Mrs. Cornelius II came to be known—on a par with the time when she lunched at the old Ambassador Hotel with her wastrel son, Reggie, and his new, second wife, Gloria Morgan. Had Gloria received her pearls yet? she wanted to know. Reggie was shamefaced; dearly though he wanted to give Gloria pearls, he could not afford a string worthy of her. For answer, Alice commanded the maître d' to bring her a pair of scissors—and snipped off roughly $70,000 worth of pearls from the ropes that festooned her neck.

"There you are, Gloria," said Alice complacently, "all Vanderbilt women have pearls."

In the case of the Vanderbilts, the old Wall Street saw—"from shirtsleeves to shirtsleeves in three generations"—seemed likely to be proven true.

For by 1900 another Vanderbilt was in on the spending spree: Grace Wilson Vanderbilt, wife of Cornelius III, whose marriage had so displeased his father that he had been cut off with a scant $1 million, later increased to $7 million through a gift from his brother, Alfred Gwynne. Within six years, Grace's insatiable social ambition was to drive her frail, introspective husband to the bottle.

From 1901, she had set out to eclipse not only *the* Mrs. Astor but Mamie Fish and her set besides. She, too, demanded a Newport villa, Beaulieu, whose trappings included seventeen automobiles, thirty horses, fifteen stable boys, a coachman, maids, footmen, an English butler, and an English nanny. From the first, the race was in her favor. The daughter of a wealthy banker, she had mixed in European Society from the age of eleven, and was a special favorite of Edward, when Prince of Wales. Thus she had acquired a know-how that other hostesses only assimilated by degrees: the correct way to board a yacht, how to keep a sauce béarnaise from curdling, how to serve wines properly *chambré*. Her son, Cornelius IV, early learned to field deftly such questions as, "Should the former governor of New York be seated on the right of the hostess and the former ambassador of Great Britain on her left, or vice versa?"

Not only did Grace Wilson Vanderbilt act regally; she felt royal in her bones. "Poor dear Marie Antoinette," she often remarked. "I feel so sorry for her. If the revolution ever came to this country, I would be the first to go." By the winter of 1902, she was one jump ahead of all New York Society; on a visit to the United States, Prince Henry of Prussia, Kaiser Wilhelm's brother, made a beeline for Grace's box in the Diamond Horseshoe. The Prince might lunch with Pierpont Morgan and breakfast with Mrs. Darius Ogden Mills, wife of the head of the Bank of California—but dinner was reserved for Grace Wilson Vanderbilt alone.

Never seen in public without her bandeau and diamond stomacher, Grace embraced entertaining with a missionary fervor. When her husband inherited 640 Fifth Avenue, Grace set 600 laborers to work on a remodeling job, including a ballroom duplicating that of Versailles and the installation of thirty-three bathrooms. Then she moved in for the kill. In one year alone, she received 37,000 guests—and her social secretary, Miss Henderson, kept a card index that listed all their likes and dislikes, down to their favorite bedside authors and favorite cigarettes. She became famous for her Worth and Paquin dresses, some so heavy with jet and pearls they could not be hung, but were folded, in blue tissue paper, on twelve-foot shelves, and for her 500 pairs of shoes, all with matching handbags. Her dinner table, which seated sixty, was packed out every night of the week, with a single dinner featuring $200 worth of hothouse fruit.

It was a rare year in which entertaining cost her less than $250,000, but Grace had battled her way to the top. No one would ever question who was *the* Mrs. Vanderbilt now.

* * *

For the Johnny-come-latelies among America's financial and industrial barons, the identity crisis was even more acute. Overnight, following the Civil War, their fortunes had changed, when a floodtide of immigrants—Germans, Irish, Jews, Slavs, Scandinavians—began the great trek to the mines and farms and foundries west of the Alleghenies. Quite suddenly, men who recalled only dirt-poor, shirtsleeved beginnings were powers in the land.

By 1901, Henry Clay Frick, who had then turned fifty-one, had undergone only thirty months of formal schooling in his life; he had begun working as a bookkeeper in a whisky distillery. But now he was a millionaire, the King of Coke, a cool, withdrawn man, who slapped no backs and told no salesmen's stories, the man who had fired the coke ovens of Pennsylvania for the Age of Steel, who had profited by buying coke ovens and coal mines at knockdown prices in the financial debacle of 1873. Edward Townsend "Little Sunshine" Stotesbury was in a similar dilemma. At fifty-two, he looked back forty years to rock-bottom beginnings as a $16-a-month bank clerk—a far cry from his current status as the head of Drexel, the Philadelphia bankers, and a partner in J. P. Morgan and Co., New York.

There were other fish out of water: Peter Arrell Brown Widener, a butcher's boy until a Civil War government contract led to mutton that spelt a $50,000 profit, which was parlayed in turn into a $100 million fortune. There was J. Pierpont Morgan himself, a banker of frightening mien, with his black, blazing eyes, his bulbous nose aflame with acne rosacea; to meet his gaze, said the photographer Edward Steichen, was "like confronting the headlights of an express train bearing down on one."

None of these men qualified for—or were interested in—membership of "The 400." How then could they display their new-won affluence in a way that befitted Rainbow People?

From the turn of the century, Joseph Duveen, the stocky, ruddy-faced, gray-eyed art dealer who had helped stage-manage King Edward's coronation, set out to give them guidance.

From his bases at 21 Old Bond Street, London, and, by 1912, the place Vendôme, Paris, and New York's Fifth Avenue, Duveen, whom the aesthete Harold Acton regarded "as smooth as a jaguar licking itself in the sun," understood his new-found millionaires very well. He recognized their hunger for prestige, so that offering any article for its true value was to at once diminish them. He knew that men of dynamic ambition must be top dogs in the world of collectors, too. Thus, for almost forty years—he died, as Lord Duveen of Millbank, in 1939—he drove up prices in the art world to heights never before known.

His prime technique was rivalry; he kept Frick vying so bitterly with Henry E. Huntington, nephew of Collis P. Huntington, the railroad king, over the acquisition of Gainsborough portraits that prices rocketed into the Raphael class. In one deal alone he sold Huntington, who had married his uncle's widow, Arabella, three full-length Gainsborough portraits for $775,000—in truth a bargain, for Frick had paid $300,000 for just one Gainsborough. One astonished art dealer always recalled Duveen, in an inner room at Old Bond Street, crouched on his knees before a Rembrandt, muttering over and over, "I can't let you go." He was screwing himself up to put the bite on Frick.

Such rivalry could prove contagious. Another leading dealer, Schuyler Parsons of New York and Newport, once sped to San Francisco to inspect four antique Chinese vases on behalf of Peter Widener's son, Joe. If Parsons liked their color, he was to phone Joe Widener for authorization to buy. But Gump's, the great San Francisco art store, was holding them on a twenty-four-hour option for another client, who next day offered $50,000. Thereafter, the bids escalated sharply for three days and nights, until Parsons, on Widener's behalf, bid $105,000. On the fourth day, the rival client clinched a bid for $110,000.

Had Widener not upped his bids for objets d'art he had never even seen, the price would have remained rooted at $50,000.

Early in life Duveen had mastered the art of flattery. "Make sure that stuff goes by White Star Line," he once instructed his bookkeeper. "We don't want any more mistakes"; from the corner of his eye he had spotted White Star's owner, Thomas Ismay, browsing through the salesroom. When Ismay ventured, "The others are just as good," Duveen disagreed vehemently. "The White Star Line is the only properly managed one among the whole lot!" His "surprise" when a gratified Ismay bought several thousand pounds worth of bibelots and revealed his identity was, recalls his nephew, James Henry Duveen, a masterly improvisation.

An unabashed con man, Duveen, according to Kenneth (later, Lord) Clark, late director of the National Gallery, rarely knew the names of the painters at whose pictures he blew ecstatic kisses. In this he was at one with his clients; Pierpont Morgan, after asking, "Who is Vermeer?" was happy to pay $100,000 for a painter of whom he had never heard. Duveen's manner was that of a huckster in the marketplace. "Greatest thing I ever saw! Will give you the biggest price *you* ever saw!" was a sample of his technique. "If I had the Sistine Chapel I could sell it tomorrow half a dozen times over" was another favorite lament. This was language that men like Peter Widener, who bought his Rembrandts like pairs of socks, a dozen at a time, could wholly understand.

Just as the Vanderbilts felt the compulsion to build white elephants, so Duveen's clients were seized by the magpie instinct. Like them, Henry Clay Frick was building a $5 million Fifth Avenue palace, determined to make that of his bitter rival, Andrew Carnegie, "look like a miner's shack"; the problem was to fill it. New York's earliest interior decorator, a lesbian actress named Elsie de Wolfe (later Lady Mendl), was hired to oversee the second story for 10 percent of the cost of the furnishings, but in Paris, where they met, the King of Coke, who was late for a golf game, could spare her barely half an hour.

A table priced at 350,000 francs? "All right, I'll take it." A console at 400,000 francs? "All right, buy it." In thirty short minutes, even at 10 percent, Elsie became, in her own words, "tantamount to a rich woman."

The same mania possessed Morgan. Through Duveen, he bought the famous Garland collection of Chinese porcelain, and then, in 1906, the great Hoentschel collection of eighteenth-century French decorative art. Dabbling in books with one Thackeray manuscript, he eventually acquired whole libraries, which overflowed into a library building and then into a warehouse on New York's Forty-second Street. But even Morgan's holdings paled beside those of the press baron, William Randolph Hearst. In all, Hearst accumulated $50 million worth of art treasures, some of them, never uncrated, occupying two acres of cellar space: statues, urns, carved gilt ceilings, confessionals, battle flags from Siena, Cardinal Richelieu's bed, even a Spanish Cistercian monastery, which was shipped to San Francisco stone by stone but never reassembled.

Duveen's markups were as shrewd as the man himself—exactly what the traffic would bear. From the canny oil tycoon, Calouste Gulbenkian, called "Mr. Five-Percent," from the size of his stake in the Iraq Petroleum Company, Duveen exacted a profit of no more than 25 percent. With others, who were spending to purge their systems, the sky was the limit; the $500,000 Mazarin tapestry that had graced Westminster Abbey during King Edward's coronation had cost Duveen $50,000. (Morgan, like Widener, bought his tapestries wholesale, enquiring, "How much for the stack?") A large *Holy Family* by Andrea Mantegna, for which Duveen paid £29,500, cost the New York department store magnate, Benjamin Altman, £103,300. In perhaps Duveen's most publicized deal, Huntington's purchase of Gainsborough's *The Blue Boy* from the Duke of Westminster, Duveen's profit was an impressive $620,000.

His tips were as expansive as his manner. A $100 bill pressed discreetly into the palm of a deck steward on the liner *Aquitania* seems excessive for the era, but it secured Duveen what he wanted—a deck chair placed alongside that of Alexander Smith Cochran, the carpet tycoon. Wrapped in steamer rugs, sharing morning bouillon and afternoon tea, Duveen and Cochran were soon on the best of terms—which set Cochran back $5 million worth of European art.

He was adept at keeping the wealthy in line, with what one man called his "the-lord-hath-spoken manner"; if he was ensuring them immortality, then a proper respect was his due. To teach Huntington a lesson he would not forget, Duveen stood blandly aside when the tycoon bought a purported Romney from a rival dealer, Lewis and Simmons, for $100,000. When a £10,000, seven-day hearing in the High Court of Justice's King's Bench

Division revealed it as a portrait by an obscure painter named Ozias Humphrey, Duveen was, of course, all forgiveness, tempered with a modicum of "Don't let it happen again."

He was a master at subtly casting doubts on the authenticity of any purchase not made through Duveen. This so affected William Randolph Hearst when Duveen dismissed out of hand two allegedly Rossellino bas-reliefs of angels that he trumpeted despairingly, "If those angels aren't right, then nothing is right!"

Most, for all their wealth and power, came obediently to heel. Industry knew Frick as the hardest of men, one who had not hesitated, in the Homestead, Pennsylvania, steel mill strike of July 1892, to cross swords with the Amalgamated Association of Iron and Steel Workers, calling in 300 Pinkerton operatives for a shoot-out that left fourteen dead and 163 severely injured. Yet in Duveen's hands he was as modeling clay, tamely submitting to Duveen's creation, abetted by the British interior designer Sir Charles Allom, of a special room based on ten decorative Fragonard panels, *Roman d'Amour de la Jeunesse*, for £205,000, more than £20,000 a panel.

Thus both parties achieved a meeting of minds. In his lonely Fifth Avenue château, Frick sat surrounded by the trappings Duveen deemed appropriate: more than 200 works of art—Rembrandts, Goyas, Renoirs, Van Dycks, pictures that he dared not move an inch without Duveen's say-so. In this sumptuous setting he himself enjoyed the simple pleasures of a parvenu, seated under a Baghdad baldechin, leafing through the pages of *The Saturday Evening Post*, while an organist, imported each Saturday afternoon, meandered through such homely favorites as "The Rosary" and "Silver Threads Among The Gold."

There was a darker side to this. More than 3,000 miles from New York, in a rambling Tuscan villa called I Tatti, near the village of Settignano, a bearded Jewish-Lithuanian refugee from Boston, Massachusetts, Bernard Berenson, born in 1865, was, as he himself phrased it, part of "a vast circular nexus of corruption that reached from the lowliest employee of the British Museum right up to the King." At the center of that nexus, Berenson charged, was Duveen himself.

In a sense, Berenson, together with his wife, Mary, and his longtime amanuensis, "Nicky" Mariano, had charted his own path to self-betrayal. As a poor Harvard graduate, he had come to the notice of Mrs. Isabella Stewart Gardner, a prominent Boston hostess, intent on assembling a priceless collection of art at her home, Fenway Court. Roaming through Europe as her chief adviser, Berenson, as early as 1886, became obsessed with authentication: to establish definitively for the first time who had painted what. Beginning with the sixteenth-century painter Lorenzo Lotto, he had published his first short list of authentic Venetian paintings in 1894. But this was the point of no return. If Berenson was going to draw up dogmatic lists, then dealers like Duveen—no less than Felix Wildenstein and René Gimpel, in Paris—needed him on their team.

The insidious temptations were all too obvious. In 1900, Berenson, still a penniless scholar, first chanced on, and rented, I Tatti. Four years later, the Berensons were in New York, in pursuit of what Mary called "the bigger game"—not only Mrs. Gardner, but also J. Pierpont Morgan, the men of the Metropolitan Museum of Art, and Henry O. Havemeyer, the multimillionaire sugar refiner. It was this highly publicized trip that, in 1906, brought Duveen to his door.

It was, as "Nicky" Mariano was to attest, a love-hate relationship from first to last. For sixty years, it was Berenson's "infallible eye" that gave works of art their price tag in the marketplace, the certificates of authenticity for which Duveen pressed increasingly and for which the Svengali of the salons was prepared to pay 25 percent of the sale price. Thus, as early as 1909, when I Tatti's lease was up, Berenson was able to realize the £6,000 needed for an outright purchase.

Poised on the razor edge of probity, Berenson was always ambivalent regarding his role. He despised the Fricks and the Morgans—"the squillionaires," he called them—yet, like them, he reveled in luxury. To him, the dealers' world was "a real inferno," yet out of that inferno came the lucre that subsidized the three-year enlargement of I Tatti, the building up of a 40,000-volume library, and the grooming and landscaping of fifty acres of gardens, where the soothing sound of running water was always audible. Here, where pictures awaiting authentication were massing like examination candidates, Berenson daily held arrogant court at the luncheon table, surrounded by such sycophants as his resident painter, Derek Hill—"The light on your beard is too heavenly. I simply must capture it."

Mary Berenson, a vast and jolly woman, was far less inhibited. "I love opening letters. They might contain a check," she would exult, and Berenson shuddered palpably; Berenson was never heard to mention money. "I enjoy the spending of *money immensely,*" she confided to her journal, and the italics are her own; she reveled, too, in the sporadic visits of Duveen. "It's like drinking champagne," she gushed, to which Berenson responded with one dour monosyllable, "Gin."

A vital cog in Duveen's sales apparatus was "The X Book," a record of all the pictures bought on the advice of "Doris," as Berenson was code-named, its pages numbered in Berenson's own hand. Yet he was called on for far more than mere authentication. By Duveen—and by Wildenstein and Gimpel, and Henry Walters, the Baltimore collector, who paid him a $75,000-a-year retainer—he was expected to hunt up potential sales in advance.

The technique was cut-and-dried. Berenson would learn of a picture for sale, then visit to inspect it. A first letter would alert Duveen of its existence and request a cable regarding reservation. A second might deal with a specific query of Duveen's: was the subject of the picture "too painful"? The "squillionaires," who had come up the hard way, while desiring, as Berenson put it contemptuously, "to gloat over the object as a scalp or trophy," wanted pastoral piety, not grim realism.

Only once this canon was satisfied, did a third letter, with Berenson's official authentication, follow on.

And Berenson, like Duveen, drove up his own price. At first he had worked on a fixed percentage—which in one year alone amounted to £38,000—but this was at the mercy of market fluctuations, and I Tatti, a rich man's folly, had still to be maintained. As a result, Berenson demanded a new arrangement, with which Duveen dared not quibble: a guaranteed £10,000 a year, plus 10 percent of all Italian sales.

Was he free from taint? Though he was to split with Duveen, as late as 1938, for passing off a Titian as a Giorgione, the weight of evidence suggests that he was not. "I can assure you," Duveen would tell prospective clients, "that the stock of Giovanni Bellinis is absolutely inexhaustible," a suspect statement at least, and there were other suspicious pointers. A painting that Berenson listed in 1896 as a *Madonna and Child* designed and superintended by Andrea del Verrocchio had, by the time Duveen sold it to the cable tycoon Clarence Mackay, become an authentic Verrocchio. When art critics caviled, it was abruptly reduced in status to "Style of Verrocchio."

Then again, *The Madonna and Child With Saints*, which Berenson certified as "a late work" of Giovanni Bellini, was later reclassified as "G. Bellini and Workshop." And when John Walker, director of the National Gallery of Art in Washington, tried to talk the collector, Rush Kress, into subsidizing the gallery's purchase of a fifteenth-century painting, Fra Filippo Lippi's *The Adoration of the Magi,* Kress would have none of it. Unless the painting could be ascribed to Fra Angelico, Fra Filippo's master, the price was entirely too high.

Walker was in despair—for years earlier Berenson *had* gone on record to certify it as a work executed by Fra Angelico himself. He journeyed to I Tatti to find Berenson contrite. "I know I was wrong," he admitted mournfully. "The painting is not by Fra Angelico. It is really by Fra Filippo Lippi."

In vain, Walker consulted all the relevant information in Berenson's library, for a crucial purchase was at stake. He had almost given up when the sage of Settignano broke silence. "Johnnie," he said, smiling gently and stroking his luxuriant beard. "I do think that just before he died Fra Angelico may have painted one or two of the figures. . . ." Honor was satisfied; the painting, now in the National Gallery, bears the label: "By Fra Angelico and Fra Filippo Lippi."

Berenson was to survive Duveen by exactly twenty years; he died in 1959, aged 95. But the last laugh was with Duveen. All his life, the bankers had allowed him a revolving credit of £1,200,000—yet when he died he left no debts, £3 million in the bank, despite a $10 million loss in the Wall Street crash of 1929, and an inventory worth £2 million.

The Rainbow People had paid—and would go right on paying.

* * *

On September 25, 1909, when King Edward had just returned from Marienbad to Balmoral, a new musical, *The Dollar Princess,* starring Lily Elsie and Joe Coyne, featuring lyrics by the rising young composer Jerome Kern, opened at Daly's Theatre, on London's Leicester Square. The title caused no raised eyebrows among knowledgeable theatergoers. For most, Dollar Princesses had been a fact of economic life for fully forty years.

Unlike America, English high society was suffering no crisis of confidence; "To be an Englishman," as Ogden Nash was to put it later, "is to belong to the most exclusive club in the world," and none were more conscious of this than King Edward's circle. Their stately homes, in fact, had no problems that a healthy infusion of sound American dollars could not solve.

For some, the danger signs had long been apparent. The Duke of Sutherland might still pin £1,000 banknotes to his wife's pillow while she slept, but he was sensible of change; his Stafford House was one of the first great London mansions to go, long before Grosvenor House and Dorchester House gave place to opulent hotels. As early as 1899, Lord and Lady Warwick had set the fashion for turning estates into limited liability companies, registering life interests in their estates and collieries as Warwick Estates Limited, with a capital of £120,000. But many more turned to the Dollar Princesses for subsidy. By 1915, *Titled Americans,* printed and revised annually in New York, listed fully 454 American women who, abetted by their fathers' checkbooks, had crossed the Atlantic to no mean advantage.

Among them were forty-two American princesses, nineteen viscountesses, thirty-three marchionesses, forty-six ladies, the wives of knights or baronets, sixty-four baronesses, no fewer than 136 countesses, but only seventeen duchesses. (The going rate for dukes was $3 million.) These "black-pudding" marriages that so tickled King Edward were a trade freely acknowledged in fashionable circles. "If among your clients you have . . . a lady who is willing to purchase the rank of peeress for £25,000 sterling, paid in cash to her future husband," ran a *Daily Telegraph* advertisement aimed at family solicitors in February 1901, "I shall be pleased if you will communicate with me. . . ."

Titled Americans went further still; not only were ladies who had triumphantly made the grade listed, but all those noblemen still available to aspirant Dollar Princesses, such as the twenty-year-old Duc d'Uzès, son of King Edward's boon companion—"his mother is the heiress of the celebrated Veuve Cliquot, of champagne fame." There were tips for aspirant fathers-in-law, too: "The Earl of Ava's entailed estates do not, owing to mortgages, yield their nominal income of $100,000."

As early as 1895, one Californian calculated that over thirty-five years titled Europeans had siphoned off $200 million from the United States through matches with American heiresses, with seven Californians alone accounting for $20 million. Some aristocrats made a virtual profession of conferring their titles in return for bed-and-board; Count Axel de Wichfeld, a penniless Dane, first married Mabelle Swift, the Chicago meatpacking heiress, with a guaranteed £300,000 a year, and later "Fifi" Widener, madcap daughter of Joe, whose traveling luggage at once erupted in a rash of coronets.

Dollar Princesses who had nobled their titles early on sometimes gave a helping hand to those still in search. Minnie Stevens, daughter of a New York hotelier, was smart enough, on reaching Europe, to trade on the Prince of Wales's patronage of her father's Fifth Avenue hotel; after a Sandringham invitation and a brief status as Edward's mistress she settled for marriage with Arthur (later Sir Arthur) Paget, one of the chosen circle, a grandson of the Marquis of Anglesey. A large-hearted girl, Minnie saw to it that her friend Alice Cornelia Thaw, a $10 million Pittsburgh heiress, was in turn settled—for all of five years—with the Earl of Yarmouth, son of the sixth Marquis of Hertford.

At the same time, Yarmouth's friend, the Duke of Manchester, who had announced publicly that he must "either marry an Astor or a Vanderbilt or throw in the sponge," failed to carry off May Goelet (who became Duchess of Roxburgh), but was luckier with Helen Zimmerman, a railroad tycoon's daughter from Cincinnati. It was none too soon; just before the wedding, Manchester went bankrupt for $135,000.

It was fortunate that Helen's papa, Eugene Zimmerman, owned not only railroads but coal and iron lands and Standard Oil stock, for paying off Manchester's debts was just for openers. Helen had £10,000 a year in her own right, but much more was needed before they could live according to their rank—to say nothing of their very costly triumph in 1904, when the King and Queen Alexandra accepted their invitation to Kylemore Castle in Ireland.

The words "His Majesty Accepts" were to deplete Zimmerman's bankroll by $150,000; not only did the railroad station have to be enlarged and redecorated to receive the King ($3,900), but to climax the royal visit souvenir presents must be offered ($10,000). Possibly Zimmerman thought it cheap at the price; along the way he had even bought them the castle for $350,000.

Typical of the public reactions of the day was the New York *Tribune*'s headline, when the sewing machine heiress, Isabelle Singer, wed the young Parisian, Duc Elie Decazes: SHE PAYS ALL THE BILLS—HE THINKS HIMSELF CHEAP AT THE PRICE.

The most notorious, and most shamefully used, of all the Dollar Princesses was the lovely and languishing seventeen-year-old Consuelo Vanderbilt, daughter of William Kissam and Alva Smith Vanderbilt Belmont. Ruthlessly disregarding her daughter's love for Winthrop Rutherfurd, an eligible thirty-year-old New York bachelor, Alva masterminded a marriage with "Sonny," the arrogant twenty-four-year-old ninth Duke of Marlborough, an arranged match as fraught with scenes as any Victorian melodrama. "I don't ask *you* to think. I do the thinking, you do as you are told," was Alva's strident refrain; until the wedding ceremony, Consuelo was literally locked in her room with a guard stationed outside.

The future of Blenheim, Marlborough's ancestral seat, was now secure. On that same day, a document that transferred to him $2,500,000 of stock in the Beech Creek Railway Company—on which the New York Central guaranteed an annual payment of 4 percent—ensured that Blenheim's fourteen acres of roofs could be releaded and central heating installed. On their first meeting, the Dowager Duchess of Marlborough made it crystal clear to Consuelo what was expected of her: "Your first duty is to have a child, and it must be a son, because it would be unthinkable to have that little upstart Winston become Duke."

Life with a husband as mean in purse—on their Roman honeymoon he forbade her to enter antique shops lest the Vanderbilt millions up the price—as he was in spirit—at Blenheim he constantly hid objets d'art to tease the staff—ultimately proved too much for Consuelo. In 1908, they separated for good; by then the well-being of Blenheim had cost the Vanderbilts some $10 million.

The fatality rate among Dollar Princesses was undeniably high. Fully forty of them at length sued for divorce and almost always on the same grounds: ill treatment, extortion, and desertion. But of all the cases recorded, none so reached the depths of banality or the heights of the ludicrous as completely as the eleven-year union of Count Marie Ernest Paul Boniface de Castellane-Novejean—"Boni" to his friends—and Anna Gould, daughter of railroad tycoon, Jay, whose fortune was originally based on the manufacture of a sure-fire mousetrap.

Born in 1867 at his family seat, the Château de Rochecotte, in Provence, Boni, from the first, adhered wholeheartedly to the maxim of Anthony Trollope: "The society of the well-born and the wealthy will as a rule be worth seeking." From the spring of 1894, in Paris, Boni sought it in the person of the woefully plain Anna, "whose swarthy face would not have caused comment if seen peering out of a wigwam."

For that matter Boni himself, as pictured by Alice Keppel's daughter, Violet, was equally an acquired taste: "He had fuzzy pink hair, set rather far back on his forehead, a fair drooping mustache, heavy-lidded sleepy eyes, and the staccato walk of an automaton." On the beach at Deauville, he was a sight not easily forgotten: a footman in a red bathing dress walked ahead, removing the pebbles from his master's path before testing the water with a thermometer. A second footman followed on, carrying Boni's peignoir and the leash of his dog Bou-Boule. Finally Boni himself, glorious in a yellow bathing suit, his toenails painted coral, would enter the water for a few slow, condescending strokes, before retiring to his Pompeian bathing cabin.

His marriage to Anna, after a year's assiduous courtship, at the Goulds' Fifth Avenue home on March 4, 1895, was tantamount to a license to print money. "If American wives endow us with their wealth," was Boni's philosophy, "we, for our part, give them . . . besides a name, something which their money is powerless to purchase—a tradition and a taste."

From their marital home on the Avenue Bosquet, Paris, Boni was swift to pay a call at Guiraud's tapestry shop in the Faubourg Saint Honoré. Here he was so overcome by the marvelous Gobelin tapestries "in tones of blue and pink" that he scattered the 250,000-franc asking price all over Guiraud's floor. It was small wonder that he soon recorded, "By this time every dealer was on my track. The hunt was up!"; even in the Faubourg Saint-Honoré, the spectacle of a nobleman scattering thousand-franc notes like a drunken matelot was sufficiently rare. Soon Boni was off to fresh fields: to Charles Wertheimer's Bond Street salon, where a Reynolds portrait simply begged for a home, and a Gainsborough, too, proved irresistible. Boni, like Oscar Wilde's Lord Darlington, could "resist everything except temptation." In a few London days the tills of the Denver and Rio Grande Western Railroad were poorer by a million francs.

Back now to Paris, where a Van Dyck portrait of the Marquise de Spinola at Sedelmeyer's art gallery was crying out to be bought for 120,000 francs—as was Rembrandt's *Man With A Fur Cap,* at Sammary's—a snip at 100,000 francs. "I was by this time intoxicated with the power of purchasing," was how Boni summed up this heady addiction.

For a mere 80,000 francs, Wertheimer's dredged up another treasure, a sixty-foot fourteenth-century carpet, which had disappeared from Lisbon Cathedral to surface in the vaults of Lord Rocksavage. This was truly Boni's day, for before the shopkeepers had put up their shutters for the night, Jacques Seligman had parted with a superb buhl clock, and Stettiner's with a dinner service of apple-green Sèvres.

A man whose talent for spending other people's money amounted to genius would not stint if a party was in the offing, and on Anna's twenty-first birthday, Boni rose nobly to the occasion. As devoted to detail as his friend, César Ritz, he first hired the Tir aux Pigeons, the trapshooting pavilion in the Bois de Boulogne. The best place to secure Venetian lamps was, of course, Murano, and for good measure Boni ordered 80,000 of them, dispersing them among the trees, above the broad walks and avenues, "where they glittered in the pale similitude of transparent fruits and innumerable fire-fly lights." Since this was an evening occasion, inevitably there would be dew, but Boni overlooked nothing; Belloir, the upholsterer, was attending to that, with a generous fifteen kilometers of carpeting. None of Boni's 3,000 guests—of whom 250 had been invited to an "intimate" dinner party preceding the fête, in a pavilion adorned with 250,000 long-stemmed roses—would suffer from wet feet.

It was a spectacle Parisians would long remember. Along the broad highways sparkling with Venetian lamps, sixty footmen in scarlet livery were massed for optimum effect in tight knots of color. Some guests, as uninhibited as Boni himself, made contributions of their own; Camille Groult, the vermicelli millionaire, arriving with his wife in an open country cart, chose the onset of the firework display to release twenty-five large white swans. Panic-stricken by the whoosh of rockets and the bedlam of a 200-strong orchestra belting out Offenbach numbers, the birds wheeled wildly, swooping low, to the mounting dismay of eighty picked ballerinas, whose gyrations were mirrored in the waters of the lake.

At a conservative estimate, the evening would cost $250,000 of hard-won Gould money.

As a man who had found it hard to get by on £530,000 a year, King Edward saw Boni as a kindred spirit—just the man, he thought, to take the racing yacht *Britannia* off his hands for £10,000. But Boni had plans of his own. It was beyond his powers to commission a Rembrandt or a Gainsborough, but given the bottomless Gould purse he was in the market for something showier than *Britannia,* namely the 1,600-ton steam yacht *Valhalla,* which mustered a crew of 100, as well as the Castellane's personal suite of valets, lady's maids, manicurists, and secretaries.

To show Edward there were no hard feelings, Boni did follow his suggestion that he should commission and build a racing yacht, the *Anna,* which he accompanied to Cowes for Regatta Week. This, of course, involved a party on board for Edward, though on a relatively modest scale: a Japanese orchestra was imported from Montmartre, and 4,000 tea roses were hastened down from London.

But the true test of Boni's talents as a host was yet to come. The ancestral seat at Rochecotte proving too pedestrian, he snapped up the estate and château at Marais, which were then on the market; here he envisaged a miniature zoo, where "gigantic Nubians wearing plumed red turbans" wandered among "glowing flower beds, holding jaguars and sinuous black panthers in leash." Like many of Boni's fantasies, this was never to be realized; he had to rest content with outfitting the footmen with white coats and pale-blue breeches to harmonize with the château's reseda-colored interior.

For his main efforts—and Anna's millions—were now directed toward the creation of a palace at 40, avenue du Bois de Boulogne, where 300 decorators, metalworkers, sculptors, and plumbers were busily at work on a marble masterpiece: a building harking back to the days of the Bourbons, its magnificent double staircase leading on one side to an immense Salon des Arts, on the other to a 600-seat theater, where Boni, in a new role as impresario, would stage new plays and modern operas. Even the kitchen area would be in white marble, so that the trains of the ladies he took on conducted tours would sweep over the floors "with a sound almost exactly similar to waves breaking gently on the seashore."

It was at No. 40 that Boni staged his famous Flower Dinner Party for 250 guests, followed by a Flower Ball—"Why should flowers be always *inanimate*? So many women have their floral counterparts." Thus the Duchesse d'Uzès came as a red carnation, the Duchesse de la Rochefoucauld as a cornflower, Anna as a scarlet poppy, and Princess Daisy of Pless as a sprig of jasmine. For Boni, such an entertainment was small-scale stuff; his soirées normally involved 2,000 guests, with the hired help on hand to form "a revolving aureole of powdered wigs."

Boni was really an interior decorator manqué; even Elsie de Wolfe, who could command $500,000 for large-scale commissions as early as 1905, thought him a perfect "metteur en scene," skilled in the use of thick ropes of old-fashioned cabbage roses. His plaint was that so many guests who should have known better proved so painfully insensitive. At No. 40, even the marble failed to match up to his standards, but one visitor, finding a panel had been painted over, was crass enough to ask: "What on earth possessed you to *paint marble*?" Boni had to put him in his place. "The marble happens to be too crude for my taste," he replied coldly.

It was the same when King Carlos of Portugal, of all people, on a visit to Marais, totally ruined Boni's color scheme. After the shooting party, Boni had besought all the ladies to change into tea-gowns that would not clash with his resedas, blues, and creams, and all had complied. Then the plump and jovial King chose to appear in a smoking jacket of pillar-box scarlet. It was a gaffe that left Boni pale and speechless for the rest of that evening.

Nonetheless, he congratulated himself that he was "the best investment that the Goulds ever made!" He had, after all, gritted his teeth and sired three sons, Boni, George, and Jay, who were habitually clothed in ermine, and just on the side his drafts on Anna's bank account had passed the $12 million mark in half that number of years.

This, together with his flagrant infidelity, was to bring about Boni's comeuppance.

For Anna, that despised meal ticket, was cannier than he knew.

There was no lack of "good friends" to alert her as to Boni's escapades with Madame Henri de Rothschild and Madame Léon de Jauze, and many, many more. Thus Boni, quite unsuspecting, arrived home at No. 40 one night to find Anna entertaining a young American who had just arrived in Paris. "Let me introduce you to an old friend of ours from New York," said Anna excitedly. "Mr. Herbert J. Perkins," and Boni found himself shaking hands with a handsome stranger in full evening dress, who said, "Happy to make your acquaintance, sir," in the approved Fifth Avenue manner.

After accepting a breakfast invitation, Perkins soon departed and Anna explained her dilemma. Perkins was an F.F.V.—one of the First Families of Virginia—who had recently inherited a large fortune and had come to Europe to have fun, knowing nobody except Anna. "*I* know nobody," Anna complained, "but you do—you know everybody, Boni. Do take him in hand and introduce him about and make him enjoy himself—we've known him at home since he was a child."

Boni was all eagerness. Lately Anna had been tightening her purse strings, but if Perkins had money and wanted introductions, things could be evened up nicely. The first step was to arrange an honorary membership of the Rue Royale Club. Next Boni took him to the racetracks at Longchamps and Auteuil and shamelessly begged for loans—which were freely granted with a "Whatever and whenever you like, my dear Count." Once more Boni had unearthed a cornucopia, and soon Perkins was introduced to both Madame de Rothschild and Madame de Jauze and learned more of Boni's peccadilloes and was made privy by the boastful Boni—"*Foi de gentilhomme,* don't breathe a word of it to anyone"—to letters from these and many other ladies.

That was in December 1905. On Twelfth Night 1906, Boni had a distinct hint that all was not well; he and Anna were dining with the Comtesse Robert FitzJames in her flat in the rue Constantin when a guest asked idly how he had passed his day. "I've been to the Chambre," Boni replied, for he had represented Castellane as a deputy since 1898.

To his consternation, Anna cut in icily, "I don't think Boni has been to the 'Chambre.' The word has two meanings, and I think he prefers a 'Chambre' as a bedroom to a place of legislation."

A troubled silence fell, until it was Boni's lot to draw the Twelfth Night "bean" and toast the guests with the old formula: "The King drinks." Near at hand a woman gave an audible stage whisper, "King today—dethroned tomorrow."

Yet another Dollar Princess had become heartily sick of her investment. On the night of January 26, Boni returned home at 6 P.M. to find No. 40 in pitch darkness; after cutting off the electricity at the main, Anna, his sons, and even the servants had decamped to the Hotel Bristol. Only the boys' tutor, the Abbé Cagnac, reading by the light of a solitary candle, was left to tell him, "She will never return."

Only later—when Anna, who afterward married the Prince de Sagan, sued for divorce—did Boni learn that Herbert J. Perkins, who gave evidence on oath, had been a personable private detective whom Anna had bankrolled to obtain the evidence she needed.

Boni, being Boni, kept his end up. Creditors might seize the *Valhalla*, Guiraud's Gobelins would pass to the head of the House of Morgan, and the Metropolitan Museum of Art, New York, would acquire his Rembrandt; despite all this and the slights that Anna inflicted on him—"My Light That Failed," he called her, echoing Kipling—Boni remained unbowed. For twenty-six years thereafter—he died in 1932—he got by as an antique dealer, advising the new-rich like Nellie Melba on matters of taste, banishing second-rate Louis Seize from their lives and their living rooms.

To the end he was determined to put into practice a suitably Rainbow aphorism coined by Montesquieu: "It is bad enough to have no money, but it would be much worse if one had to deprive oneself of the comforts of life into the bargain."

* * *

It was Princess Daisy of Pless, formerly Daisy Cornwallis-West, who first noticed the danger signs. That was on February 10,

1909, following an official luncheon at the British Embassy on Berlin's Wilhelmstrasse; she and King Edward were sitting side by side on a low sofa, the King drawing deeply on a Henry Clay cigar. Quite suddenly he coughed convulsively, slumping against the sofa back; the cigar rolled from his fingers. In the pale face, the eyes grew staring and dilated; he could not breathe. Both the Princess and Queen Alexandra tugged vainly at his too-tight collar, and the thought flashed through Daisy's mind, "My God, he is dying; oh, why not in his own country."

All at once, he came to, unfastening the collar on his own; later, after his physician, Sir James Reid, had placed him on a special inhaling machine, he seemed to recover. "Please God, this dear, kind, able monarch is not in for a serious illness!" Princess Daisy recorded in her journal. He was not, just then, nor was he dying, but he had barely a year to live.

There were other signs, unperceived by the public, watched with concern by the Queen and the Royal Household. He wheezed, a painful grampus wheeze, whenever he climbed stairs. At luncheon or dinner, even at the opera, he would fall disconcertingly asleep as if a coma threatened. His face was unnaturally drawn; sometimes, fleetingly, he discussed the possibilities of abdication. In Paris, on March 7, 1910, watching Edmond Rostand's *Chantecler*—which bored him stiff—at the Théâtre de la Porte Saint Martin, a chill set in, which worsened into bronchitis. Two days later, in Biarritz, he collapsed, taking to his bed in the Hôtel du Palais.

At Sandringham, toward the end of April, the east winds swirling in from The Wash were treacherous and bitter; inspecting the home farm and pedigree stock, with all his old punctilio, he coughed and gasped painfully. On May 5, for almost the first time, he failed to meet Alexandra, who had hastened back from Corfu, at Victoria Station. "I must fight this!" he repeated doggedly, still, even now, insistent on giving formal, frock-coated audiences. On Friday May 6, at Buckingham Palace, after receiving Sir Ernest Cassel and taking a light tray-luncheon, he once more collapsed while playing with two pet canaries in a cage by an open window. That restless, indomitable heart was giving out.

Now there was little the doctors could do. Oxygen, strychnine, tyramine, ether were all in vain. Only morphia was successful in allaying the massive pain. Still he sat in a chair, resisting all efforts to coax him to bed, protesting, "No, I shall not give in; I shall go on; I shall work to the end."

By Tuesday, May 10, a day of bright morning sun, he was waning rapidly, although still striving for "business as usual," propped in an armchair. Outside the Palace, thousands on their way to work—clerks, costermongers, charladies—paused briefly, keeping a short silent vigil, though there was nothing to be seen. At noon, their death watch had been relieved by others: the gleaming carriages and motorcars of the fashionable, whose world he had epitomized. No one saw another visitor, who slipped in by a side entrance; in a largehearted gesture, the Queen had sent for Alice Keppel before it was "too late."

Soon after 5 P.M., there was one last cheering item of news for him to hear, a whisper from the old pleasure-bent past; his horse, Witch of the Air, had won the spring Two-Year-Old Plate, the 4:15 at Kempton Park, by half a length. "I have heard of it, I am very glad," he told the Prince of Wales, who brought the news. He was to speak no other coherent words or absorb any other conscious thought.

Rain fell softly. Outside the Palace, where headlights flitted across the teeming pavements, a vast crowd shuffled uneasily under umbrellas and newspapers—many of the people in full evening dress, bound for the Savoy or the Gaiety, though somehow this seemed the place to be. In the courtyard, a gifted young reporter, the *Daily Chronicle*'s Philip Gibbs, paced restlessly, lighting cigarette after cigarette; from an inner archway a carriage rolled by, and in the lamplight he glimpsed the tear-stained faces of the Prince of Wales and his wife, Princess Mary of Teck. It was 11:45 P.M.

In the outermost foyer of the Palace, Gibbs sought for late news. Choking back tears, an equerry announced, "Sir, King Edward died two minutes ago."

Appropriately, it was at the Carlton, the hotel that Ritz had created in his image, that two young diplomats, Harold Nicolson and Archibald Clark Kerr, heard the news. They were still dining when a waiter approached them. "The King," he said quietly, "is dead," before switching off Ritz's apricot-pink table lamp.

In the United States, it was as if a president had died. On Broadway, theater orchestras at the Winter Garden, the Casino, and the Criterion spontaneously struck up "God Save the King," and everybody stood in silence. Stock exchanges all over the country suspended business. On Wall Street, flags flew at half-mast; the offices of Pierpont Morgan dripped black crepe.

Only the very young, like nine-year-old Sonia Keppel, Alice's daughter, could not fathom the shroud that had descended on the capital: the drawn blinds everywhere, the dimmed lights, the black ribbon that must be threaded through her underwear. Her mother lay in bed, prostrate, staring at her "without recognition," and Sonia burst into tears, running to her father, the Hon. George, to sob out, "Why does it matter so much, Kingy dying?"

An era was ending as it had begun—with pomp and panoply. At the state funeral, on May 20, more than 28,000 red-coated troops—arms reversed and colors dipped—lined the route from Westminster Hall, where Edward had lain in state, to Paddington Station, where the cortège journeyed by train to St. George's Chapel, Windsor Castle. Behind the khaki-colored gun carriage, drawn by jet-black horses, followed, as was the custom, a riderless horse, Edward's favorite charger, military boots reversed in the stirrups. Trotting poignantly in the rear was a small white terrier, whose collar bore the inscription: "My name is Caesar. I belong to the King."

It was a pageant such as Edward, in life, would have relished—showy, spectacular, larger than life. Never before had nine kings marched together in one funeral procession—including England's new monarch, forty-five-year-old King George V, Kaiser Wilhelm of Germany, the weak, willowy King Manuel of Portugal, who had reigned only two years, the dashing playboy figure of King Alfonso XIII of Spain—along with forty-four crown princes and enigmatic figures like the Archduke Franz Ferdinand of Austria, green plumes fluttering from his helmet, all of them marching with awful finality to the strains of the "Dead March" from *Saul*.

The Rainbow People waited another month before paying their own special tribute—at the Ascot Race meeting, midway through June. They overdid it, of course, as they overdid everything, but this again would have appealed to the King's sense of spectacle. In the week that came to be known as "Black Ascot," gray toppers and colorful silk dresses were nowhere to be seen. Instead, old cronies like the Duke of Portland and Sir Ernest Cassel were clothed from head to foot in black: black silk top hats and black frockcoats, black trousers, black ties, black waistcoats. In their black-gloved hands they held tightly rolled black umbrellas. "The ladies," thought Cecil Beaton, "must have seemed like strange giant crows." Their black dresses were trimmed with long black fringes, they carried black lace parasols, and their wide-brimmed black hats, some of them two yards in circumference, were waving mounds of black ostrich feathers mingled with black tulle. It was a fitting tribute to the "Tum-Tum" they had known and loved.

In a sense it was Alexandra who spoke his epitaph. At first, as he lay on his deathbed, his face "happy and composed" above the collar of a pink shirt, she had, she told Frederick Ponsonby, "been turned to stone, unable to cry, unable to grasp the meaning of it all."

Then her old sparkling sense of humor broke through to aid her and she recalled all the years when her "naughty little man," avidly pursuing his "little toys," had been sighted now in Paris, now in Cannes or Biarritz, before once more moving on.

"Now at least," she told Lord Esher, "I know where he is."

3 / PORTRAIT OF A TRIBE:
The Rainbow People

The King was dead, but in spirit the King lived on—far, far longer than he could have anticipated. Not until Saturday, March 15, 1975, when the Greek shipping magnate, Aristotle Onassis, known to his crowd as "Daddy-O," died in the American Hospital at Neuilly, outside Paris, was that spirit finally extinguished. In the interim sixty-five years, it was alive and well in the keeping of the Rainbow People—and by 1941, James McKinley Bryant's Cafe Society Register was to list 3,000 of them—all of whom had at least one thing in common. In 1975, there was scarcely one of Edward's circle, if alive, who would not have been a welcome guest aboard Onassis's yacht, the 1,700-ton *Christina*. In 1910, had they been in existence, the Onassis set would have been boon companions aboard Edward's 5,500-ton *Victoria and Albert III*.

For they were truly an integral tribe, in whom a gifted anthropologist, a Desmond Morris of the day, would have noted more than a score of distinct characteristics: the ancestors of today's Preppies and Sloane Rangers. Some of them, the purest Rainbows, exhibited all those characteristics, and a few more besides. With others, the quasi-Rainbows, the field narrowed down. Embodying one main characteristic, they more resembled the "Humours" of Ben Jonson: a character representing one individual passion or propensity. Still on the periphery were those sorely tempted, the mini-Rainbows: those lacking the self-confidence, the money, or the opportunity, sometimes all three, to go the whole outrageous hog.

All, in essence, although consenting adults, had never ceased to be spoiled children, as capricious as Edward VII or Onassis himself. Most—though not all—could at times prove impossible to live with.

To thwart them in any way was to provoke a mammoth tantrum. Victor Herbert, the plump jolly composer whose musical *Mlle. Modiste* was the Broadway hit of 1905, might have composed their theme song in his showstopping number, "I Want What I Want When I Want It." For inevitably when a Rainbow person wanted anything, he or she wanted it there and then.

In 1942, at the height of World War II, King Farouk of Egypt, learning that a new inamorata favored Chanel No. 5, rang for his personal pimp, Antonio Pulli, long after midnight, to bespeak the biggest bottle of the perfume he could find. When Pulli replied that in five hours the shops would reopen, Farouk raged, "I don't care if you have to break down doors. Get it now!" It was the same with Alfred de Rothschild, one Saturday morning at Seamore Place; the living-room carpet, he told his aide, Felix Joubet, was a shabby disgrace. When Joubet agreed to replace it in the coming week, the languid Alfred was all steel: It must be done today. At 11 A.M. Joubet sped to Harrods department store to summon a team of carpet layers—who for the sake of speed tacked down the new carpet on top of the old.

Other members of the tribe were yet more exacting. Dmitri Mantacheff, the 6' 6" Siberian oil baron, whose income verged on £25,000 a day, always assumed—correctly—that when he visited Paris, Pierre Cartier's jewelry shop at 13, rue de la Paix would stay open all night. How else could Mantacheff buy a £3,000 bracelet for his girl of the evening at 4 A.M?

As Loelia, former Duchess of Westminster, recalled of her husband, the second Duke, who was nicknamed Bendor after a Derby-winning stallion, "Every passing whim had to be obeyed as if it was a divine command." This was the thinking that prompted Henry de Vere Clifton, the London property magnate, to retain permanent suites at both the Ritz and the Dorchester hotels, eight blocks distant; he explained to the Ritz's hall porter, Victor Legg, "If I'm passing down Park Lane and feel tired, I've got somewhere to go." Or, equally, William Randolph Hearst, on his 600-square-mile estate, San Simeon, in California, instructing an architect to construct a terrace to bolster up a two-mile stretch of fruit trees. When the architect asked why, Hearst was succinct: "I might want to pick one of those tangerines."

A man with the power of life and death could, of course, call his own tune. In 1917, the year of the Russian Revolution, Tsar Nicholas II, dropping into Truefitt and Hill's world-famous hairdressing salon on London's Old Bond Street, decreed that a pretty newcomer, Christine Drew, attend to his manicure. In vain, the management explained that Miss Drew was a counter assistant, not a manicurist; the Tsar was implacable. Nobody but she should work on the Imperial cuticles. For Miss Drew, thereafter, it was uphill all the way; adopted by the peerage, who were lavish with jewels, she lived in splendor in her own house in Paradise Walk, Chelsea.

Such men saw any reverse as a direct challenge to their persona. On one occasion, M. C. Borden, the cotton king, returning to New York aboard his steam yacht, *Little Sovereign*, found himself overhauled on the water by Cornelius Vanderbilt III's *Winchester II*. Promptly, Borden ordered his captain: "Don't stop at the yacht club landing, go on to Seabury's Yard—I want to order a faster yacht." Press baron James Gordon Bennett, Jr., an exile in France since 1877, once entered Maxim's, a Monte Carlo restaurant, to find the terrace tables were for drinkers only. Bennett, intent on dining al fresco on what was his staple diet, a well-grilled mutton chop, took what for him was unusually restrained action; drunk, his progress through the restaurant was marked by an orgy of tablecloth tugging, leaving a devastation of overturned food, wine, and crockery in his wake. Before the day was out he had bought the restaurant, fired the manager, and handed the bill of sale to his favorite waiter, an Italian-born Egyptian named Ciro. "Now you own the place," he commanded. "Get those luncheon tables back on the terrace and go cook my chop."

Thereafter, like Miss Drew, Ciro's Restaurant, at Galerie Charles III, never looked back.

Even "Diamond Jim" Brady, by temperament a placid man, could prove a tartar when his blood was up. On one occasion, his determination to sample a new dish was such that young George Rector, the restaurateur's son, was plucked out of Cornell University and sent all the way to Paris to join the staff of the Café Marguery and pirate their secret recipe for fillets of sole. Two months of fifteen-hour days brought the final revelation: a blend of shrimps and mussels in white-wine sauce with fines herbes.

When young Rector arrived back in New York, "Diamond Jim" ate nine helpings in silence, then delivered his verdict: "George, if you poured that sauce over a Turkish towel, I believe I could eat all of it."

As a tribe they automatically expected the best, and nothing but, in every field of life—a sure stimulus to the Royces and the Ritzes. Charles Ritz, son of César, understood this purism very well, as when he upbraided a *commis* for slicing the toast too thickly: "A poor man may spread his caviar thin, but *our* people want to taste caviar." At times, Rainbows found it hard to explain this fastidiousness to outsiders. Asked how he justified a Rolls-Royce, Bill Ackroyd, personal assistant to the couturier Hardy Amies, could only reply, "You feel such a fool without one." To ensure that his head gardener and fourteen underlings understood exactly how to lay out the flower beds at his Kentish home, Port Lympne, Sir Philip Sassoon bought a stack of Cartier cigarette cases in differing shades, to be used as a color chart before planting. This choosiness extended even to the hired help. When Aline de Rothschild sought a hall porter, she first enquired among her Parisian friends: Did they know of any impoverished nobleman who could fill the bill?

Few men summed up the credo better than one of their favorite novelists, Michael Arlen: "All I want of the world is very little. I only want the best of everything and there is so little of that."

Yet the Rainbow People never ceased to be fascinated by how the other half lived. Alfred de Rothschild always disliked March because it was "the end of the strawberry season," and Leonora, his sister, wondered how it was that people got dead leaves in their parks. Mamie Fish, late in life, saw, for the first time, a woman knitting and exclaimed spontaneously, "Oh, to have the time to do that!" Old John Jacob Astor, who took a genuine interest in his staff, once asked his coachman, William, "Where do you expect to go when you die?" "Why, sir, I have always expected to go where the other people go," William replied, leaving the old man profoundly unsettled. A heaven lacking green baize doors had never once occurred to him.

The Rainbow concept of the simple life was always pitched to the luxury level—a constant throughout the time they held sway. As far back as 1901, "Diamond Jim" Brady was planning a rural weekend retreat for himself and Edna McAuley: "I ain't gonna get anything elaborate—just twenty-five or thirty rooms and a bit of land, say 300 acres." In the twenties, Mrs. Eva Stotesbury, the freest spender Palm Beach, Florida, ever knew, defended the gold-plated plumbing fixtures in her Bar Harbor, Maine, home by explaining, "It saves so much polishing, you know." In the thirties, Prince Alexis Mdivani, first husband of the Woolworth heiress, Barbara Hutton, was well satisfied with the modest $10,000 outlay that brought Jack Harris's band from London to Paris for Barbara's twenty-second birthday: "We didn't think it fitting to spend too much money in these times." As recently as 1968, the Austrian armaments king, Fritz Mondl, showing this writer round a nine-room spread at Cap d'Antibes, responded to a compliment: *"This?* This isn't the *house!* This is just a little place where we change our clothes for the beach."

Their one abiding fear—one they had wholeheartedly shared with King Edward—was boredom. They dreaded that a day would come when Byron's lines would be proven true:

> Society is now one polished horde,
> Form'd of two mighty tribes, The Bores and Bored.

This fear was near-pathological, as the composer Cole Porter was to confess: "I have spent my life escaping boredom, not because

I am bored but because I do not want to be." In later years, when fame was his, Porter would imperiously command friends like the actor Monty Woolley, "Amuse me!"—preempting the right to cut short the conversation if his informant proved less than scintillating. And just as with King Edward, it was easier to weary them than to divert them. Intellectual conversation was out—"As a class, we did not like brains," Lady Warwick once stated flatly—and most books were suspect. In Palm Springs, California, bookstores charged a flat rate for shelves of books, provided the interior decorator approved the jackets—just as Edward VII, when furnishing Sandringham, instructed Hatchard's bookshop to provide books "suitable for a country home." Good music was suspect, too, as no one demonstrated more pointedly than the uncrowned King Edward VIII. "We enjoyed that very much, Mr. Rubinstein," he told the great pianist firmly at one party, after two brief Chopin extracts, dismissing him out of hand, then, once Noel Coward had taken over the keyboard with "Mad Dogs and Englishmen," stayed on into the small hours. "It's a very odd thing about George and music," he once pronounced of his nephew, George Lascelles, seventh Earl of Harewood and managing director of the English National Opera. "His parents were quite normal—liked horses and dogs and the country."

One factor, above all, helped to stave off boredom: the never-ending pursuit of novelty. "What do you have that's new and beautiful today?" Grace Wilson Vanderbilt would enquire of the clerks at Tiffany's, on Fifth Avenue, the sempiternal question posed by all the Rainbow People. Some took advance precautions against the malaise: at his villa at Californie, on the heights above Cannes, the Russian Prince Cherkassy employed forty-eight gardeners to change the flower beds overnight and thus surprise him each dawn. On principle, "Diamond Jim" Brady changed the furnishings of his home on Eighty-sixth Street every September, from cellar to attic. Others never quite knew when the craving might seize them. The eccentric Marchesa Casati, the former Luisa Amon of Milan, who sported tiger-skin top hats or inverted golden wastepaper baskets, once invited a friend on an urgent shopping expedition; she felt an overwhelming desire for "something orange." The entire day was passed in every type of shop—except a fruiterer's—until at last she ran it to earth in an antique shop: a Fabergé cigarette case of orange enamel. Exhausted but content, she returned home.

As the economist Thorstein Veblen put it, "New ways of consumption must be devised from season to season, a never-ending game of invention and excitement must be pursued." Thus the five Dorn brothers, millionaire oilmen of Midland, Texas, once decided that what they needed most in life was a refrigerator that when opened produced a perfect ready-mixed dry Martini. Given Texan know-how, they finally licked the problem, and out came, in due order, onion or olive or lemon peel, a spray of vermouth, and prechilled gin. For three blissful days and nights they threw parties around the clock, until the painful truth dawned slowly: Each time they opened the refrigerator, they did not necessarily *want* a dry Martini.

This quest for novelty led inevitably to what Dixon Wector was to call "sophisticated silliness, especially fun with fauna." Chicago's C.K.G. Billings, the public utilities millionaire, once hosted a dinner at Louis Sherry's restaurant at Fifth Avenue and Thirty-sixth Street at which all the guests, attired in riding costume, dined on horseback, sipping their champagne through long rubber tubes connected to ice buckets stowed in the saddlebags. James Paul, of Philadelphia, had much the same concept in mind when he threw a "Butterfly Ball" for his daughter, Mary Astor Paul; at a given moment, 10,000 exotic Brazilian butterflies were released from a canopy to flutter among the chandeliers. No one had taken into account that the chandeliers were hot—or the disenchanting spectacle of a dance floor littered with 10,000 dead butterflies.

Novelty was responsible for another aberration: what a psychiatrist might have called the Out-of-Season Syndrome. The London Ritz knew that the breakfast table of the Aga Khan, the spiritual head of 20 million Ismaili Moslems, was never complete without green figs and mangoes, so they had them flown in from Bombay. On the glamorous Rome Express, running from London to Naples, the passengers, as a matter of course, ex-

Betty and Ena Wertheimer by John Singer Sargent.

The roulette room of the Monte Carlo casino in 1902.

A shooting party circa 1900 with King Edward VII (*seated centre*), Consuelo Duchess of Manchester (*on his right*) and Alice Keppel (*front row, second from left*).

Edward VII (*third from left*) and, on his left, Lady Arthur Paget (Minnie Stevens) at a Scottish house party shortly before his accession.

Lillie Langtry by Downey.

Mr. and Mrs. Willie James in fancy dress, 1910.

Cowes Regatta, July 1909.

Black Ascot, 1910.

...telier César Ritz.

(*Below*) Peacock Alley in the Waldorf-Astoria, New York, and (*above*) the hotel's famous maître d'hôtel, Oscar Tschirky.

Diamond Jim Brady in 1913.

(*Above right*) Harry Lehr.

Mamie Stuyvesant Fish with her daughter Janet (*left*) in July 1914.

s.Cornelius Vanderbilt, 1939.

Edward and Letitia Stotesbury at the Palm Beach New Colony Club, 1937.

e Breakers, Cornelius Vanderbilt's seventy-room 'summer cottage'.

Kate Meyrick welcomed home from Holloway prison, 1930.

Santos Casani and partner dancing the Charleston on a taxi in London's Kingsway.

pected fresh green peas in November; the solution was to buy them in Brindisi from Corfu shippers and race them to Calais via the Indian Mail. Out-of-season strawberries at £1.25 per dozen—a *commis*'s weekly wage—featured regularly on the winter menus at London's Savoy, as did plovers' eggs, at a guinea apiece, a bargain compared with those James Gordon Bennett, Jr., imported from the Orinoco at $400 a dozen. At Monte Carlo, the teetotaler King Farouk's insistence on fresh raspberry juice all the year round was a sore trial to the Hôtel de Paris, for the juice had to be freshly squeezed, not served from a carton or a bottle. But the Out-of-Season palm undoubtedly went to the Russian Count Apraxine, on a January visit to the Hôtel du Cap d'Antibes. Each winter night, ten fresh strawberries, priced at ten gold francs apiece, were dispatched to his salon. First the Count called for a fork. Then he crushed the fruit to a pulp. He inhaled the fragrance deeply, like a man savoring frankincense or myrrh. Then he sent them back to the kitchen and went to bed.

All through their life-span, the name of the game with the Rainbow People was ostentation. It manifested itself in small ways, as well as in great: in the gold-tipped cigarettes and diamond-encrusted holders of Solly Joel, racehorse owner and impresario, in the nonchalant way that Count von Zernsdorff, at Monte Carlo Casino, lit his cigars with thousand-franc notes, valued at £50. Who you were was how you looked, and Cole Porter's wife, Linda Lee, with her tinted hair and riding in a yellow Rolls-Royce phaeton with an Old English sheepdog perched beside the chauffeur, was worth more than a passing glance—as were her living rooms, with platinum wallpaper, zebra-skin carpeting, and red-lacquered chairs upholstered in white kid. Who you were was where you stayed, which was why the novelist, Arnold Bennett, uncertain of his billet in Munich, told his publisher: "I can't remember the name of the hotel but look for the biggest and most expensive—I'll be there."

Thanks to the fortunes involved, American Rainbows were always slightly ahead of the pack and were vigilant to remain so; as Philadelphia's A. Atwater Kent once told his wife sternly,

"Mabel, you aren't spending enough money." No such accusation could have been leveled against the tobacco baron, Thomas Fortune Ryan, who died worth $135 million. When his wife asked diffidently for a rose garden, Ryan's response was to buy the $1,250,000 Fifth Avenue mansion of Henry Yerkes, the traction king, next door, level it to the ground then call in the nurserymen. The Carrara columns of the grand staircase were retained as an arbor. "They would have been expensive to build," Ryan reasoned.

Such ostentation never caused the Rainbows one twinge of shame. When Mrs. Claude K. Boettcher, one of Denver, Colorado's, ten best-dressed ladies, arrived in Palm Beach, she was taken to task by an eastern grande dame for wearing diamonds in the morning. "Oh no, my dear," she was reproved, "you mustn't. One simply doesn't wear diamonds in the daytime." "I thought not, too," agreed Mrs. Boettcher, all honey, "until I had them."

Seeking novelty, fleeing boredom as Francis Thompson fled the Hound of Heaven, they were a restless breed. The most unstable by far was Bendor, second Duke of Westminster, afflicted, as his Duchess put it, by "mental St. Vitus' dance"; in five years of marriage, Loelia Westminster rarely spent more than two nights under the same roof. On one occasion, between marriages, Bendor had a party of forty guests—none of whom knew one another—at his country seat, Eaton Hall, Cheshire. It was an occasion so dismal that two of the more resourceful guests organized a telegram summoning them back to London. Just as their train moved out of Chester Station, the compartment door flung open and in jumped Bendor. "Oh, how clever of you!" he enthused. "Wasn't it an awful party?"

"I hate a room without an open suitcase in it," Zelda Fitzgerald, the novelist's wife, confessed. "It seems so permanent." She might have spoken for them all; permanence was something to banish from their lives. There was not one second in twenty-four hours that one of the Duke of Sutherland's four Rolls-Royces was not parked on the driveway with its engine turning over; "instant readiness" was the Duke's unfailing motto. There were many like him. Always escaping ennui, the Cole

Porters shuttled from London to Paris to Venice, on to New York, and then back again. As valet to Count Axel de Wichfeld, Ernest King recalled that the Count, the former Mabelle Swift, and an entourage of twenty-nine went to and from London and New York six times a year with 176 trunks, some of them large enough to house a full-grown man. Charles Dean, valet to the dashing Prince Serge Obolensky, who had married Alice Astor, journeyed with them to at least seven ports of call each year; in twelve years' service, Dean made twenty-eight Atlantic crossings, each time supervising ninety-nine pieces of luggage.

Age or youth seemed to make no difference. Not until he was past forty did Society's chosen playwright, Frederick Lonsdale, find staying in one place intolerable, but thereafter the virus was well-nigh incurable; once, arriving at New York's Pier 90 off the *Mauretania*, a £500 return trip, he was met on the quayside by his agent. "What have you come over for?" the agent asked.

"I'm damned if I know," Lonsdale replied. "I think I shall go back again." He did, too, boarding the first ship to leave the harbor.

For a tribe so peripatetic, they were almost never on time. With Rothschild representative August Belmont, this was deliberate; punctuality was for peasants. If invited for dinner at 8 P.M., Belmont arrived at 10 P.M., coincident with the finger bowls. With others, like Queen Alexandra, it was but one more facet of a disorganized existence: Hearst's mistress, the gifted comedienne, Marion Davies, customarily arrived at a theater ten minutes before the final curtain. Napier Sturt, the second Lord Alington, was normally hours, even days, late; once, missing a train from Paris to Venice, he hired a taxi instead. Alice Astor Obolensky usually traveled to dinner parties with her personal maid, Isabella Boyack, in the back seat with her, struggling into her evening clothes and fixing her makeup as the car sped on its way. Lonsdale himself was such a byword for unpunctuality that a luncheon party for ten that he had planned at the Colony Restaurant, New York, never materialized. Not one of his guests had credited he would remember the invitation, let alone be there on time.

For almost all of them, an entourage was important: the

Rainbow People could never, ever, be alone. Marion Davies normally had twenty hangers-on in attendance, but on a trip to Europe she would take at least twenty-six, so that solitude was never her lot. Even in the small hours, Frederick Lonsdale would linger on, talking with a hotel's hall porter, the liftman, or the night waiter rather than retire to bed. "Modern snobbery does not admit of solitude," noted the Society editor of the London *Daily Sketch,* Patrick Balfour, in 1932. "It is held to spell failure." He noted, too, that the average Society woman was "not the unwilling victim of this system. She manufactures it, because she knows that, were she to be left alone, she would no longer exist."

Rather than see her party guests depart, the madcap American actress, Tallulah Bankhead, would turn friends into prisoners, locking their hats and coats in closets and hiding the key to prevent them saying good-bye. Others, like the London hostess, Emerald (Lady Cunard), had ruthless recourse to the telephone, phoning friends at 3 A.M. to discuss a character in Balzac. (A love of books was Emerald's one non-Rainbow characteristic.) When her lady's maid protested, "But, my lady, he'll be in bed and asleep," Emerald would retort, "At two o'clock? Do you think he goes to roost with the chickens?"

This dread of loneliness, like a child's fear of the dark, was a visible token of their insecurity. For the Rainbow People, even the wealthiest of them, were basically vulnerable; when a friend asked Barney Barnato, the diamond magnate, whether he was really worth £20 million, his answer was revealing: he would need at least another £5 million to feel safe. "Really, I am a poor man," Andrew W. Mellon would protest, though his tax return for 1922–23 suggested a $4 million-a-year income, derived from his stakes in Gulf Oil, aluminum, Bethlehem Steel, Pullman, and Westinghouse, to name but a few. Yet Mellon, like most other moguls, needed Duveen, a haughty salesman in a cutaway, to reaffirm his status, through an art collection worth $50 million. Others relied on such arbiters as Oscar Tschirky of the Waldorf-Astoria, or Olivier Dabescat, of the Paris Ritz, whom Harold Nicolson defined as "blending with a masterly precision the ser-

Portrait of a Tribe: The Rainbow People

vile and the protective, the deferential and the condescending." If such maître d's hovered solicitously, the Rainbows were secure for one more day, still part of an exclusive circle that nodded and smiled to one another and knew the waiters by name. As Oscar Wilde had truly said, "To be in Society is simply a bore, but to be out of it is simply a tragedy."

At one and the same time, Joseph Hergesheimer noted, "they were . . . mature and immature, possessing an amazing knowledge of the surface of things together with a helpless ignorance in the face of reality." The most trifling setbacks shattered their composure; Valentine Charles Browne, Lord Castlerosse, the gargantuan gossip columnist of Lord Beaverbrook's *Sunday Express,* often spent out £160 a year to replace golf clubs broken in fits of childish rage at the eighteenth hole. They were happiest in fancy dress costume, a surefire evasion of reality; a die-hard like the photographer Cecil Beaton might go for ten days at a stretch, exchanging one outré costume for another before collapsing into bed at dawn. His young friend, Lady Diana Manners (later, Lady Diana Cooper), was almost never seen in conventional costume; she shrank from life behind a veil of Greek draperies, Eastern djibbahs, and Romanian peasant shirts, at other times disguising herself as a costermonger, a black swan, and as Diana the Huntress, with two greyhounds on a leash.

Often hard and cynical, at other times they were as naive and wide-eyed as children pressing their noses against a toy shop window. A shrewd restaurant manager, Filippo Ferraro of the Berkeley Hotel on Piccadilly, cleverly traded on this when he set a team of *commis* to work, in full view of the street, on a new dish called *Fraises Mimosa:* an eye-catching process of rolling strawberries in powdered sugar, sprinkling them with port, rolling them in sugar again, drenching them with Benedictine, Curaçao, grapefruit juice, and raspberry sauce, topping the finished confection with sliced oranges and powdered cinnamon. The response from the first party of six was immediate: "The rest of the dinner doesn't matter, but we must have those strawberries we saw being prepared from our window at The Ritz."

No caterer dreaming up a children's party could have worked

things better, and the palates of many Rainbows were indeed still nanny-oriented. Few hotels aside from the Savoy and Claridge's were acceptable to Frederick Lonsdale, yet faced with a deluxe menu he settled for boiled eggs or cold chicken. The incomparable Mario Gallati, whose Caprice Restaurant, off Piccadilly, was a magnet for gourmets, knew even so that the Aga Khan would plump for plain roast mutton and plum duff, sundry de Rothschilds for treacle tart, and the oil magnate, Nubar Gulbenkian, son of "Mr. Five Percent," for bacon and eggs and lager.

On the surface, at least, the self-interest of the tribe amounted to megalomania. "He says if he [Bernard] had his life to live over again," Mary Berenson recorded in her journal in 1911, "he would try to marry a woman who had no other thoughts or interests but himself." This was only par for the course; when a cookery columnist asked Nubar Gulbenkian the ideal number for a dinner party, his reply was, "Two—me and a damned good head waiter." Once "Rhapsody in Blue" and "An American in Paris" had achieved international renown, George Gershwin's own ego-trips took some beating. "You've got Gershwin with you, so drive carefully," he would caution anyone offering him a lift, and on an overnight train journey, he peremptorily assigned the upper berth to pianist Oscar Levant: "Upper berth, lower berth—that's the difference between talent and genius."

If truly honest, thought Elsie de Wolfe, all of them would inscribe on their own tombstones: "To the one I love the best." On a transatlantic crossing aboard an ocean liner, W. Somerset Maugham, in conversation with Lillie Langtry, felt totally out of his depth, baffled by the actress's constant references to someone called Freddie Gebhard—actually a playboy New York champagne salesman. When Maugham confessed that he had never heard of Gebhard, Lillie expostulated, "But he was famous on two continents." "Why was he famous?" Maugham wanted to know. "Because," Lillie responded magnificently, "I loved him."

As with most spoiled children, the determination to shock was never far from the surface. When Nancy Langhorne Astor patted the paunch of the overweight Lord Castlerosse, remarking, "If that was on a woman we should know what to say," the peer replied with a lascivious wink, "Half an hour ago it was." Tallulah Bankhead more than got her own back, when the second Lord Alington, her lover, who was escorting his mother, cut her dead in a London night club. "So, Lord Alington," she purred, as she passed his table, "you can't recognize me with my clothes on?" Emerald Cunard was outraged that her rebel daughter, Nancy, served champagne in glasses shaped like a phallus—which, of course, was why Nancy did it. The cabaret star Beatrice Lillie, arriving by taxi at London's Savoy with her Pekingese, Ming-Ki-Poo, was upbraided by the driver who found a spreading puddle on the leather seat. "Now then," he demanded, "what do you mean by letting your dog mess in my taxi?" To the consternation of the doorman, Bea, pressing a handsome tip into the cabbie's hand, confessed, "I did it."

Like sassy children, too, they excelled in the put-down, mostly witty, sometimes spiteful and wounding—another mark of insecurity. "Why, Mr. Arlen, you look almost like a woman," gushed Edna Ferber, spotting the author at a fancy-dress party with a shepherd's crook, to which Arlen responded gravely, "Why, Miss Ferber, so do you." Beatrice Lillie was a past mistress of the art. "Can I drop you somewhere," she asked a bore as a party was ending, "over the George Washington Bridge, for instance?" and she squelched the hostess of another tedious evening, "I've had a lovely party, but this wasn't it." Even tycoons were not immune from temptation. When Hearst had the temerity to cable James Gordon Bennett, Jr., enquiring whether his New York *Herald* was for sale, Bennett fired back: "Price of *Herald* three cents daily. Five cents Sunday."

Sometimes a put-down had racist implications. Importuned for a dance by a Jewish banker in the bar of the Palace Hotel, St. Moritz, Liz Dupont replied: "If you don't go away I'll push you right back into the Old Testament." But more often it was intended to puncture pomposity. When Berenson's friend, the musicologist, Francis Toye, remarked, "You know, I discovered Verdi," Honolulu's leading hostess, Louise Dillingham, shot back,

"How curious—I've heard Verdi's music all my life, but this is the first time I've heard of you." When the Vicomte d'Alte, the minister from Portugal and a regular summer visitor at Bar Harbor, Maine, consistently served only white port at his dinner parties, one British blue blood asked scathingly, "What do you do with your red port?" "What the servants don't require," replied the Vicomte coldly, "I sell to the British nobility."

For the tribe, life was governed by two sets of rules: one that applied to the common herd, the other to Rainbows alone. It was an accepted myth that Rainbows got away with things. When a water shortage beset the Carlton Hotel, Cannes, it never occurred to Castlerosse to suffer along with the rest; ordering 800 bottles of Vichy water to fill his bath, he charged them to Beaverbrook, who was staying in the same hotel. When the actress Gertrude Lawrence faced imminent bankruptcy in 1935, she hit on what seemed an infallible way to reassure her creditors. Along with a reporter from the London *Evening News,* she first inspected a Rolls-Royce in the Conduit Street showrooms, then progressed to trying on a mink coat in Elsa Schiaparelli's Grosvenor Street salon. There followed an impressive order for a silver-fox cape—since *Evening News* readers were not to know that these were four-year-old skins being remodeled.

No one was more astonished than Gertie when her creditors foreclosed and she and her maid, Dorothy, evicted from their Portland Place flat, faced bankruptcy to the tune of £25,000.

At all times the Rainbow People lived by a tacit code of their own. Insincerity was accepted as the basis of all social relationships, for they abided by Oscar Wilde's dictum, "The first duty in life is to be as artificial as possible." "Explaining oneself is the refuge of the weak," Harry Lehr ajudicated, on behalf of "The 400." "It always puts you at a disadvantage." In a later age, Emerald Cunard agreed: "The whole structure of society falls if you start to be sincere." Directly linked to this was the cult of personality, the creation of a new persona for public consumption. Thus the worthily named Florence Nightingale Graham emerged as the beautician, Elizabeth Arden; the Melbourne-born diva, Helen Porter Mitchell, became, by 1918, Dame Nellie Melba; a sea captain's daughter, Jessica Dermot, was transformed into the actress Maxine Elliott, mistress of Edward VII and Pierpont Morgan, with her own theater on New York's Thirty-ninth Street, and an Armenian merchant's son, Dikran Kouyoumdjian, quite understandably became Michael Arlen.

As Noel Coward defined it, in a crash course he gave a bewildered Cecil Beaton aboard a transatlantic liner, nothing less than the creation of an entirely fresh image was called for: "You must appraise yourself. Your sleeves are too tight, your voice is too high and precise." And Coward confessed, "It's hard, I know. One would like to indulge one's own taste," at the same time stressing that one never could. "I take ruthless stock of myself in the mirror before going out. A polo jumper or an unfortunate tie exposes one to danger."

Tolerance of infidelity was a marked feature of their lives. Diana Cooper positively encouraged her husband Alfred's extra-marital dalliances; once, at Lady Cunard's, his suggestive advances to a pretty girl were so apparent that Emerald suggested that Diana might like to take him home. "Why?" said Diana, mystified. "He's not bored yet, is he?" During one weekend house party, when Alfred suggested escorting Ann Charteris to bed, Miss Charteris, wary of a scuffle in the shrubbery, suggested that another guest might accompany them. "Oh, no, don't spoil it," Diana cried, hastening them on their way.

Sir Oswald "Tom" Mosley, although serenely married both to Cynthia Curzon and, later, to Diana Mitford, Lord Redesdale's daughter, doggedly pursued Blanche Barrymore, wife of John, the actor, his stepmother-in-law, Grace Curzon, and a Parisian mistress called Maria. Most wives seemed more concerned that their husbands' mistresses should do them credit. Mrs. Philip Lydig, the former Rita de Acosta, one of the best-dressed of the Newport, Rhode Island, belles, was shocked to learn that her husband was supporting a French ballerina whose taste in clothes was execrable. "I can't have you going around with a creature who looks like that," she protested, and at once furnished an introduction to her dressmaker.

Even so, incompatibility, a by-product of divine discontent, was equally a fact of life among the Rainbows. By 1936, in an effort to straighten out who was—or had been—who, *Fortune* magazine published a marital anthology of the Palm Beach crowd, noting that the former Marjorie Merriweather Post, whose fortune derived from the Postum Cereal Company and the General Foods Corporation, was in fact Mrs. Marjorie Merriweather Post Close Hutton Davies. Equally, the former Mona Strader, daughter of a Kentucky horse trainer, was currently Mrs. Mona Strader Schlesinger Bush Williams. In a sense, *Fortune* had jumped the gun. On her death in 1973, Marjorie was then Marjorie Merriweather Post Close Hutton Davies May. At roughly the same time, Mona was Mrs. Mona Strader Schlesinger Bush Williams Bismarck di Martini, achieving a grand total of three millionaires in thirteen years. It was Mona who went on record in the Depression that she had heroically cut her dressmaker's bill to $20,000 a year.

"As for money," Lady Warwick summed up as tribal spokeswoman, "our only understanding of it lay in the spending, not in the making, of it." In all the venues they frequented, and in every decade, this was true. An impecunious young manicurist in the London Savoy's hairdressing salon, Madeleine Gal, early noticed a trait that was foreign to her: her clients never counted their change. At the Palm Beach Restaurant, Florida, two canny restaurateurs, George Lamaze and Wilson Mizner, acting on a hunch, doubled all their prices overnight, so that even bread and butter cost $1 per head and celery and olives cost $1.50. To their glee, they found their clients never even noticed—and, once they did, openly boasted of the prices they paid.

What was lacking above all was any sense of balance. Few were as wholeheartedly profligate as Count Andor Festetics of the Austro-Hungarian Empire, who would not only lose £5,000 at the racetrack but scatter gold sovereigns all over the paddock, exhorting all those who tried to retrieve them, "Keep them, I've finished with them—I'll get some more tomorrow." More typical was big-scale splurging hand in hand with piffling economies; the pretender to the Spanish throne, Don Jaime, would cheerfully drop £1,000 at Monte Carlo Casino, yet cram his pockets with Ciro's bread in order to feed his chickens. Cloakroom attendants at hotels and restaurants were especially resented. Bendor, Duke of Westminster, who died worth £16 million, was proud that he saved £300 a year by going hatless, and it was noted that Aristotle Onassis thriftily left his overcoat in the back seat of his car.

The Rainbows were renowned for thinking golden. One American tycoon told Eric Asprey that his most urgent need was a gold toothbrush fitting into his waistcoat pocket, to clean his teeth after business lunches, and Asprey obliged with a nine-carat gold telescopic handle and pure bristle head, all reduced to the size of a pill box—a best seller, like their adjustable nine-carat gold collar stiffeners. Playwright Moss Hart always recalled his first "golden" meeting with Cole Porter in the bar of the Paris Ritz. It was Christmas, 1933, and Hart had brought, along with a letter of introduction, a small package from the dancer George Hale: a red leather satin-lined box from Cartier's, containing two gold garters initialed "C. P." To Hart's astonishment, Porter lifted his trouser legs, removed the gold garters he was wearing, replaced them with the new ones—then tossed over the originals as a *pourboire* for bartender Frank Meier.

It was the kind of throwaway gesture at which the tribe excelled. On his first visit to the North London home of the beautician Helena Rubinstein, the interior designer David Hicks asked her what colors she had in mind for her living room. For answer the imperious Helena lifted her purple ribbed silk Cristobal Balenciaga dress, then, with a pair of scissors, sliced a strip from the hem.

"Please weave tweed to this exact color for the walls," was how she wound up the consultation. The prodigality of ruining a $1,000 dress to make her point would never have occurred to her.

For guilt, in the sense of being overly blessed with this world's goods, was an emotion unknown to the Rainbows. Once identity crises were overcome they never doubted that their place was at the top of the heap, as unselfconscious as latter day Bourbons or Hapsburgs. "A man with a million dollars can be just as happy nowadays as if he were rich," Ward McAllister reflected. What mattered was to travel from the cradle to the grave with style and panache.

It was Hearst's New York Society columnist, Maury Henry Biddle Paul, "Cholly Knickerbocker," who best delineated their values: "Nobody cares a damn who you sleep with. In this world, it's who you're seen dining with that counts."

4 / THE WORLD OF LITTLE DAVID:
"All Wars Fought, All Faiths Shaken"

On June 23, 1914, just six weeks before the cataclysm of World War I engulfed first Europe and then the world, he came of age. Two weeks later, on July 7, dapper and diminutive (5' 6") in white tie and tails, he attended his first ball at the town house of Lord and Lady Londesborough. Two days later, he recorded in his diary that he had "become fond of dancing and loved going out." By July 10, he had had no more than eight hours sleep in the preceding seventy-two. Four years after the death of his grandfather, Edward VII, the Rainbows had found a new pack-leader: the twenty-one-year-old Edward Albert Christian George Andrew Patrick David, the new Prince of Wales. Both family and friends, to save time, called him "David."

Although in no sense a worthy successor, David had always adored his grandfather. He had relished the stories of Edward's compulsive philandering and the old man's characteristic mingled aromas of brandy, cigars, and *eau du Portugal;* at Sandringham, in his company, there was a sense of peace and liberation he never knew with his father, the gruff and chilly King George V. Tragically, history was all too soon repeating itself; the stifling soul-destroying routine that had driven Edward into a lifelong search for pleasure would wreak the same mischief with David, a weaker character by far. When Lord Derby once suggested to George V that his regimen was unnaturally strict, the King allegedly replied, "My father was frightened of his mother; I was frightened of my father; and I am damned well going to see to it that my children are frightened of me." It was to prove a royal recipe for disaster.

As a child, onlookers noted, David almost always looked sad. His eyes rarely seemed to focus on those of his interlocutor. "My father doesn't like me," he remarked on one occasion. "I'm not at all sure I particularly like him." What he disliked above all was the negative atmosphere of constant correction, such as the sailor suits with the pockets sewn up so that he could not put his hands in them. At Osborne, once Queen Victoria's summer residence on the Isle of Wight and later a naval preparatory college, and then at the Royal Naval College, Dartmouth, he had chafed against the discipline and protocol; he had shown what his tutor from the ages of eight to twenty, H. P. Hansell, had called "quick intelligence but little concentration." At Oxford, where the slang of 1912 transmuted the "Prince of Wales" to "The Pragga-Wagga," he had for the first time chosen his own friends, and like his grandfather's, few of them had been to the manner born. When a Socialist undergraduate had argued that the monarchy was obsolescent, David, helpless with laughter, burst into "The Red Flag" to his own banjo accompaniment.

By contrast, an Osborne cadet unwise enough to address him as "Your Royal Highness" was punched on the nose for his pains. What David wanted, as he stressed in all his years as Prince of Wales, was freedom from "the tyranny of starch."

At times plagued by melancholia, he rarely smiled. His nervous mannerisms were akin to facial tics; he would tug at his tie, twist his neck like a man whose collar was too tight, grasp his right wrist in his left hand. In the Great War for Civilization, as the Victory Medal styled it, he had sought a frontline role in vain—"What I cannot permit," the Secretary of War, Field Marshal Lord Kitchener, told him, "is the chance of your being taken prisoner." To David this was especially bitter; all his life, problems were most readily evaded by headstrong, impulsive action.

As restless as his grandfather, he was, by contrast, young and lithe and physically always on the go. His concept of luncheon, a hastily snatched apple, would have made Edward shudder, and so, too, would the sheer physical energy he expended: shooting, beagling, golf, tennis, hunting, the soccer field. His passion for dancing amounted to a mania; a tango normally lasted four minutes, yet David was once a fixture on the dance floor of the London Ritz for three tangos that dragged on for thirty-five minutes apiece.

This was in a sense symbolic; David was the pacesetter of an age in flux. On the surface, at least, master and man were returning from the Western Front in 1918 to the same scene they had left four years earlier: the same conventions of dress, the same houses, the same social routine. Yet the old system of prestige could never have quite the same power or meaning again. To the old guard among the Rainbows on both sides of the Atlantic—Grace Wilson Vanderbilt, Sir Ernest Cassel, Mrs. Eva Stotesbury, Alice Keppel—the pursuit of pleasure still had the same materialist connotations: the great houses, the retinues of retainers, the fleets of cars, the Old Masters, and the yachts. But Edward's generation, the Rainbows of the 1920s, were less concerned with great possessions.

His set numbered many of the "New Poor," women who had opened their own dress and accessory shops—women like Mrs. Dudley Coats, whose "Audrey's," in Davies Street, retailed embroidered handbags, and Poppy Baring, whose dress shop, "Poppy's," displayed the latest fashions. The currency of their age was enjoyment, this and the cult of youth. More frivolous even than the Edwardians—and more snobbish—their money was lavished on spur-of-the-moment parties, on stunts and hoaxes, and dancing through the nights and down the days. "New dancers must grow up," *The Queen* rationalized, "to replace the million and a half who sleep forever on the battlefields, and a further million and a half who, lame, blind, disfigured, and paralyzed, still fill a thousand hospitals."

The dances seemed to change with the seasons, the tom-tom throb of jazz replacing the lilting Strauss waltzes, and David took pains to master them all. By 1919, the Maxine, the Boston, the turkey trot, and the bunny hug were already slightly passé; in vogue, briefly, were the Maxina, the Baleta, the Hesitation Waltz, and the one-step. (Only the fox-trot was there to stay.) Dancing without gloves—too costly at around four shillings a pair—was now acceptable, and so, too, was smoking, mostly Turkish and Egyptian cigarettes, while sitting out.

The rhythms of the jog trot and the vampire have long died away, in a way that the reverberations of the Charleston can never do. It was launched, around October 1923, by a young chorine from Bound Brook, New Jersey, Bee Jackson, a performer at such clubs as Gilda Gray's Rendezvous and the Question Mark, who first glimpsed the dance as a high spot in Lida Webb's show *Running Wild* at New York's Colonial Theater. A high days and holidays dance, which originated on the islands of Beaufort County, on the South Carolina coast, its caperings had been known to the Beaufort Negroes for generations, but for Bee Jackson this was "a brand-new dance, a sensation, something that would bring me to the attention of the managers."

And not only to the managers of New York's Silver Slipper and Club Richman, but swiftly to the notice of managers as far afield as Florida, Havana, Paris, and London. One of the earliest converts was David himself; one afternoon a week, at the Café de Paris, he took lessons on the deserted dance floor to the music of a gramophone. The Charleston was suddenly the biggest of business; at 90 Regent Street, Santos Casani, a monocled bantamweight man resembling Erich von Stroheim, had until then been running a two-floor dancing academy with fourteen instructors, averaging ninety lessons a day. Now, as David's zest set the seal on the Charleston's popularity, Casani's daily Charleston lessons alone totaled 280—at a guinea for three lessons—and Casani was buying gramophone needles 50,000 at a time, changing both records and needles fourteen times an hour. To demonstrate the sheer zing of this pagan rhythm, Casani once hired a taxi and with a partner Charlestoned on its roof down the length of London's Kingsway.

It was an age ripe for sensation—any and every sensation. The very smartest aberration was drug-taking; even before World War I, opium dens had thrived in Paris, and cocaine and morphia had not been uncommon. A *Punch* cartoon of 1911 had shown two matrons at a garden party, discussing another of decadent appearance: "If only it were chloral; or even morphia. But laudanum, my dear—laudanum is so frightfully middle-class." Though David was to resist this temptation—unlike his brother, Prince George, later Duke of Kent—drugs were increasingly a part of the London scene. Lady Diana Cooper, like most of her crowd, indiscriminately sought highs on morphia, chloroform, and even a mixture of brandy and sal volatile.

On both sides of the Atlantic, mores were changing at the frenetic speed of the new Jazz Age. Divorce was now an accepted fact of life. In the United States, the rate was rising steadily, from one in ten, in 1914, to one in six by 1928. By 1927, mandatory residence in Reno, Nevada, was reduced from six months to three, though to save themselves trouble, rifting Rainbows had always favored a Paris divorce. Nor was the situation more stable in Britain. From 1918 onward, divorces increased steadily, until by 1928 the annual rate was 4,000, 80 percent of them undefended.

"Here was a new generation grown up to find all gods dead, all wars fought, all faiths in man shaken," wrote F. Scott Fitzgerald, the novelist who gave the Jazz Age its name, an age that historian Frederick Lewis Allen was to call in retrospect "an era of tremendous trifles," when "the outside world, so merciless and so insane, was shut away for a restless night." Since David and his set were by nature tremendous triflers, they had come into their own.

Rarely had the art of the trivial been cultivated so assiduously. There was, briefly, a craze for the pogo stick, said to have emanated from France: a pole with a crosspiece at the bottom to secure the feet, and a strong spring to facilitate jumping. The upper part of the pole was grasped with both hands. A "Stars' Pogo Race," when two musical comedy players, Mona Vivian and Reginald Sharland, raced each other down the street outside London's Hippodrome Theatre, was deemed to be headline material, for both David and his cousin, Lord Louis Mountbatten, were adept performers. That was in 1921; by 1923, a new and less exacting craze had swept first the United States, then Europe—Mah-jongg.

This was a Chinese game, played with chips and domino-like ivory or bamboo counters, at which the Rainbows excelled; Lady Diana Cooper, Olga "Oggie" Lynn, and Tallulah Bankhead all vied with one another to call "pung," "Quong," or "Chow," when particular sets were completed, or talked cryptically of "The East Wind," "The North Wind," and "Red and Green Dragons." Rainbows like Mrs. Eva Stotesbury bought sets priced at $500 and enrolled themselves in the Mah Jongg League of America. And along with Mah-jongg and the Charleston, other fads and fancies came and went, as transient as winter sunshine: face-lifting, a fashion set by the American actress, Fanny Ward, though her neck, noted the columnist, Beverley Nichols, "was a perfect maze of scars"; the fashion for dark sunglasses with white rims, and beach pajamas of bright printed cottons; for lilliputian dogs, like those of the cocotte Gaby Deslys, who swathed her Chihuahuas in dark Russian sables; for artificial sunlamps; and, above all, for slimming. The gourmandiserie of Edward VII was now old hat; it was fashionable to emulate David's bird-like appetite. In a *Punch* cartoon, a lady in a doctor's consulting room, asked whether she drinks at meals, replies, "Don't be silly, doctor, I don't even *eat* at meals!"

A new figure on the American scene was the analyst, glib with his Freudian fulminations on masochism, inferiority complexes, sadism, Oedipus complexes, and the uninhibited sex life. Of course, Rainbow women like Mrs. Harrison Williams and Mrs. William B. Leeds, wife of the tin-plate king, had to go one better; they went to Paris or Vienna to have their "ids," "egos," and "libidos" pronounced upon. Another fad, persisting into the thirties, was to simulate Bohemianism, renting a studio in Chelsea or Greenwich Village to give "amusing" parties and use everyday implements in an unconventional way: spreading butter with a cutthroat razor or drinking tea from a brandy glass. Some Rainbows jibed at this; Diana Cooper had secretly envied the over-the-top life-style of Lady Cunard's rebel daughter, Nancy, until she went to help clear up after a party at Nancy's studio at 8 Fitzroy Street: "Champagne bottles broken at the neck to save the trouble of drawing the cork, pools of blood and vomit, frowsty, unmade beds, a black velvet divan thick with dust." The Bohemian life, Diana decided there and then, was not for her.

In London Society, stunts and hoaxes were now a way of life, as if a latter-day Harry Lehr had become Master of the Revels. The acknowledged past master was Horace de Vere Cole, an Old Etonian, then past fifty, with an imposing mane of white hair and sparkling blue eyes; disguised as "the Anglican Bishop of Madras," Cole had once descended on the old school to confirm a bunch of Etonians. A professional prankster, he passed his nights haunting houses, armed with bell, candle, and shroud, but his days were also given over to the really hard graft of a full-time funny man.

On one occasion, posing as the Sultan of Zanzibar, he ceremonially inspected Cambridge University. As a brother-in-law of the Chamberlain family, with many parliamentary connections, his favorite ploy was to challenge an M. P. to a race down Whitehall—then slip a gold watch into the M. P.'s pocket and set up a cry of "Stop, thief!" His finest hour came when he reviewed H.M.S *Dreadnought* at Weymouth on behalf of the Emperor of Abyssinia. His party, which included the novelist Virginia Woolf and her husband Leonard, clambered aboard the Admiral's pinnace, all of them robed and wearing coffee-colored makeup, conversing in a gibberish patois based on the phrase "Bonga-bonga," their hoax rewarded, on departure, by a twenty-one gun salute.

On both sides of the Atlantic, it was preeminently the decade of bad manners. Driving in open cars, David's set delighted in the childish game of "Beaver"; the first to spot a bearded man and yell "Beaver!" scored a point, though a red beard, or "Beaver Royal," scored five. At other times they indulged in an adolescent game of Follow-My-Leader, two dozen strong, along the counters of Selfridge's department store, and once, with the help of sixteen gallons of gasoline, literally "set the Thames on fire" at Henley. Above all, wherever Rainbows were gathered together, there was always an excuse for a party.

"There were," wrote Evelyn Waugh, in his telling satire of the time, *Vile Bodies*, "Masked Parties, Savage Parties, Victorian Parties, Greek Parties, Wild West Parties, Circus Parties, almost-naked parties in St. John's Wood, parties in flats and studios and houses and ships and hotels and night clubs, in windmills and swimming baths." And this brief catalogue only scratched the surface. There were parties at which David appeared as a Chinese coolie—his impassive face strikingly effective—along with Winston Churchill as Nero, and parties at which Cole Porter appeared as a youthful David, in Eton collar and knee pants. There was Mrs. Rosemary Sandars's Baby Party at London's Rutland Gate, where everyone arrived with dolls and comforters, swigging gin from their feeding bottles. There was another Cole Porter party, aboard a docked barge on the Seine, when Stravinsky took a flying leap through a laurel wreath and Picasso created "instant art" from children's toys.

Given the perfect gimmick, such parties took care of themselves, and no one was more adept at dreaming them up than Elsa Maxwell, an overbearing and overweight one-time nickelodeon pianist from Keokuk, Iowa. An inspired organizer of charity drives in World War I, the surest passport to international society, Elsa, who dominated the party scene for three generations (she died in 1963), was really a female Harry Lehr—not an unjust comparison, since Elsa was as blatantly butch as Lehr was gay. An early success was her Parisian As-You-Were-When-The-Autobus-Called Party, when the guests, knowing only that a charabanc would call at an unspecified hour, came in whatever attire was theirs when the horn tooted. Thus one woman arrived with only one side of her face made up, a man clad only in shaving soap and a hotel towel, and several women with half-fastened skirts.

Then there was Elsa's Come-As-Somebody-Else Party, at which the hostess impersonated Herbert Hoover and Mrs. G. F. Vanderbilt Bishop Manning; her Come-As-The-Person-You-Like-Best-Or-Least Party, which Elsa graced as the French Premier, Edouard Herriot, and the stag party she gate-crashed by posing as Albert Einstein. This undoubted talent for what she called "offering escape from plush-lined boredom" paid handsome dividends all her life: it was the Harry Lehr pattern all over again. Elsa organized the parties; others, like the wealthy fortune hunter, Jay O'Brien, footed the bills, and there were other perks besides. At Maxim's, on the rue Royale, no bill was ever presented to Elsa, even when a dinner party for eighteen was involved; at the Waldorf-Astoria, from 1931 onward, she lived rent-free. In postwar years, despite her Michelin-tire proportions, she rated fourteen free dresses a year, valued at $1,100 each, from the couturier Jean Dessès. Sponging shamelessly on her wealthy friends, and duly sponged on in turn, she was, as one critic phrased it, "a preacher whose invocations, not of hell but hedonism," fetched her hearers to "a pitch of hypnotic frenzy"; a monstrous woman in every sense "who had never been any closer to life than a dinner table."

But there were many other party-givers aside from Elsa. Diana Cooper favored motorized midnight treasure hunts, when a cavalcade of fifty cars set off, their occupants disembarking at intervals to prowl the pavements, sometimes on their hands and knees, in search of elusive clues scrawled in chalk—a will-o'-the-wisp chase that might lead from the Achilles Statue in Hyde Park to the Tate Gallery, thence to the Pensioners' Garden in Chelsea and a pillar-box in Woburn Square. It was as good an excuse as any for staying out until 4 A.M.

Incredible sums were lavished on costumes and decorations. Mrs. Florence Hwfa Williams, a survivor from the Marlborough House set, once paid the French couturier, Paul Poiret, £70 to disguise her as a macaw: a short, tight maillot, wings of purple chiffon, and a curved parrot's beak secured to her forehead. At another party, Mrs. Irene Stewart, wife of the motor magnate, materialized as a cocktail, wearing a white, glass-shaped chiffon skirt and a green velvet cap decked out with a cherry and an olive. At one of Diana Cooper's favorite parties, thrown by the Ronald Trees at Ditchley Park, a huge tent of white muslin was erected on the terrace, and decorated by the fashionable designer, Oliver Messel, with Negro heads sporting feathered hats and ropes of pearls. Also on the agenda were fireworks and flowers by Constance Spry; the ladies, by request, wore red and white, and Messel himself arrived in a white suit and a red tie, his eyelashes painted silver. "Bugger ought to be thrown in the lake," muttered a scandalized peer.

Even the twenties saw ruinously extravagant parties, in the Boni de Castellane tradition of a quarter of a century before. At one, given by Paul Poiret, 300 guests watched the dawn break over his garden in Faubourg Saint-Honoré, attended by black slaves serving dishes at tables seventy-five feet long. An actor, his costume shimmering and shaking with thousands of pearls, recited near-inaudible poems—thanks to the eldritch chattering of a minimenagerie of parrots, cockatoos, and monkeys. Among them the guests ate 300 lobsters—one apiece—and drank 900 liters of champagne, while Poiret, from the splendor of a throne, surveyed his little empire serenely. Not surprisingly, his rival, Jean Patou, attempted to go one better: walls, ceilings, trees, even twigs were draped in eye-dazzling silver foil, and at the climactic raffle, the winners, like it or not, drew a live lion cub.

But costume parties were by no means the prerogative of Parisians. For New York's Beaux Arts Ball, the peak of the social calendar, held first at the Astor and later at the Waldorf-Astoria, Mrs. S. Stanwood Menken, the star performer, pondered for almost 364 days and nights before deciding what this year's costume would be. No such delicious uncertainty marked the parties given by William Randolph Hearst and Marion Davies at Marion's ninety-room Santa Monica beach house. Whatever Marion's guise—often it was Little Lord Fauntleroy—Hearst stuck doggedly to impersonating the one figure in history he hero-worshipped: Napoleon.

Not all British parties were so costly: the keynote was eleventh-hour improvisation. Parties featuring stuffed animals, such as golliwogs or bulldogs, were hugely popular, as were Gate Crashing Parties, when the Bright Young Things, as the London press called them, rampaged through Mayfair in evening dress, invading any function to which they had not been invited. At one Sign of the Zodiac Party, the Sitwell brothers, Osbert and Sacheverell, with crowns of stars three feet high, wore black and gold as the Heavenly Twins, and Cecil Beaton, in gold and silver with a horned mask, was Aries. More confusing was Captain Neil McEachern's party, when Brian Howard, a well-known homosexual-about-town, went as the Duchess of Portland, Oliver Messel as Tallulah Bankhead, and Tallulah herself as the tennis ace Jean Borotra, in a beret and white flannels.

No matter what the costume, the masquerade must never cease; night after night the parties must go on, and David, or "The Little Man," as his set called him, attended far more of them than his censorious father deemed proper. Another of the set, who yet found his charm resistible, dubbed him "Peter Pan." But many among the Rainbows would have echoed Peter's cry: "No one is going to catch me and make me a man. I always want to be a little boy and have fun."

* * *

All through the twenties, David was on the move. He was the British Empire's "traveling salesman," Prince Charming in plus fours, beloved for his tow-colored hair and diffident smile, whose travels began in 1919 with a goodwill visit to Canada and a side trip to the United States, where young Rainbows were soon copying his burgundy carnation in his buttonholes. A year later, he was in New Zealand and Australia; in 1921, in India. On occasion, a wild streak was noticeable: in Budapest, after a bender on Imperial Tokay, he stood at his hotel window letting fly at the street lamps with a shotgun, and the police had to clear the pavements. In nightclubs he was insistent on standing in for the jazz drummer. Yet the crowds took him to their hearts.

When he returned to America in 1924, he socialized more widely; he was seen at the races in Belmont Park, in August Belmont's box, and the Clarence Mackays gave a dance for him at their Versailles-style residence. Frank Crowninshield's New York magazine, *Vanity Fair,* was enchanted by him and came up with some spoof statistics: he had been photographed 2,754,911 times, laid 7,003 cornerstones, survived 2,431 hunting accidents, been proposed to by 4,187 girls, kissed 2,329 blondes, and downed 19,218 quarts of champagne. "Hats off," *Vanity Fair* wound up, "to the indestructible Dancing Drinking Tumbling Kissing Walking Talking and Sleeping—but not Marrying—idol of the British Empire."

His father's verdict, if harsh, was percipient: "After I am dead the boy will ruin himself in twelve months."

The "not marrying" parenthesis was a shrewd shaft, for David had a lifelong quirk: He was fated to fall in love only with married women. From 1918 to 1934, the love of his life was to be Freda Dudley Ward, who was twenty-five when they first met, romantically, in a cellar at the height of a London air raid. The disaffected wife of a Liberal Member of Parliament, Freda, whom Lady Cynthia Asquith disparaged as "a pretty little fluff," was in reality a woman of acute intelligence, the fulcrum of David's life—exactly as Alice Keppel had been Edward's.

"I don't want to be King," David had told Elsa Maxwell as early as 1927, "I wouldn't be a very good one," and it was almost as if his choice of married women—for divorcees were barred from even the Royal Enclosure at Ascot—was his subconscious means of making that accession impossible.

Between public engagements, his life was often aimless. From his bachelor quarters at York House, St. James's Palace, he would stroll to the Turkish Baths on Jermyn Street, to idle away the hours, before gravitating to Alfred Dunhill's, though unlike his brothers, Prince George, Prince Henry (later, Duke of Gloucester) and Prince Albert (later, King George VI), he firmly refused the privilege of the Royal Pipe Drawer. What the average customer was offered was good enough for him. As much of a dandy as his grandfather, he would then drift on to the Piccadilly Arcade emporium of the shirtmakers Ralph Hawes and Freddie Curtis, who had opened up in 1913; since David had been an early customer, 12,000 others were now on their books. A new Hawes and Curtis line that he favored was their comfortable backless evening dress waistcoats, in eighteen varieties at three guineas apiece; their best silk evening dress shirts retailed at four guineas, and David would order them six at a time, returning them at intervals for laundering.

From Hawes and Curtis he would move on, as Edward had

done, to his tailor, Henry Poole, in Savile Row, the recipient of fully thirty-six royal warrants, then finally to his hatter, James Lock, of St. James's Street. Once, the staff recalled, he arrived with a coke (bowler) hat in a paper bag, announcing laconically, "The bloody thing doesn't fit." A few minutes in the kiln room, and this was righted; leaving his paper bag behind him, David departed.

These were his daytime diversions; his evenings and nights were devoted to Freda.

Each day when in London, punctually at 5 P.M., he called at the Dudley Ward home at 42 Great Cumberland Place, often staying to dine or take Freda out to dinner. If a public engagement prevented this, he returned later that evening. When Freda took a summer house at Sandwich, in Kent, David did the same. If Freda was invited to other people's parties, David was there, too.

Every Thursday night saw a scramble for tables at London's exclusive Embassy Club at 6–8 Old Bond Street, a long, underground room with beige, mirror-lined walls and red velvet banquettes; on this night, the table on the left of the door was sacred to David alone, so to be present at one and the same time was a kind of accolade. (Only four other men, his brother Prince George, his cousin, Lord Louis Mountbatten, Bendor, Duke of Westminster, and King Alfonso XIII of Spain, were equally favored.) Normally, David arrived unannounced, at 11:45 P.M., along with the same party of friends bearing neo-Wodehousian names, "Fruity," or Major Edward Dudley Metcalfe, "Burghie," otherwise Vere Anthony Francis St. Claire Fane, fourteenth Earl of Westmorland, "G," or Brigadier Gerald Trotter, David's assistant comptroller, and Freda. He seldom ate, although London's 1921 Licensing Act decreed that unwanted sandwiches must be served with drinks after 11 P.M. and glasses removed by 12:30 A.M. This way of life David had come to accept; until 12:30 A.M., he would drink champagne then switch to brandy camouflaged by teacups.

Those Rainbows privileged to secure tables—Nubar Gulbenkian, Prince Aly Khan, son of the Aga, the Countess of Portarlington, an Australian so rich she was reputed to live on the income from her income, Lord Louis Mountbatten and his wife, Edwina, who had inherited the bulk of the £7,500,000 left by her grandfather, Sir Ernest Cassel—followed the same routine.

The man sifting the grain from the chaff in this *beau monde* was of strictly peasant stock: Luigi Naintre, an Italian once rejected for Savoy service by César Ritz on account of his fractured English. A small, sharp-eyed man, the image of Arturo Toscanini, Luigi had learned his English the hard way, as a six-shilling-a-week footman to a Hampstead doctor; moving on to Romano's, in the Strand, then to the east room at the Criterion, he had bought out the Embassy's owner, the showman Albert de Courville, for more than £18,000 in 1923. Now, assured of David's patronage, his autocracy was absolute. Prosperous tradesmen, well able to afford Luigi's *Mousse de Homard à la Darryane* (a lobster and cream confection with paprika, garnished with fried oysters) and his champagne at twenty-five shillings a jug, would still eat screened from the quality by the bandstand. Rainbows owing them money might otherwise have their enjoyment marred.

It was the same with the Embassy's bandleader, the arrogant and talented Bert Ambrose. A request from David was at once a command; a request for a rhumba, along with a £5 note, merited consideration; a request accompanied by a pound note saw it stuffed contemptuously back into the dancer's top pocket. Pound notes were for taxidrivers and cloakroom attendants, not for David's favorite bandleader, already, in 1927, pulling down £10,000 a year.

For where Prince Charming went, the carriage trade would follow, and the staffs took infinite pains to humor his whims. Police raids to check branches of the licensing laws were not uncommon, even at the Kit-Kat Club, off the Haymarket, whose membership included thirty peers; between 1924 and 1928 alone, sixty-five clubs were prosecuted. Victor Legg, now head porter at the London Ritz, has recalled how he and other staffers sat on a Kit-Kat sofa all through one raid, swinging their legs, while David crouched ignominiously beneath. In 1928, the Quaglino brothers, whose restaurant in Bury Street he favored, went further still; they built a private annex for David to dine without evening dress, freed from "the tyranny of starch."

A hit song of the time ran, "I danced with a man who's danced with a girl who'd danced with the Prince of Wales," and proof that his presence could switch a nightclub dramatically from the red to the black came with the Café de Paris on Coventry Street. Opened in 1928 by Martin Poulsen, Luigi's Danish former head-waiter, and modeled—inexplicably—on the Palm Court of the ill-fated liner *Lusitania,* the Café swiftly fell on hard times, despite such comely hostesses (working for £2 a week and their supper) as Estelle O'Brien Thompson (later, Merle Oberon) and Nora Turner (later, Lady Docker).

When the club was £10,000 in the red, Poulsen, despite the remonstrations of his business associate, Henry Stephenson, rang David at York House. "Your Royal Highness," he reminded him, "you promised me that if I ever opened up my own place you would pay it a visit."

"Well, where are you?" David asked, and Poulsen told him.

"When do you want me?"

"As soon as possible, Your Royal Highness. Things are desperate for me."

David was practical. "If I am going to be of any use to you, Poulsen, you want time to tell people that I'm coming and also let the news get around generally."

"Would next Wednesday, the extension night, be convenient?" Poulsen pleaded, and David confirmed that it would.

Poulsen took a gamble. With the help of an Embassy mole, he secured Luigi's top-secret address book of club members and sent telegrams to 400 of them, guaranteeing a free evening at the Café de Paris. Then, on the morning of Wednesday, July 31, 1929, disaster threatened. A pipe in the Rialto Cinema, sited overhead, had burst and water was sluicing down the famous semicircular staircase onto the dance floor. Working with sandbags to stem the flow, stretching canvas tightly over the floor, and rubbing in French chalk, Poulsen contrived what he thought was an apology for a dance floor.

About 300 Embassy Club members took up their invitations, setting Poulsen back a further £2,000—but where was David? The evening seemed to stretch forever, but at last he came—along with the bookmaker, Lord Graves, Brigadier Trotter, Audrey Dudley Coats, a Society beauty, and Freda. To Poulsen's consternation, he was no sooner settled at the right hand banquette than he took to the dance floor.

He danced for more than twenty minutes nonstop. Then he beckoned Poulsen over. "Yours is the best surface on which I have ever danced," he told the incredulous Dane. And Freda, tiny, dark, and composed, smiled, too. If David was happy, then so was she. Things were as simple as that in Rainbowland.

* * *

As much as any of her American contemporaries—Mrs. Harrison Williams, Alice Astor Obolensky, Nonnie May Leeds—Freda Dudley Ward exemplified the New Woman. Although denied the vote until 1929—only Englishwomen over thirty had won that right in 1919—she knew a freedom of style and fashion quite alien to her corseted, chaperoned predecessors.

She was pictured in tight-fitting cloche hats, for these were universal, though by 1927 the crowns were marginally shallower, the brims larger. Her lingerie was provocatively feminine, featuring ice-cream shades of coffee, pistachio, and strawberry, a natural successor to the crepe de chine petticoats and "underwear as delicate as cobwebs" that the Maison Lucile of Lucy, Lady Duff-Gordon had pioneered at the turn of the century. Her skirt lengths could have been charted almost by graph. By 1920, they were nine inches off the ground, and climbing higher; by 1927, they had reached the knee and there they would stay until 1929. Her shoes were high-heeled, even for dancing; heels were at first curvy, in the Louis XIV style, though squatter, Cuban heels, for sports and walking, were fashionable from 1922. Ornate pearl and diamanté buckles were the modish evening wear.

As Edward Rayne, whose parents' Waterloo Road shoemakers had always catered for the theatrical profession, explains: "Until female emancipation, exciting shoes had only been worn by actresses and ladies of easy virtue." By 1920, Rayne, who merged with the New York firm of Delman in 1961, had undergone a sea change. At 58 New Bond Street, their three-guinea models in new and exciting materials were precisely what Freda and her kind were seeking: sea-leopard, ostrich, zebra, dolphin, and Siberian pony.

It was a fertile field to till; fortunes were to be founded on finding favor with women like Freda Dudley Ward. In 1910, a landmark year, Florence Nightingale Graham, the thirty-two-year-old truck driver's daughter from Ontario, Canada, who had rechristened herself Elizabeth Arden, had laid the foundations of her New York empire, borrowing $6,000 from a well-heeled cousin, a loan she repaid in six months. A small (5' 2") trim woman with a round, kittenish face and bright, beady eyes, she was superficially a sentimentalist, who would weep copiously all through a performance of *Madame Butterfly*. As a business woman she was as abrasive as carborundum; out of six general managers hired in four years, five had quit or been banished forever from the gleaming red front door at 691 Fifth Avenue. The fast-growing world of cosmetics soon had a word for it: "Work for Elizabeth Arden and live in a revolving door."

Her initial secret was her facial massage technique; her first face creams had been copied from those of a business partner, Elizabeth Hubbard, who went broke in 1916. An adept plagiarizer who was swift to learn, Miss Arden, on an early trip to Paris, visited four beauty salons each day to buy up creams and perfumes and study how the job was done. Ideas were not slow to formulate. By 1915, she knew what she wanted: "a face cream that's light and fluffy, like whipped cream." When an industrial chemist, A. Fabian Swanson, came up with that requisite "whipped cream," Miss Arden never looked back.

Where London was concerned, she moved cautiously—perhaps too cautiously. By 1920, she had branches in Paris and Nice, but only in 1922, twelve years after opening her Fifth Avenue salon, did she open up at 25 Old Bond Street. For the British, cosmetics had long exuded a delicious aura of sin, like Rayne's "exciting" shoes; the choice had been limited. There was Willie

Clarkson's Lillie Powder, named after Mrs. Langtry, tinted with minute quantities of carmine and sienna, admixed with talc and melted lanolin. Aside from this, there were also Sarah Rachel Leverson's "rachel" face powder, a shade still known today, and Mrs. Frances Hemming's South Molton Street salon (later the House of Cyclax), whose clients arrived, to sample three shades of rouge, heavily veiled, through a backdoor entrance, like the habitués of a high-class brothel.

By the time Miss Arden hit the London scene, a formidable rival, six years her senior, was already firmly established there: a petite (4' 10"), implacable Pole, with an accent as thick as borscht, named Helena Rubinstein.

From her first salon in Melbourne, where Nellie Melba was an early client, Miss Rubinstein had stormed London as early as 1908, renting the twenty-six-room Mayfair mansion of Lord Salisbury on Grafton Street. In New York, by contrast, she was a late starter; her West Forty-ninth Street salon opened only in February 1915.

For five years, from 1915 to 1920, Arden and Rubinstein waged a bitter no-holds-barred battle for the complexions of Freda and her liberated sisters. It was still considered "fast" to powder one's face in public, and lipstick was a more dubious commodity still; Arden's first British advertisements, in 1922, were for face powder and eyelash dye only. Ten years would pass before 1,500 lipsticks were selling in the London shops for every one sold in 1921.

Though Rubinstein scored some creditable firsts—the matte look, the first colored foundation and face powder, waterproof mascara, a perfume called Heaven Scent—the subtle edge was with Arden. From a modest $200 trial sale to Harrods department store, she was to become the world's biggest cosmetic manufacturer; by the thirties, almost 400 Rainbow women a day were flocking to 691 Fifth Avenue, half of them to sample the "Vienna Youth Mask," an application of diathermy techniques to the face, costing $200 for six treatments. From a $17 million business in 1914, the U.S. market alone had topped $141 million by 1925.

Such profits enabled both rivals to achieve a Dollar Princess's dream; Miss Arden married and divorced Prince Michael Evanloff, while Miss Rubinstein, in 1937, married Prince Artchil Gourielli–Tchkonia, who generously lent his name to a shaving cream. Both, when they died—in 1966 and 1965, respectively—left multimillion-dollar empires.

In this same era, at 5, rue Cambon, Paris, another martinet was wreaking a quiet revolution in the world of coiffure, experimenting on such complaisant Rainbows as the Princess de Faucigny-Lucinge, the former Baba d'Erlanger, and the Hon. Mrs. Reginald Fellowes, the former Daisy Décazes. Born the son of a Polish shoemaker in 1884, Antek Cierplikowski, known always as Antoine, was, from 1905, to hairdos what Ritz had been to hotels: a quiet and dedicated revolutionary. From the first, he worked closely with the great milliners like Reboux, whose clients such as Lady Michelham and the Princess Odescalchi bought sixty hats at a time. Early recognizing that short hair, like the shorter skirt, was an outward sign of freedom, Antoine was the first to pioneer the bob (by 1912), the shingle (by 1923), the Eton Crop (1926), all of them attuned to the close-fitting cloche, the longer shingle (1929), and the windswept look (1931). Later still, he introduced lacquer hairsprays, the poodle cut, frosted nail varnish, the lilac rinse—tried out on the hindquarters of his Borzoi, then adopted by Elsie de Wolfe—the V-line, the Amphora, the *jeunesse*, and the beehive.

Such chic did not come cheap: at "Antoine's Fountain," as his circle of five spouting washbowls was called, special hairdos for clients like Sarah Bernhardt and Mistinguett were priced at $100 even before World War I. But most felt it was worth it; snug in one of Antoine's pale-blue peignoirs, soothed by peony-red carpets and silver blue walls lined with Modigliani paintings, more than one pampered client was heard to murmur, "I feel as though I'm at home, only here I have no servant problems." A certified eccentric who slept each night in a crystal bed, Antoine always had the last word. A desolate cry of "Please, Antoine, don't cut that curl!" was countered with a reproving, "Madame, you don't tell your surgeon when to amputate."

In the world of haute couture, after much trial and error, a total break with the past was equally in store for the Rainbow women.

Many had sought to wrest the palm from the House of Worth, whose crinoline, created for the Empress Eugénie in 1860, had, in effect, become the firm's albatross. In the boom years they had ridden high, favored by Lillie Langtry, *the* Mrs. Astor, Consuelo, Duchess of Marlborough, and Nellie Melba, but none of these women in 1920 were now trendsetters.

One man who had early seen the shape of things to come was Gaston Worth, younger son of the firm's founding father, the Englishman Charles Frederick; not only had most great ladies of the Empress's time got past the latest fashions but many could not even pay their bills. As Gaston put it to Paul Poiret, the young designer he lured from the couturier, Doucet: "We are like a great restaurant which would refuse to serve anything but truffles. It is therefore necessary for us to create a department for fried potatoes." Even princesses, he pointed out, "occasionally take the bus when they go out, and they walk in the street like the rest of us."

But though Poiret admired Gaston's taste and created for him many of the peeresses' robes for Edward VII's coronation, he could not stomach the perpetual feud between the progressive Gaston and his old-fashioned brother Jean Philippe. By 1903, he had opened his own salon on the rue Auber.

A plump, self-indulgent boulevardier, who "ran through several fortunes like a small boy running through flower beds," Poiret was boldly innovative. By dispensing with the corset and emphasizing the brassiere, he paved the way for the New Woman's new shape. Yet as early as 1910, he in part defeated his purpose by shackling her legs with his hobble skirt, a fashion scarcely practicable for promenading the streets, let alone boarding a bus.

But practicality was Poiret's bête noire. His forte was for colors that were "like a blow in the face"; his triumph was an invitation from Margot Asquith, the wife of Britain's Liberal Prime Minister, to hold a fashion show at No. 10 Downing Street—which the resentful British press promptly rechristened "Gowning Street." His slender, high-waisted tube dresses, the onset of the androgynous look, were nothing if not striking, featuring lampshade tunics, Turkish trousers, and fur-banded hems. Yet as the twenties dawned, Poiret became increasingly the prisoner of his own legend. Year in, year out, his clients looked like Asiatic princesses or Tartar priests, vibrant in scarlet and black, resplendent with gold tassels like a prewar hussar.

Where a Frenchman had so successfully dramatized the world of haute couture, an Englishwoman was not slow to follow, and at No. 23 Hanover Square, London, Lucy, Lady Duff-Gordon, sister of the lurid romantic novelist, Elinor Glyn, showed a kindred talent for the gorgeous and the gaudy. Her mannequins, with names like Gamela and Hebe, were a novelty in themselves, as were Lucile's creations. The old terminology of "the black velvet" and "the pink silk" were out; Lucile's were "Gowns of Emotion," with such palpitating titles as "When Passion's Thrall is O'er," "A Frenzied Song of Amorous Things," or "Red Mouth of a Venomous Flower."

One of Lucile's star pupils was Captain Edward Molyneux, a dapper ex-officer who had both won a Military Cross and lost an eye in World War I; in 1919, aged twenty-eight, Molyneux took the courageous step, like Worth before him, of opening up in Paris, at 5, rue Royale. For Rainbows, Molyneux advocated classic simplicity; his women were distinguished by their inimitable two-pieces and tailored suits with pleated skirts, and their small, white-glazed collars. Though the couturier Hardy Amies was to recall him as "totally uncozy—a *very* dry martini cocktail," Molyneux, too, knew the value of publicity; with Elsa Maxwell, he opened two Paris nightclubs, Les Acacias and Le Jardin de Ma Soeur, both inspired showcases for Molyneux evening gowns. In a salon on the avenue Montaigne, Madeleine Vionnet, a worried-looking, unobtrusive woman, was working toward the same end—"the dress does not hang on the body but follows its lines . . . when a woman smiles the dress must smile with her." A dressmaker's dressmaker, who won the plaudits of such fellow craftsmen as Jacques Worth and Pierre Balmain, Vionnet won fame for her flared skirts and cowl necks, above all for her classic bias cut.

All these essays toward a greater simplicity were now crystallized, as so often happens, by the one designer who sensed instinctively what the New Women of Little David's world were seeking: a style to go with freedom. This unlikely Pygmalion, the greatest transformer of the twentieth century's Rainbow women, was, in fact, a country girl, born in 1883 in the Auvergne, deeply ashamed of both her peasant origins and her illegitimacy, Gabrielle Bonheur "Coco" ("Little Pet") Chanel.

With her huge, intense black eyes, flat cheekbones, snub nose, and overlarge mouth, hers was essentially a gamine appeal—and this was, perhaps, part of her secret. It was as if, a fashion reporter commented in 1920, one were seeing "clothes which an amazingly artistic and talented woman had had made for her own use alone, by a dressmaker who worked solely for her." Coco herself summed up in a way that Mademoiselle Vionnet would have approved: "The skirt must walk with the girl."

Cecil Beaton might cavil at her "chic poverty," but poverty was a condition Coco understood very well. Orphaned at twelve, she had been raised in cheerless frugality by two maiden aunts on a farm near Vichy. In her early twenties, after unrewarding stints as a clerk in a hosiery store and as a music hall performer, she fell in with Chasseur Etienne Balsan, playboy son of a wealthy industrialist, whose mistress she became. By 1910, she had fallen in love with his best friend, Arthur "Boy" Capel, a wealthy English polo player; their relationship thus became a tolerant menage à trois. Since Coco had a latent talent for designing hats, Boy furnished the money to set her up in her own millinery shop in the rue Cambon, behind the Ritz, a few doors from "Antoine's Fountain."

By the summer of 1913, Coco had branched out; again financed by Boy, she opened a shop at Deauville, on the rue Gontaut Biron. Here, for the first time, she experimented with couture: an original, suggestive of a sailor blouse. The line was loose and, in the Poiret fashion, required no corset. When the war erupted and fashionable society moved south, Coco and Boy moved with them—to Biarritz, to open a full-scale maison de couture, whose dresses were priced at 3,000 francs (then, roughly £150).

In 1916, a disgruntled textile manufacturer, Jean Rodier, showed Coco a material that had never been used and that he believed never could be: a beige-colored, machine-made woollen material called jersey, originally created for sportsmen's underwear. But Coco saw its potential. Women had earned the right to be comfortable, to move freely. Her first jersey chemise dress followed Poiret, in allowing the foot to show, but went further: she disengaged the ankle altogether, removed the waist, and "changed the look of the street scene forever."

Already, in the same year, her ateliers in Paris and Biarritz were employing 300 workers. By 1919, she was poised to give the New Woman what she wanted. Not only had she upgraded jersey; she had made velveteen chic, as well as cardigans, pleated skirts, and tricot sailor frocks. Many of her fashions were spur-of-the-moment improvisations to suit her own convenience. Either at Cannes or Biarritz—the accounts vary—she hit on a pair of sailor's pants as the most practical way of boarding a yacht, and went on to adopt their striped maillots, their pea jackets, and their berets. One chilly day at the Deauville racetrack, she borrowed a turtleneck sweater from a jockey and sashed it with a kerchief. Within a week, all Deauville was in turtleneck sweaters.

The "little black dress" became her international trademark, but Coco inspired many others. She popularized the turned-back jacket cuff, the *Garconne* look, though softening it by turning neckties into pussycat bows; she made costume jewelry and the beige trench coat fashionable. Proletarian materials like corduroy and rabbit fur became the rage; Coco decreed it so.

Her concepts were basic to the wardrobes of generations of Rainbow women, like Broadway star Ina Claire and each and every Rothschild: draped turbans, blazers, sling pumps, strapless dresses, gypsy skirts, embroidered silk blouses with accompanying shawls, the fashion of wearing pearls over a sweater.

In her gray, beige, and gold rue Cambon showroom, she was a formidable taskmistress, often working until 2 A.M. for weeks before a collection, turning out 2,000 originals a year. Herself an indifferent seamstress, she cut to perfection, with her special collection scissors threaded on a long white tape hanging round her neck. She worked with her hands with a living model, while a trepidant staff hovered and passed the pins. To perfect a suit she would take it to pieces as much as twenty-five times—"a suit only looks good when the woman who wears it looks as if she had nothing on underneath." Criticisms, delivered in her catarrhal, chainsmoker's monotone, were always barbed: "Make the sleeve a bit bigger—it looks like a stovepipe." Or, "What are those buttons? They look incredibly hideous—they look like poisoned chocolates."

Ironically, she was not only dressing exclusive Rainbows; through copies she was dressing the world. "I am not an artist," she would insist. "I want my dresses to go out on the street." And onto the streets they went in thousands: easy to copy because of the straightforward design, cheap to produce because of the standard fabric. Even a copy of a Chanel could claim its cachet. Private customers paid anything from $500 to $700 for an original; buyers, intent on knockoffs, would pay closer to $1,500.

From 1920 onward, she was perfuming the world as well; it was this year that saw the launching of Chanel No. 5, which guaranteed her financial independence for life, an estimated $15 million. As publicity-oriented as Molyneux or Poiret, Coco had approached the Riviera perfume house of Rallet for a fragrance that she could market under her own name, and in due time, the chief chemist, Ernest Beaux, came up with ten tiny sample flaçons. Coco, sniffing in due order, stopped in delight at Sample No. 5.

The blend Beaux had achieved was unique, through juxtaposing classic odors: a large dash of aldehydes (an intermediate between alcohol and acid), contrasting with such old-fashioned fragrances as jasmine, rose, and violet. By the late twenties, the perfume, along with four others—Bois des Isles, Gardenia, Russian Leather, and No. 22—bearing the classic black-and-white labels, was being marketed by Pierre Wertheimer's House of Bourjois, who paid Coco 2 percent royalty on every bottle sold.

As a rich woman in her own right, Coco had scant interest in marriage. Although she was, for six years following the death of Boy Capel in World War I, the mistress of Bendor, second Duke of Westminster, she brushed aside all his pleas to become the third Duchess. "When I had to choose between the man I loved and dresses," she confessed later, "I always chose the dresses." No matter that Bendor lavished on her a textile mill and an entire suite at Eaton Hall in which to plan her collections; Coco remained heart-whole. Yet it was typical of the Rainbow twenties that a peasant girl from the Auvergne should dictate to High Society what they wore and when, that a premier English duke should court her as his bride, and that a companionable evening was once spent at the rue Cambon by Coco, Bendor, and his engaging young friend, who lounged ungracefully in a low armchair and begged her, "Do call me David."

Just as in Edward's time, the new freedom—some called it license—of the age had its critics. To John Galsworthy's Soames Forsyte, Society was now "one vast ugly shoulder-rubbing petrol-smelling Cheerio." A hatter to the London nobility, Frederick Willis, dolefully saw the cloth cap of the Socialist leader, Keir Hardie, as "a symbol of the shape of things to come." When Alice Keppel and Mrs. Willy James were present, expressions like "deevy" and "expie" still lingered on in London drawing rooms, but the new slang of David's day was harsher, often pejorative: things were "joy-making" or "blush-making," according to one's predilections, or could be "lousy," "foul," "putrid," or, alternatively, "wizard" or "king." An adult human being was "a top," "an egg," or "a fruit," who if suffering from "an inhibish" was automatically "a dud."

Yet the twenties saw the real welding of the old families and the new-rich, which Edward's reign had signposted. The new-rich, admittedly, had the money; the old families were skilled in spending it. And this was no less true in the United States. The phenomenon was first noted on a bitter February night in 1919, in the downstairs dining room of the Ritz Hotel, New York, when Maury Henry Biddle Paul, who penned the "Cholly Knickerbocker" column for Hearst's *Journal*, was struck by the disparity of a dinner party sextet: Mrs. Gouverneur Wellman, a grande dame; Joe Widener, the millionaire Philadelphia racehorse owner, whom Philadelphia mainliners had never acknowledged; Laura Corrigan, an arriviste and onetime waitress from Cleveland, Ohio; an architect, Whitney C. Warren, Jr.; and "one assorted pair of Goelets."

"Society is going out to dinner, out to night life, and letting down the barriers," mused the enraptured Paul. "It's like a seafood cocktail, with everything from eels to striped bass." This novel grouping he dubbed "Café Society"—and though the queen of etiquette, Emily Post, might dismiss them disdainfully as "an unclassifiably mixed group of restaurant and night club habitués," the fact remained that the power of "The 400" was waning. Harry Lehr was in exile in France; Mamie Fish had died in 1915; Tessie Oelrichs had gone insane; and Alva Belmont had repented and embraced good works. New York Society had at last caught up with Edwardian England.

It was still, in many ways, an age of transition. Whether to immortalize oneself by a portrait in oils or a posed photograph in a Tiffany or Asprey frame, set slightly atilt on the grand piano, was still a nice point to ponder. A small select tribe of practitioners in both these arts was still on hand to preserve the Rainbows in perpetuity—at a price.

Most Society portrait painters had set up their easels well before Edward's funeral. Since 1910, Sir John Lavery and his beautiful wife, the former Hazel Martyn, of Chicago, had been fixtures at Cromwell Place, South Kensington, where Sir John, a short, bald, ruddy-cheeked man with twinkling brown eyes, had a studio "with lots of room to splash about." Unlike many of his fellow Academicians, Lavery had come up the hard way. As an orphan in Glasgow, Lavery, who had fled from Ireland to abort attempts to turn him into a priest, even vied with the starlings for the crusts scattered in the public parks; from a blind-alley job as a billiard marker, he had learned the rudiments of his craft by touching up portraits in a photographer's studio. Rejected seven years running by the Royal Academy, he was finally elected R. A. in 1921.

Even a painter who as early as 1910 commanded £300 for a

portrait had inevitable setbacks. David, who sat for him on two occasions, proved an easy subject, free with intelligent questions, as did Lillie Langtry and Diana Cooper. But the actress Mrs. Patrick Campbell proved impossible to satisfy; "Ah, you do not paint me *con amore!*" she charged, and flounced out halfway through the session. Sarah Bernhardt, in 1912, also proved intractable; "I could see that fifty years would have to come off if I was to please," Lavery admitted. After one silent two-hour sitting, the Divine Sarah commented only, "Ce n'est pas mal," and never returned. The dividing line between truth and flattery had always a tightrope quality. One peer, surveying the completed portrait of his wife, burst out, "What is this flat-chested modernity that I see? Where is the snowy amplitude of her Ladyship? No, Sir John Lavery, that does not represent my wife!"

To regulate their lives, Society painters needed an inflexible self-discipline. "You start going to lunch with Lady Cunard . . . and you're done!" Ambrose McEvoy would warn his fellow artists in his high, shrill voice, but no one stood more in need of his own counsel than McEvoy, a man who could no more refuse a dinner invitation than a commission. His life became as overcrowded as his tiny studio at 107 Grosvenor Road, where he executed about 200 portraits in oils between 1900 and his death, in 1923: Brian Howard, Hazel Lavery, Consuelo Marlborough, George Gould, Henry E. Huntington, all of them charged with an air of subtle melancholy. Fair-haired, alert, and overstrung, McEvoy worked in asphyxiating heat, hemmed in by hangers-on from whom he feverishly canvassed opinion. "Do you think it will come?" he would enquire repeatedly, his eyes starting from his head with anxiety. Those with the stamina to survive 100 McEvoy sittings and the wherewithal to meet his £600 fee would ultimately be rewarded.

A new arrival on the Society scene was McEvoy's friend, Augustus John, whose habits provoked the nickname "Disgusting John," almost a caricature of a Murger Bohemian. A Welsh solicitor's son, who liked to claim kinship with the gypsies, John took pains to conform to the popular artistic stereotype: shoulder-length russet hair offset by jade-green earrings, a black slouch hat, red tie, and baggy green corduroys. All his life he was beset by a drinking problem that he never quite overcame; from the same houses where he might set up his easel by day, he was often, on party nights, borne out unconscious by liveried footmen. "John had the drinks," the writer L. A. G. Strong recorded in his diary. "His friends had the headache."

As an artist he was in a class—and a price bracket—of his own. For a portrait of his wife, Dorelia, John, in 1910, netted £225, and even Tallulah Bankhead got off cheaply with £1,000 in the 1920s. (The cellist, Madame Guilhermina Suggia, had stumped up £3,000.) Working nonstop on portraits of Joe Widener, Elizabeth Arden, and the Marchesa Casati, John's sheer force of style lifted him above the potboiler class; puffing on a noxious bubbling pipe, his piercing blue eyes sometimes only an inch away from his sitter's face, pacing, grunting, stamping his foot, this "burly and debauched Christ," as Harold Nicolson saw him, amazingly survived until 1961, when he died aged eighty-four.

The doyen of all the portrait painters, the living link between Edward's era and David's, was John Singer Sargent, born of American parents in Florence in 1856, who lived on at his home, 31 Tite Street, Chelsea, the onetime studio of James McNeill Whistler, until 1925. Though some commentators saw him as no more than a sycophant with a palette, this did him far less than justice; sitters like the Duke of Portland and the Wertheimer sisters, Ena and Betty, were subjected to a hard-eyed, warts-and-all scrutiny rarely surpassed in the era. "It's positively dangerous to sit to Sargent," remarked one timid aspirant. "It's taking your face in your hands."

At Welbeck Abbey, at the turn of the century, Sargent, a tall, gangling man with bulging bloodshot eyes, who chain-smoked Havana cigars, devoted a whole month to one portrait of the Duchess of Portland, rushing at the easel, as the Duke recalled him, "with strange Spanish oaths," finally after two weeks, to the Duchess's immense distress, slashing the portrait to ribbons and embarking on a clean canvas. He must, he apologized profusely, paint "something alive." But with the years, the commissions piled up so thick and fast as to overwhelm him—Lady Agnew, Henry James, Sir Philip Sassoon, even David himself, though he held no charms for Sargent. "He's a very dull young man," he told a fellow artist sepulchrally.

Thus Sargent becme the victim of his own talents. Now appointments with "the Van Dyck of Tite Street" must be made six, even twelve months ahead. At times he had commanded 1,000 guineas a portrait, but now, working at breakneck speed, he had settled, by 1920, for fixed fees: $500 in the United States, 100 guineas in England. At the Hyde Park Grill, he allowed himself exactly thirty minutes for lunch; on the tablecloth, a relentlessly ticking watch marked the time span and all food, from soup to cheese, must be served simultaneously. Then it was back once more to his upstairs studio at No. 31, waiting for his "man," a sandalled Venetian gondolier named Nicolo, to usher in the afternoon's first sitters.

Society photographers were expected to flatter, and even the earliest exponents knew it; in Edward's day, the Bassano studio in Regent Street, which he patronized, was *the* favorite among the twenty-eight London photographers to whom Queen Victoria had issued the royal warrant. One of Edward's most intimate friends, the Parisian-born Adolph, the Baron de Meyer, part Scottish, part Jewish, was an early master of the art, though insisting, of course, that he was not a professional, merely a talented amateur. Even before World War I, de Meyer and his wife, Olga, found good reason to migrate to New York; an era that was to see dachshunds stoned in the streets, when King George V was swift to change the family name from Saxe-Coburg-Gotha to Windsor, was chary of foreign origins. One of de Meyer's few peers was Leonard Green, a 6' 2" schoolmaster's son from Gloucestershire, who in 1924 opened the Lenare Studio at 28 St. George Street, Mayfair; these two, above all, ranked as the Sargents of the lens.

Early pioneers like Hugh Cecil, of Dover Street, who rejected all clients whose social standing was not up to scratch, had a phrase that summed it up: "doing a de Meyer." For the blue-eyed baron, who also dyed his hair blue for reasons of harmony, and always donned a hairnet before ducking under the camera's tarpaulin, was the first quintessentially romantic photographer: the first whose 8" × 10" photographs were always shot with a backlight behind the filter, "always iridescent and opulent," never impersonal or one-dimensional. His was a talent that Alfred Condé-Nast, who in 1909 took over the magazine *Vogue,* was delighted to hire for $100 a week—then an unheard-of sum for a Society photographer.

De Meyer's was, par excellence, a Rainbow world. His office and studio at 59 East Fifty-second Street, where he and Olga retired to bed under mink coverlets, was a misty nirvana, shielded from reality by silk gauze drapes. His women sitters, of course, wore elegant dresses, but de Meyer had to heighten this effect; he bathed them in halos of shimmering moonbeams, he buried them in torrents of lilac, lilies, and freesias. They posed with one hand on their hip, the other extended with little finger crooked— easily spotted by what Cecil Beaton called "their gaping goldfish mouths." Theirs was a world of tapestries and console tables, of brocade pillows and ostrich fans, where women like Rita Lydig, Elsie de Wolfe, the Vanderbilts and Whitneys, posed "as though swimming in a glass of champagne."

In essence, the secret of all these photographers was simple: The hard work was done *after* the photograph was taken. The use of a soft lens in the enlarger rather than in the camera, and a large plate negative, enabled the retouchers to get to work with paper stumps and lead to create a soft highlight. Old hands like Dorothy Connor, for fifty years a retoucher with the London-based Dorothy Wilding studio, learned in time, if a background was too gray, to use orange ink behind the head, bleeding it away to give a "a hint of glow."

For them, all the world was a stage, to be pictured in a flattering peach-fuzzed light. When de Meyer left *Vogue* in 1922 to work first for *Harper's Bazaar* and then to freelance, his natural successor was Edward Steichen, a formidably tall and bearded man, whose tenure lasted fifteen years. But though Steichen experimented from the first with the strobe camera and infrared, his ladies, hugging ropes of pearls to their bosoms, coyly patting ostrich fans, were almost twins of the de Meyer ladies, though with one difference: Steichen ladies sometimes smiled; de Meyer ladies remained in a twilit trance.

In 1927, another nobleman entered the New York scene: the

son of a Baltic-Russian father, Baron George Hoyningen-Heune, a tall, bald man nicknamed "The Egg," whose speciality was haughty heads with chiseled profiles, swathed in silk turbans and festooned with pearl earrings. For him, every sitting was as complex as a chess game, at which Heune, chin in hand, would brood for long, silent minutes like a contemporary Spassky before vanishing beneath the tarpaulin—until lunchtime rewarded his sitters with a gourmet buffet of smoked salmon, *poulet en gelée,* and vintage champagne.

One early Heune protégé was the young Cecil Beaton, perfectly at home with his 3A Folding Pocket Kodak until Condé-Nast bullied him into buying an 8″ × 10″ camera like Steichen's, a tool with which he never felt "quite at ease." As histrionic in his approach as many of his sitters, the nimble Beaton would even clamber onto mantelpieces to achieve a more startling angle, and his eighty-year-old nanny, who acted as his prop girl and light holder, soon came to accept such bizarre backdrops as walls covered with cardboard egg crates, floors gleaming with wet cement, and models posed with whisk brooms and ladders.

Increasingly, Beaton's lenses were focused on the small tight world that was David's own: a world where Chanel or Molyneux dressed the women and Henry Poole or Charles Wetzel the men, people who hailed one another as convivially in the Embassy Club as in the bar of the Carlton at Cannes or in the Waldorf-Astoria's Peacock Alley. Many were English, but were equally made welcome in the New York apartments of such cosmopolites as Scuyler Parsons, the art dealer, or the jeweler, Jules Glaenzer, the head of Cartier, New York. The bulk of them belonged to the booming world of show business, for David, like his grandfather, was a rabid musical comedy fan. When the musical farce *Stop Flirting!* opened at London's Shaftesbury Theatre in May 1923, David not only sat through it ten times but enrolled its two volatile young American stars, Adele and Fred Astaire (born Austerlitz, in Omaha, Nebraska), into the York House set.

Few of these initiates had been weaned on silver spoons, but to David, fleeing from "the tyranny of starch," this was all to the good. Gertrude Lawrence, then starring in the revue *London*

Calling!, whom Diana Cooper described as "so common one feels that she has nits in her hair, so kitchen-maidy," was the daughter of a drunken music hall performer and had begun her life belting out the refrain of

> Oh, it ain't all honey, and it ain't all jam,
> Walking round the 'ouses with a three-wheel pram . . .

at her mother's musical evenings. Yet, on many occasions, Gertie was a guest at David's parties where, despite "the solemn old Palace," there was "never anyone who was dull or stuffy," but "international tennis champions, the newest blues singer, a guitarist who was all the rage in Paris." Beatrice Gladys Lillie, from Toronto, Canada, labeled herself "lace-curtain Irish," but as the star of *The Nine O'Clock Revue,* she was welcome, too. Walter John Buchanan, better known as "Jack," had known equally hard times; when his father, a Scottish auctioneer, died with a crippling load of debts, his mother made ends meet by opening a Glasgow boarding house, scrubbing her own steps at night to avoid the neighbors' prying eyes. But as the star of *Battling Butler,* whose shirts were tailored by Hawes and Curtis, Jack was on first-name terms with David. George Gershwin, a Brooklyn boy with a broken nose, had started out as a $15-a-week song plugger at Remick's, the music publishers, but after "Rhapsody in Blue" he was another York House man—like Noel Coward, star and part-author and composer of *London Calling!*

Coward's mother had also kept a boarding house, and Coward, a "stage brat" from the age of twelve, had known such poverty that later in life he admitted filching the tips left under the plates for teashop waitresses. Now he would sit up half the night playing piano accompaniment to David's ukelele.

The only well-born trouper of the set, Tallulah Brockman Bankhead, a congressman's daughter from Jasper, Alabama, was habitually the worst-behaved, though she strove for restraint, not always successfully, in David's presence. It was in 1923 that Tallulah, named after a waterfall in the highlands of Georgia, first hit London in a series of indifferent plays that yet won her star status among the gallery girls: the first of the Queen Bees. Along with her tossing waves of honey-colored hair, her prowling, lioness walk, went a voice that one critic likened to "a man pulling his foot out of a bucket of yoghurt," but the low, throaty tones beguiled millions and were made throatier still by the smoking of four packs of Craven A cigarettes a day. "She had the honesty of the very rich," Virginia Graham was to recall. "She just couldn't give a damn," for Tallulah herself made no secret of her defiance of established custom.

She drank as immoderately as she smoked—Old Grand-Dad bourbon when she could get it—and she sniffed cocaine on the side. She needed drugs to wake up, drugs to drop off, drugs to kill pain or kill time. Her most torrid love affair was with Napier Sturt, the second Lord Alington, but there were many more transient liaisons—she was, she claimed, "as pure as the driven slush." When an admirer ventured, "I've heard a lot about you . . ." Tallulah assured him, "It's all true." To her, everyone was "Dahling," and for the simplest of reasons—"Because, dahling, I meet so many people and simply can't remember all their names."

Checking her irresistible urge to strip herself naked—but not to turn cartwheels—she was the life and soul of many of David's parties, determined to see things through until dawn—"And the first one to fall asleep is a shit. I can say shit, dahling; I'm a lady."

* * *

All through the 1920s, the Rainbows were drawn to the bright lights like moths to a flickering candle. Rarely had the night exerted such a mystical appeal. The hour when the milk vans cruised the streets was the earliest for sleeping. When New York's Mayor Jimmy Walker, himself no slouch when it came to a party, imposed a 3 A.M. clampdown in 1928, one outraged girl summed up what everybody felt: "Go home at three o'clock? Why, that ruins the whole evening!"

On the face of it, American Rainbows faced an intractable problem. To be sure, the British were forbidden to drink after

12:30 A.M., or, on one weekly extension night, after 2 A.M. But Americans, after the Volstead Act for the enforcement of the Eighteenth Amendment went into effect on January 16, 1920, were forbidden to drink at all. The era of Prohibition had dawned.

But for the Rainbows, this was sheer bliss: a heaven-sent opportunity to cock a snook at authority, any and every authority. The children spoiled rotten were in their element; no pleasures could compare with those that were strictly illicit. Overnight, their world embraced new and even dangerous elements: at its most decorous, the fashionable dinner party, launched on a flood tide of contraband cocktails, or the debutantes' balls, where dowagers swept imperiously into the ballroom followed by liveried chauffeurs staggering under a consignment of champagne from a trusted bootlegger. And the deb of the day was seldom parted from her dainty little diamond-flecked gold flask.

From the first, the Rainbows set the pace in defying Prohibition, and partly as a result of this defiance a near-impenetrable maze of organized crime grew and flourished: the rumrunners, pitching against the waves, outside the twelve-mile limit, nightly transferring their cargoes to fast cabin cruisers, the illicit stills, turning out bathtub gin by the barrel, the hijacking of beer-running trucks on interurban highways by hoods armed with Thompson submachine guns, Alphonse "Al" Capone, who controlled 10,000 Chicago speakeasies, as the new illicit drinking dens were called, purring through the streets in a black armor-plated limousine with bulletproof windows.

But even Chicago paled beside New York, which had seventy nightclubs alone—some highly exclusive, like the Sutton, on Fifty-seventh Street, where guests came nightly to hear Beatrice Lillie, or The Trocadero, where the Astaires were the featured dancers. And these were augmented by an estimated 32,000 speakeasies, most of them sited in the cellars of midtown brownstone residences, where Rainbows claiming to be "friends of Mr. Sweeney" customarily underwent scrutiny from behind a curtained grille until the strong-arm man on the door was satisfied. In later years, their names were a nostalgic litany recited by all those who had survived their dubious liquor unscathed: the Hotsy Totsy, run by the mobster, Jack "Legs" Diamond,

Tony's on East Fifty-third Street, the Clamhouse, the Sligo Slasher's, Frank and Jack's, Phyllis's Twenty-One West Forty Third. In this driest of eras, New York had never been wetter.

The uncrowned "Queen of the Nightclubs" was a brash, blond, husky-voiced forty-year-old from Waco, Texas, Mary Louise Cecilia Guinan, known always as Texas Guinan, a onetime rodeo stunt rider, Broadway chorine, and silent screen star in cut-price sagebrush epics like *Little Miss Deputy*. Four years after Prohibition became established fact, Texas fell in with a former taxi driver turned rumrunner, Larry Fay, who notched up a statistic or two: He owned twelve trunks of Savile Row clothes, acquired in England, and was arrested forty-nine times in the forty-four years that he lived. Impressed by her breezy insouciance at a show-business get-together, Fay hit on a new gimmick: a Mamie Fish of the boîtes de nuit, a performer-hostess who would trade insults and wisecracks with the carriage trade. The result, the El Fay Club, which opened in 1924 on East Forty-sixth Street, became part of nightclub history.

First-timers to these plush premises, which opened promptly at midnight, received their biggest shock with the cover charge: $11 a head. (On subsequent visits, it scaled down to $3, rising to $5 on Saturday nights.) Scarcely less daunting was their first glimpse of Texas. Perched on a tall stool in the center of the main room, dazzling in diamonds and sequins, armed with a clapper and a police whistle, she greeted all new arrivals with a love-tap on the head from a wrought-iron fan and a husky ingratiating drawl of "Hello, sucker!"

Her genial contempt for the Rainbows and their world—all of them, from Lady Diana Cooper to Peggy Hopkins Joyce, the ex-Follies girl who collected millionare husbands like a philatelist dealing in stamps—could hardly have been made plainer.

She was out to rook them and all of them knew it—and cheerfully returned for more. A fair estimate for an evening with Texas was $300, and as a safety valve all customers receiving a check were armed with small wooden mallets to pound their tables in protest. But any serious complaint over the total was met with a steely, "You had fun, didn't you?"

In this clip joint ethos, everybody—save the suckers—profited handsomely. And with reason: the suckers paid $25 for a pitcher of Rhine wine, spiked with seltzer, masquerading as champagne, $1.50 for a bottle of mineral water, $2 for a plate of chow mein, $1.75 for bacon and eggs. Souvenirs from the handsome glass showcases, usually dolls or flasks of perfume, cost $25. This arithmetic explains why each one of Texas's seventy-eight hostesses, all of them as lightly clad as a spider in a web, averaged take-home pay of $100 a week—after selling $22,000 of showcase merchandise over five weekday nights. (Their "presents," of course, went back in the showcase.) Doorkeepers and headwaiters took home much the same; hatcheck girls averaged $60; even taxidrivers steering prospects to the premises netted 10 percent of what the client spent. With average takings of $1,200 a night, Texas, over ten months, parlayed a modest investment into a million-dollar fortune.

She was as hypnotic as a cheerleader, the first to hit on the bright idea of grabbing applause even before it had been earned. Escorting a hostess onto the floor, she would urge, "Give this little girl a big hand."

Then, when the applause had died down, "She is a good little girl." More tumultuous applause. "She never goes any place without her mother." Renewed applause. "But her mother will go anywhere"—bringing the loudest applause of all.

To a world where staid, bald millionaires played leapfrog on the dance floor, and "butter-and-egg men," as Texas called the dairy produce moguls, doled out $50 bills to every hostess, David inevitably gravitated on his 1924 tour—arriving at 3 A.M. along with Edwina and Louis Mountbatten and Major "Fruity" Metcalfe. Even Texas seemed momentarily nonplussed, halting the music before he entered, to caution them: "Pals, the Prince is coming. Don't gawk. Let him have a good time. He's bored by curiosity. Even his horses throw him to take a good look at him. Let him be one of us."

As, of course, he was, chatting, laughing, drinking, dancing, reciting a banal long-forgotten rhyme for the benefit of the audience, recounting party-piece anecdotes concerning Edward VII like any young cabaret MC.

Like all shooting stars, Texas's glory was brief. When federal agents raided and then padlocked the El Fay, she moved on, to the Del Fay, the 300 Club, the Club Intime, and to Texas Guinan's Salon Royale. By 1926, she was back in vaudeville, out to cash in on her own notoriety.

About this time, her London counterpart, Mrs. Kate Evelyn Meyrick, was in deep trouble.

Not that the genteel, Dublin-born Kate Meyrick, the estranged wife of a specialist in nervous diseases, would ever have dubbed her clients "suckers." To the writer Robert Bruce Lockhart, she would have made "an admirable matron of a nursing home"; on the rare occasions she consented to dance, it was always to a decorous refrain like "The Blue Danube." Of her six daughters, all of whom went to the exclusive girls' school Roedean, three married into the peerage; her two sons attended Winston Churchill's alma mater, Harrow.

Yet equipped with what Balzac described as "a dreamy air, an innocent face, and a strongbox for a heart," Kate Meyrick was privy to every dodge known to Texas Guinan.

From partnerships in sedate tea dance clubs in the Leicester Square area, she moved on, in November 1921, to more dubious terrain: the proprietorship of the six-story building at 43 Gerrard Street, known as The Forty-Three. Two years later, she opened up the Folies Bergères, in nearby Newman Street, then The Little Club, in Golden Square, followed in 1927 by the glossiest of all, The Silver Slipper, off Regent Street, famous for its glass dance floor and its giant silver slipper pendant from the ceiling. Though she paid her waiters only five shillings a week, they habitually took home £20 in tips—not surprisingly, when her membership list included: Augustus John; Otto Kahn, the Wall Street banker; Jimmy White, the Lancashire millionaire, who staged £400 champagne parties for six Daimler-loads of showgirls; Tallulah; the exiled Prince Carol of Romania; and Jack Buchanan.

A new generation has coined an apt phrase for Kate's technique: the rip-off. All her markups were in the heroic tradition of Duveen—an average of 300 percent across the board. For breakfasts, "which began at 9:30 P.M.," £30 worth of kippers and eggs and bacon brought Kate a return of £90; £10 worth of liquor at the cocktail bar retained for £30. Champagne that cost her 12s 6d a bottle was 22s 6d in licensed hours, rising to £2 a bottle in what Kate termed "the small wild hours." In a good—£1,000—week at The Silver Slipper, she saw £500 as clear profit.

Of course, there were overheads to which she freely admitted. At least £3,700 a year went in rentals. Fitting up a new club could cost up to £10,000. A bandleader like the tubby xylophonist Teddy Brown, at The Silver Slipper, demanded £18,000 a year. Only the finest rouge, face powder, and lipstick were provided in the ladies' rooms, and one box of face powder alone cost five shillings—a waiter's weekly wage.

There were other disbursals that she never admitted. These took place on at least one afternoon a week, on a bench in the sylvan seclusion of Regent's Park, conveniently close to Kate's home in Park Square. There, a demurely dressed Kate, who usually wore a gray cloche hat and a discreet brown fur coat, had a fixed rendezvous with a burly genial man of forty-nine with deep-set eyes and curly hair. Few words might pass between them, but an envelope always did. Thus Kate Meyrick ensured the silence and complicity of Station-Sergeant George Goddard, of Marlborough Street Police Station, whose twenty-man squad was charged with the surveillance of nightclubs and restaurants flouting the licensing laws.

And Goddard more than kept his bargain. In nine years he had received no fewer than ninety-one commendations for 234 nightclub raids, yet over three years, between March 1925 and May 1928, none of these was ever directed at The Forty-Three. Leslie Jackson, an £8-a-week alto sax player at the club, still recalls the electric moment of the tip-off: "A phone would ring . . . then a whitewashed canvas and plaster screen came down like a wall . . . after we'd moved all the bottles and glasses over to No. Forty-One."

In May 1928—perhaps as part of a cover-up—Kate did receive a six-month sentence in Holloway Gaol—where "the wardresses were dears"—for offenses against the licensing laws. But even before she was released from gaol, the wheels were grinding. An anonymous letter to the Commissioner of Police, signed only by "A Peaceful Citizen," posed some cogent questions: How could Goddard, a £6-a-week station sergeant, sustain a life-style that included a £1,650 house in the southern suburb of Streatham, a £400 Chrysler, and the financing of a brother in the pawnbroking business?

Called to account, Goddard was specious: he had so many "dead cert" tips at the racetrack from friendly bookies. His superiors were skeptical: even a phenomenally lucky punter could scarcely have amassed £17,984, stashed away in two bank accounts and two safe deposit boxes. Some of this money, it was true, came as sweeteners from Luigi Ribuffi, who ran Uncle's Club, in Albemarle Street, and from Enrico and Anna Gadda, who kept a brothel at 56 Greek Street, yet more than a score of five-pound notes held by Goddard were certified by the Marylebone branch of Barclay's Bank as having been issued to Kate Meyrick.

The outcome was predictable. In January 1929, after a six-day hearing at the Old Bailey, Kate and Luigi Ribuffi were both found guilty of "conspiracy" with ex-Station-Sergeant Goddard and sentenced to fifteen months' hard labor. Goddard himself, after twenty-eight years on the force, went down for eighteen months.

For the "Nightclub Queens," it was the end of an era. On January 19, 1933, Kate died, aged fifty-six, of bronchial pneumonia, and that November, following an internal disorder, Texas Guinan died on tour in Vancouver, British Columbia. But at least the best part of her million-dollar fortune was intact; her mother, who survived her, was generously provided for. The "suckers" had been well and truly trimmed.

And Kate? By her own admission, £500,000 had passed through her hands in thirteen years, yet all that was left, when the debts were paid, was £58 18s 10d. "I am back," she had announced on her final release from prison, "at the point where I started."

The seven guineas that each of her eight children received from her estate seemed to underscore this truth. To woo and win the Rainbows she had ultimately paid a heavier price than they.

5 / THE WORLD OF LITTLE DAVID:
"A Bender as Big as the Ritz"

In David's time, the novelist W. Somerset Maugham liked to recount how he called one morning on a peer much given to nightclubbing, to enquire of his butler, "What time does his Lordship usually breakfast?" The butler's deadpan reply summed up much of the mood of the era: "His Lordship does not breakfast, sir. His Lordship is usually sick at about eleven."

Yet, by strange paradox, David and his kind, nightbirds all, were equally slaves to the sun, an obsession to recall the age when the Incas had decreed sun worship to be the official state religion. A hit London musical of the mid-thirties, *Follow The Sun,* starring American actress Claire Luce, crystallized an injunction that the Rainbows had then followed for all of ten years.

It began, Elsa Maxwell was to claim, in 1936, when Prince Pierre de Polignac, the son-in-law of the reigning Prince Louis of Monaco, invited her to lunch. "Monte Carlo," the Prince lamented, "is dying, hermetically sealed off from the tourists, who are swarming to other resorts along the entire coast. Why are we missing the boat?" To which Elsa replied cryptically, "You're not rendering proper homage to the new king."

Then, seeing his bafflement, she enlightened him, "Le soleil, the sun! Life has moved outdoors. People come to the Riviera to relax, to get away from formality. They want to play on the beach and in the water. You've got the water. Get a beach."

This, in itself, was a kind of heresy, for traditionally the Riviera round, along the 140-mile strip of coastline from Menton to Cassis known as the Côte d'Azur, had embraced February and March, sometimes part of April, but never the summer months. The advent of summer was always marked by the sight of thousands of mattresses airing on the balconies of innumerable hotels and pensions; those few visitors eccentric enough to remain longer were known disparagingly as *les hivernants*. Yet Elsa Maxwell had unerringly spotted the new and growing trend, which saw a Riviera suntan as fashionable for the first time. Whether she was paid $6,000 a year, $10,000 a year, or $20,000 a year to popularize out-of-season Monte Carlo is dubious—at different times she laid claim to all these sums—but Polignac proved a willing pupil. Although a beach proved impracticable, a new summer Casino duly opened in July 1927, as did one at Cannes in 1929, along with a giant, fifty-yard swimming pool.

Not all the locals were bewitched. The novelist Baroness Orczy was to recall bitterly how an olive grove whose "half an acre of land was worth a few shillings, rose in price in a couple of years to as many pounds," then "to as many £100-notes . . . dearer than freehold land in the City of London." Soon Monte Carlo "was getting big and bloated," reminding the baroness of La Fontaine's frog, so anxious to emulate a bull that he huffed and puffed until he burst.

This was the noontide of the great Riviera name-trains de luxe bearing the sun-seekers southward, most especially the blue-and-gold Mediterranean Express, known from 1922 as The Blue Train, whose Car 3538 had a special bathroom for David's use; the chocolate-and-cream Golden Arrow, which the French called the Flèche d'Or, whose London-based passengers boarded at Platform Two at Victoria Station promptly at 11 A.M. to make their Blue Train connection in Paris's Gare de Lyon; the age of the Mistral Express, from Paris to St. Raphael, of the Vienna-Cannes Express, and the Rome-Cannes Express. On all these trains, Rainbow passengers, like the Aga Khan and Coco Chanel, marked their superior status by their formidable quantities of Vuitton luggage: "rigid" luggage, often handmade for entire families by the Champs-Elysée's firm of Louis Vuitton, marked by the distinctive interlocked initials of the founder and curved lozenges encircling four-pointed stars. If Mabelle Swift de Wichfeld led the field with 176 Vuitton items, David, at a later stage of his life, was not far behind with 155 pieces.

The Sun Age proved a paradise for a new breed of parasite: the gigolo, literally a professional male dancing partner but often a kept man into the bargain. The type had been prefigured, as early as 1912, by the arrival at New York's Cafe de Paris of "Maurice," a dark-haired, debonair native of the New York slums, known as "the high priest of the decadent dance." His *danse des Apaches,* so abandoned that rumor had it he had once broken a woman partner's neck, prompted dowagers to shower him with $100 bills, begging him to lead them through a tango. (Often they received only a snub for their money, in the tradition of Bert Ambrose at London's Embassy.) For London gigolos, the pickings were leaner; from the Savoy or Quaglino's, they received a flat salary of up to £12 a week, gleaning perhaps a further £5 in tips. But on the Riviera, at Cannes' Carlton or Monte Carlo's Hôtel de Paris, a gigolo, though unsalaried, could make up to £1,600 in tips in a five-month season. So insidious were their attentions that Mrs. Ruthven Pratt, a Singer sewing machine heiress, left £30,000 in her will to the bodyguard, ex-Chief Inspector Stockley of Scotland Yard, who successfully kept them at bay. At the time of her death she was sixty-five.

Those who benefited most from the Riviera boom were, of course, the Rainbow architects, men like Pittsburgh-born Barry Dierks, the "Nash of the French Riviera," and his English partner, Colonel Eric Sawyer; from 1925 onward, they changed the face of the coastline. Following a remodeling job on W. Somerset Maugham's Villa Mauresque, near the tip of Cap Ferrat, Dierks and Sawyer had, by 1930, imposed a new standard of values hitherto known only to Hollywood: villas were no longer judged by the beauty of their gardens but by the size of their swimming pools.

This was in marked contrast to the English scene, where the available hired help had decreased, even in 1921, by 82,000 souls. As a consequence, the old Edwardian grandeur was giving place to the model symmetry of the eighteenth century, with such radical labor-saving innovations as tiled kitchen walls, rubber floors, percolators, electric grills and toasters, along with vacuum cleaners, central heating, more baths and wash basins, and electric light. But on the Riviera, where cheap labor was plentiful, Dierks and Sawyer could still plan such stately pleasure domes as Lord Cholmondeley's Villa Leroc, Lord Derby's Villa Sansovino, Lady Rothermere's Villa Pibonson, and actress Maxine Elliott's $300,000 folly, the Château de l'Horizon.

At first glance, the château was an impossible dream. Maxine, now retired and approaching sixty, demanded, like all of them, sun and a sea view, even though the one site available, barely fifty feet wide, lay between a sheer drop over sawtooth rocks into the Bay of Cannes and the railroad leading from Marseilles to the Italian border. But since expense, to Maxine, was no object, Dierks and Sawyer were given their heads. The rocks were blasted and leveled, and on the top was installed a swimming pool, with a chute to slide a swimmer twenty sheer feet into the sea, if such was his fancy. To isolate the château from the noise of passing trains, a huge white wall was erected on the landward side. Perched above the bay like a white Arab fort, the long low villa appeared to be welded into the solid rock.

Whether the sixteen-stone Maxine, an eater so compulsive she devoured butter by the pat, would herself use the chute, the architects didn't know, but the prudent Sawyer took the precaution of sizing up her buttocks with her dressmaker's tape measure just in case.

For both men, it was a profitable if sometimes nightmarish two-year assignment. "It won't do. Rip it out," were words that they came to dread, but in the end Maxine had achieved her sunlit heart's desire: a villa where every bedroom had its private balcony, with a bathroom shaped like a tranche of her favorite chocolate cake, its narrow end to the sea, and where, in an enormous salon overlooking the pool, she could entertain such old friends as David, Elsie de Wolfe, and Elsa Maxwell.

All this was in keeping with an age when American money, often invested according to whim, was causing whole tracts of virgin Riviera land to blossom like the rose. It was not, in fact, the tiny Casino at Juan-les-Pins—which the Rainbows called "Johnny Pang"—southwest of Antibes that first attracted Frank Jay Gould, the melancholy, withdrawn brother of the ill-starred Anna, but the hors d'oeuvres at the newly opened Hotel Lutetia nearby: a succulent display of onions stuffed with currants, red pimentoes with anchovy sauce, and quenelles of celery with horseradish. For Gould, these appetizers were reason enough, in 1927, to pump 50 million francs into Edgar Beaudouin's three-year-old Casino, and to build the splendid Hôtel Provençal, which boasted two novelties for the new breed of summer visitor: a private bathroom attached to every bedroom, along with a cake of soap. One year later, as a token of their appreciation, the French made him a Commander of the Legion of Honor.

Those lacking the means to commission a Dierks or a Sawyer bought cheaply on the open market—the dollar exchanged at fifty francs in 1926—and called on local labor for renovations. The true pioneers of this summer life-style, both of them Americans, were, as their old friend Archibald MacLeish acknowledged, "masters in the art of living": Sara and Gerald Murphy.

Arriving in France in 1921, they adapted to the European life as if they had known no other. This in itself was remarkable, for although the former Sara Sherman Wiborg, eldest daughter of a Cincinnati ink manufacturer, had spent much of her childhood in Europe, and was fluent in French, German, and Italian by the age of sixteen, Gerald Murphy's European contacts had been primarily vicarious. His father, Patrick Francis Murphy, had spent twenty-five years studying the European Rainbows' way of life to boost the sales of his fashionable New York store, Mark Cross, at Fifth Avenue and Twenty-fifth Street, the first store to feature Minton china, Sheffield cutlery, and Waterford cut glass.

From 1924 onward, the Murphy's Villa America, sited on the two-and-a-half-mile peninsula known as Cap d'Antibes, three miles distant from the seaport of that name on the Gulf of Nice, was a mecca for all those who were seeking new directions in art for the twentieth century: Ernest Hemingway, Pablo Picasso, Igor Stravinsky, the impresario of the Ballet Russe, Sergei Diaghilev. Yet curiously it was not until March 1926—the same year that Elsa Maxwell began her transformation of Monte Carlo—that the summer Riviera was truly born. In that month, Ben Finney, a fun-loving Virginian expatriate, asked a favor of the proprietor of the Hôtel du Cap d'Antibes, André Sella. Although Sella was just then preparing to close down for the season, would he be prepared to stay open if Finney threw a gala July 4 Independence Day party?

Sella agreed. If crazy Americans were ready to put custom his way, it was not his job to dissuade them.

On July 4, summoned by invitation, sixty distinguished guests arrived at the otherwise deserted hotel, among them Noel Coward, Captain Edward Molyneux, the Murphys, Sir Hugo de Bathe, the second husband of Lillie Langtry, the singer Grace Moore, and the critic Alexander Woollcott. Also prominent among the revels were a young American couple who had arrived in France two years back and to whom the Murphys had acted as friendly guardians in Paris during the previous winter: F. Scott Fitzgerald, the creator of "The Jazz Age," and his wife, Zelda.

Six years earlier, Scott's novel, the international best-seller *This Side of Paradise,* had profoundly shocked the old guard, though telling David's generation little that they didn't already know: that youth, which had seen "all wars fought, all faiths in man shaken," habitually held petting parties, which sometimes went "all the way" in the back of parked sedans, drank deeply of bootleg hooch from hip-flasks, and saw the proper state of morality as "a single standard, and that a low one."

Yet the man who had dreamed up "The Jazz Age" was ironically fated to be destroyed by it. "I never in my life saw two more beautiful people than those two when they arrived," André Sella was to recall much later. "I watched them in the course of five years become human wrecks."

Again, the seeds had been sown six years earlier—more precisely, on Saturday, April 3, 1920, a month after the publication of his novel, when twenty-four-year-old Scott, a blond, slightly built young man with green eyes, already known from his

Princeton University days as a prodigal, footloose, drunken rowdy, married twenty-year-old Zelda Sayre, a spoiled-rotten judge's daughter from Montgomery, Alabama, in New York's St. Patrick's Cathedral. Though both sought the same things out of life—success, fame, big-city glamour—both were unstable exhibitionists, each egging on the other to wilder and more tastelessly adolescent escapades.

Their honeymoon in Suite 2109 of New York's Biltmore Hotel was the Fitzgeralds' marriage in microcosm. They turned handstands in the lobby; they rode to a party with one on the roof of the taxi, the other on the hood. In the sixth row of the stalls at *George White's Scandals,* Scott, after divesting himself of his coat and shirt, was hustled out in his underwear by a posse of ushers. They rolled champagne bottles down Fifth Avenue and leaped into fountains; predictably, after several weeks of this, the Biltmore asked them to leave, and they moved on for more of the same to the Commodore. It was all part of what Scott called "the greatest, gaudiest spree in history," yet in rare moments of sobriety the truth broke through. "I should like to sit down with half a dozen chosen companions," he wrote to Maxwell Perkins, his editor at Scribner's, in August 1921, "and drink myself to death."

The tragedy was that Scott, like Bernard Berenson, suffered an irreconcilable dichotomy; yearning to be true to his own genuine creative powers, he yet wanted to coin money. And the novels, although much in vogue with the Rainbow People, just did not coin enough. The solution lay in the short stories he churned out with such deadly facility, working for forty-eight hours at a stretch, stories about willful and lovely young girls, which he despised, like "The Diamond As Big as The Ritz," yet for which *The Saturday Evening Post* paid $2,500, later $4,000. These stories, above all, were his passport to mix in Rainbow society.

The son of a wholesale grocery salesman from St. Paul, Minnesota, Scott was in fact no sophisticate but an ingrained provincial, who never ceased to view the Rainbows with wide-eyed wonder. In a classic interchange, which has been quoted ad nauseam, he once told Ernest Hemingway, "The rich are very different from you and me," to which Hemingway replied imperceptively, "Yes, they have more money." The truth was subtler; the very rich were different because they had rarely, if ever, lain awake in the small hours agonizing over money.

Try as he might, all Scott's efforts to set his life in order came to nothing. Throughout the summer of 1920, he struggled to complete a second novel, the prophetically named *The Beautiful and Damned*, in a succession of hotel rooms, while Zelda, no homebody, piled his used shirts in a drawer and went out on the town. In May 1921, in an effort to break the spell, they moved to Westport, Connecticut, vainly hoping for rural peace and quiet, but the parties went on and on regardless. "All the stories that came into my head had a touch of disaster in them," Scott was to write. "The lovely young creatures in my novels went to ruin, the diamond mountains of my short stories blew up, my millionaires were as beautiful and damned as Thomas Hardy's peasants." Within four months, infinitely wearied of Westport, Scott and Zelda were back in New York.

At Great Neck, Long Island, 1923 saw "the summer of 1,000 parties but no work"; their fun had now assumed an ugly and destructive element. Though legend was to brand Scott as a heroic tippler, in truth his alcoholic tolerance for the bootleg gin he swigged was markedly low. Now he was vanishing into New York on three-day benders; later, neighbors would spot him asleep on his front lawn. At dinner parties he crawled round beneath the table on his hands and knees, like a bibulous toddler, hacked off his own tie with a kitchen knife, or tried to drink his soup with a fork. The writer Van Wyck Brooks was to recall a typical encounter at the New York apartment of the Ernest Boyds; after the others had finished their dinner, Scott and Zelda arrived an hour late, fell asleep over the soup that was brought in for them, then awoke refreshed to telephone an order for two cases of champagne along with a fleet of taxis to take them all to a nightclub.

For neither Scott nor Zelda was there any middle ground, only the most violent of extremes; the gods had bestowed on them every gift, it seemed, bar stability. Yet by 1925, the year when Scott published *The Great Gatsby,* both were still convinced that something could be salvaged from the wreckage. The solution was to head for Paris, then for Cap d'Antibes, to share the sun-soaked expatriate life that the Murphys had perfected. It was the beginning of a new idyll, Scott believed, and he pictured it in a poignant and almost-forgotten poem:

> *There'd be an orchestra*
> *Bingo! bango!*
> *Playing for us*
> *To dance the tango,*
> *And people would clap*
> *When we arose,*
> *At her sweet face*
> *And my new clothes.*

Scott had perhaps never read the warning that Socrates, centuries earlier, had given a disgruntled Athenian: "How can you wonder your travels do you no good when you carry yourself around with you? You are saddled with the very thing that drove you away." What Scott was saddled with was a drink problem that was to prove intractable for almost all of his life; Zelda got plastered because she enjoyed it, but Scott was a potential alcoholic. After another evening's great and gaudy spree, Zelda, next morning, took stock of last night's bad behavior and sent suitable apologies to their friends. But Scott had invariably forgotten.

George Scheuer, then an apprentice bartender at the Paris Ritz, at whose bar Scott was seen more often than in his apartment on the rue Tilsit, once recalled approaching Scott before luncheon and venturing diffidently: "Mr. Fitzgerald, it cost me a hundred francs to get that man a new hat."

"What man?" asked the puzzled Scott.

"That man whose hat you smashed."

"Did I smash someone's hat?"

Indeed, he had, Scheuer explained; the previous evening, he had leaped from his bar stool without provocation and smashed in the hat of a stranger who had just entered. "If anything like that happens again," Scheuer warned, "we can't serve you in here."

"You're absolutely right," agreed the penitent Scott.

It would, of course, happen again—if not at the Ritz then at some other Paris bar or nightclub. For unlike the Murphys, Scott never came to terms with the French—or for that matter with any other European nationality. Essentially, he was a xenophobic tourist, with little more than indifferent restaurant French, and scant interest in the art, the music, and the ballet of the period: a man who would doggedly order a club sandwich in a gourmet restaurant like Voisin. In drink, he would tip an orchestra leader 1,000 francs for one tune or a doorman 100 francs for calling a cab, yet, given a few drinks more, the free spender became a truculent, drunken bully, who would chase hotel bellhops or rip out stairway rails. As Ernest Hemingway told writer Morley Callaghan: "There's no distinction in punching Scott on the nose. Every taxi driver in Paris has done it."

It was at Cap d'Antibes, that summer of 1926, that both Fitzgeralds now seemed past redemption. There was the evening with the Murphys, at the Casino at Juan-les-Pins, when Scott began lobbing ashtrays in the direction of a nearby table; another evening, at the Villa America, when he hurled a fig from the dessert bowl at the Princesse de Caraman-Chimay, hitting her between the shoulder blades, and smashed several of Sara Murphy's Venetian wine glasses. On another occasion, Zelda attempted suicide, hurling herself down a flight of stone stairs at Saint-Paul-de-Vence, because Scott was paying court to the dancer Isadora Duncan.

It was a summer that foreshadowed all their future: their 1927 sojourn in Hollywood, when Scott collected watches and jewelry from the guests at a party and boiled them up with a can of tomato soup, their moonlight flit from the Ambassador Hotel, leaving their bill unpaid. In Paris, in 1928, Scott twice landed in jail on drunk and disorderly charges; a year later they were back at Cap d'Antibes, hurling garbage over the Murphys' wall. Both were now fighting a last-ditch battle against Zelda's growing schizophrenia and Scott's alcoholism and they were losing all along the line. By 1930, Zelda would spend most of the last eighteen years of her life in and out of mental hospitals, tortured by religious mania, convinced that she was in direct contect with Jesus Christ, William the Conqueror, and Mary Stuart— "all the stock paraphernalia of insane asylum jokes," Scott wrote. Scott himself died in 1940 as a Hollywood hack writer, after earning—and spending—more than $386,000 in sixteen years.

So the bright Riviera dream of that orchestra playing "Bingo! bango!" proved illusory. The reality was more in the mocking lines of the writer Cyril Connolly, who made one of their number:

> *We're back on the old Scott Circuit*
> *On a bender as big as the Ritz,*
> *Where Gerald is shaking a Murphy,*
> *And Zelda is throwing a Fitz . . .*
> *All high on the old Scott Circuit,*
> *While Ernest is boozing in Spain;*
> *Shall we ever get back to Nantucket*
> *And wear a tuxedo again?*

* * *

In many respects, David's crowd scarcely differed at all from the old Marlborough House set. Even fourteen years after King Edward's funeral, writers, as a class, were still suspect, identified with vaguely socialist leanings. Scott Fitzgerald was one of a small hard core of Society writers whose works were not only standard reading for a lady's bedside table but whose presence was acceptable at a lady's luncheon table or cocktail party. Another of like stripe, who was welcome above the salt, was Dikran Kouyoumdjian, who, in 1919, had, for the best reasons, changed his name to Michael Arlen; the publisher William Heinemann was ready to bring out his first book, *The London Venture*, if he hit on a name the public could pronounce. A hasty glance at the London telephone directory showed that "Michael Arlen" was going begging.

A dark, dapper twenty-four-year-old, Arlen's sole concession to Bohemianism was a black slouch hat worn at a rakish angle—an effect slightly marred by his amethyst shirt studs. His family, middle-class Manchester importers, had once nourished hopes he might join the firm, but commerce and the middle-class life were not for Arlen. From the first, like Fitzgerald, he wanted the big time. The problem was how to achieve it.

Working from a small room above a shop in Shepherd's Market, Mayfair, with a £2-a-week allowance from his father, Arlen was at first groping, eking out his scanty sales writing articles for Alfred R. Orage's *The New Age*. It was Orage himself who suggested that Arlen, as an Armenian, should deliberately adopt a cleverly wrought artificial style—the literary equivalent of Paul Poiret's creations. When such impeccable literary mentors as D. H. Lawrence and George Moore supported that advice, Arlen saw his way clear.

Although he roomed in Mayfair, he was, of course, an outsider looking in, not yet welcome in the sleek and silken world of hostesses like Emerald Cunard or Florence De Peña, whose Charles Street house had witnessed, in 1922, the first twelve-hour cocktail party. Thus, denied access to what really went on, Arlen went one better: he invented a Mayfair that never was.

It was a world of gallant, perfumed degenerates, and female Don Juans lusting after bullfighters, where "the beasts walk glittering up and down the soiled loneliness of desire," peopled by fantasy girls with names like Consuelo, "a hungry girl, made to rot men," and Diavalen and Shelmerdene and Manana and Venice, all of whom drank champagne for breakfast and swore (just a little) and were bored by the silly young lords who adored them. In 1922, his first novel, *Piracy*, had much of this Arabian Nights bouquet, but whether Arlen could keep it up the critics had cause to wonder.

Arlen could. In the summer of 1923, aged twenty-seven, he settled for two months in his parents' little Manchester villa, working uninterruptedly on a new novel. Its opening sentence was: "It has occurred to the writer to call this unimportant history, The Green Hat, because a green hat was the first thing about her that he saw." *The Green Hat* and its storm-tossed heroine, Iris March, had arrived on the Rainbow scene.

Every young female Rainbow of the international set, like Daphne Vivian or Helen Lee Eames Doherty, saw herself in Iris. Iris had a yellow Hispano-Suiza and nicotine-stained fingers and was, in her own words, "a house of men," but nonetheless, as Arlen saw her, "as gallant as a boy." "It is not good to have a pagan body and a Chislehurst mind, as I have," Iris went on record. "It is hell for the body and terror for the mind." Iris, of course, married "Boy" Fenwick, who "died for purity," committing suicide on their wedding night rather than reveal that he had syphilis; at the end, after much soul-searching, Iris, who had all along been in love with somebody else, paid for such misdemeanors as an abortion in Paris by crashing her Hispano into a tree. "Above her neck her hair died a very manly death," Arlen wound up, "a more manly death than 'bobbed' hair was ever known to die."

Overnight, Arlen was a made man, the darling of the Rainbows. In appropriate fashion, he celebrated by dropping in at Cartier's, on Bond Street, to purchase a jeweled stickpin, a blue and white duck mounted on gold, and later a $27,000 yellow Rolls-Royce, which he drove to Manchester to ensure an "M.A." registration. In the lounge of the Savoy he could count green hats by the score; he was at once persona grata at David's favorite watering place, The Embassy Club, where he, too, was seen to be sporting a Hawes and Curtis backless waistcoat.

But not only English Rainbows took *The Green Hat* to their hearts; it was a smash hit in America, too. In 1924 alone, the book's U.S. sales totaled 250,000 copies; all through the Midwest, Arlen's portrait loomed in department store windows, flanked by green hats "worn bravely, *pour le sport*." For Arlen had hit on the surefire gimmick of adapting *The Green Hat* as a play, which was launched simultaneously, in September 1925, at London's Adelphi Theatre, with, inevitably, Tallulah, and at New York's Broadhurst Theater, with Katharine Cornell. Its Broadway impresario, the inimitable Al Woods, had cabled the puzzled Arlen, "Hello, sweetheart, love and kisses, how about $2,500

[D]oris Delavigne and Viscount Castlerosse at Maxine Elliott's Château de l'Horizon.

[Ed]ward, Prince of Wales, (*front left*) in drag for [a r]eview given by the officers of the battleship *[Re]pulse*, 1925.

Texas Guinan, 1929.

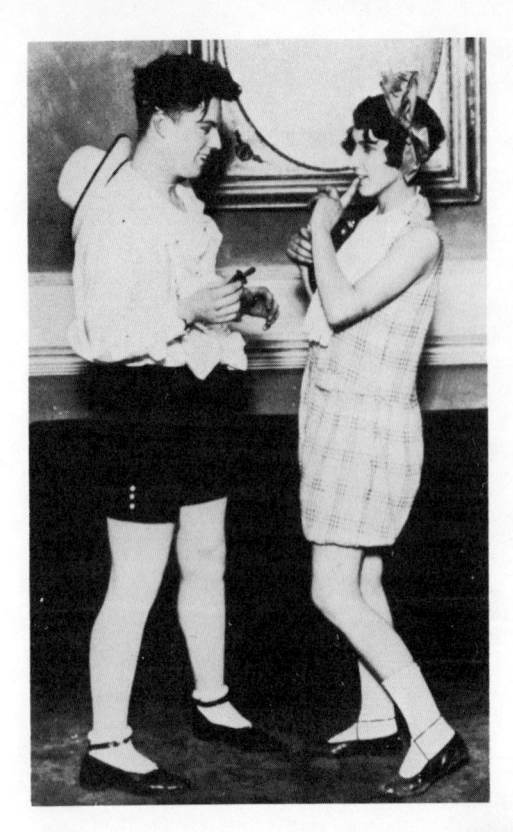

Guests at Mrs. Rosemary Sandars' Baby Party in London.

...erald Cunard (*opposite*) and daughter Nancy (*above*) as seen by Cecil Beaton.

Gertie Lawrence and Noël Coward in *Private Lives*, 1930.

Tallulah Bankhead in sultry mood.

Two 'trees': (left) Douglas Byng in Charlot's *Revue of 1933*, and Coco Chanel at a friend's Forest Ball 1938.

Chanel with her models in 1938.

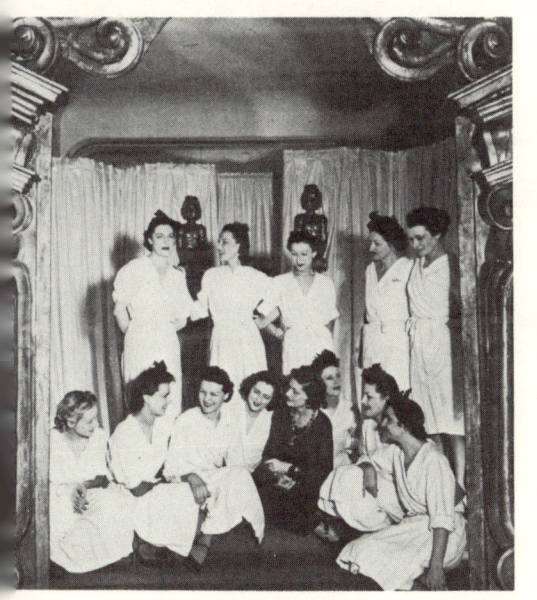

Edward, Prince of Wales, and Wallis Simpson at Ascot, 1935.

Barbara Hutton (*centre*) with Count Kurt Haugwitz-Reventlow and Lady Janet Montague at St Moritz.

The *Ile de France* about to sail on her first post-war voyage from Southampton.

The Ritz Hotel, London: tea in the Palm Court and (*below*) Michael Arlen chatting in the barber's shop.

Beatrice Lillie in wartime uniform with Sherman Billingsley at his Stork Club, New York.

Walter Winchell on the air.

Maria Callas and Aristotle Onassis on board the *Christina*.

advance royalty?" On his first day in New York, Woods called on him at the Ritz-Carlton with a case of whisky; on his second, Woods sent over a welcome-to-the-city gift, a platinum wristwatch encircled with diamonds. "I'm going to like America," Arlen told Katharine Cornell that night. "I'm going to like it very much."

He liked even more the writer Louis Bromfield's comment that "nothing quite like the opening of *The Green Hat* has been seen in New York since the Civil War draft riots." Men and women were so avid for tickets that scalpers were charging prices in excess of $100 for a single seat.

Although the New York run lasted twenty-nine weeks, not all the cast found Arlen's over-the-top lines easy to deliver. Miss Cornell's leading man, Britain's Leslie Howard, fought manfully to keep a straight face as he told his leading lady, "You are a woman with magic eyes and a soft, white body that beats at my mind like a whip," or "You are my dark angel and my tower of delight in the twilight of the world."

Yet Arlen could cope with his newfound celebrity in a way that the unstable Fitzgerald never could. Although he was earning about £20,000 a year from other trifles like *Mayfair, These Charming People,* and *Lily Christine,* he quickly cultivated a nice line in self-deprecation. "I was a flash in the pan," he told a *New Yorker* interviewer, not long before his death in 1956. ". . . and there was, by the grace of God, a great deal of gold-dust in the pan." When Rebecca West described him as being "every other inch a gentleman," Arlen took pains to circulate it widely; on another occasion, he claimed to be suffering from "pernicious Armenia." His literary career, he persisted, stroking the lambskin collar of his topcoat, could be summarized in one sentence: "Per ardua ad astrakhan."

All along, Arlen never lost sight of his one ambition: to be entirely independent and produce only one book every two years by the time he was thirty-five. Along with Atlanta Mercati, the Greek countess whom he married in 1928, he lived peacefully in his white villa in the hills behind Cannes, writing only in the forenoon, golfing or skimming the bay in his speedboat, *Swal-*

low II, each afternoon. "I have the affection of my wife, the tolerance of my children, and the friendship of head waiters," he liked to say. "What more do I need?"

It was, in effect, Arlen's generosity that launched another Rainbow favorite on a more lucrative career. Hitherto known mainly as a gifted composer of lyrics and sketches for the revues of Charles B. Cochran and André Charlot, Noel Coward had a play trying out at a fringe theater, the Everyman, Hampstead; the stumbling block was that finance was lacking to transfer it to the West End. Over lunch at the London Ritz, he broached this with Arlen—who asked no details of the play or its title, set no terms for repayment, or even expressed a desire to read the script. Instead he wrote out a check for £250 and went on giving Coward a blow-by-blow account of a new short story that *he* was planning.

The play, *The Vortex*, featuring Coward as a youngster hooked on drugs and saddled with a promiscuous mother, shocked the old guard to the core of its being. "Mr. Noel Coward," fulminated the *Sunday Express* columnist, James Douglas, "excites and titillates by shovelling up the ordure of an unprincipled smart set, exposing their nasty souls, bedizening their ugly manners, while the audience revels in a pandemonium of laxity."

This was what the profession, in a later day, would know as "a money notice."

Coward, like Arlen, was shrewd enough to fuel the sense of outrage. Without delay, he posed for a photograph of himself in bed wearing a Chinese silk dressing gown, in a scarlet bedroom decorated with nudes, wearing an expression of "advanced degeneracy." Then he followed up *The Vortex* with *Fallen Angels,* another Tallulah vehicle, which provoked an even greater storm of protest. It was, one critic charged, "vulgar, obscene, and degenerate"; the *Daily Express* was reduced to ejaculations: "Drunkenness. Drunken women. Drunken young women. Drunken young married women, both confessing to immoral relations with the same man."

This alone was reason enough for the Rainbows to take Coward to their hearts.

For a new breed of playwrights and novelists was arising, who portrayed the Rainbows as they liked to see themselves: men with an instinctive feel for the light touch and perfect timing, such as Avery Hopwood *(The Best People)*, Philip Barry *(Paris Bound, Hotel Universe)*, and S. N. Behrman *(The Second Man* and *Wine of Choice)*. Another past master was Frederick Lonsdale *(The Last of Mrs. Cheyney, On Approval, Canaries Sometimes Sing)*, who shared with Arlen and Coward the secret of employing the upper-class weapon of ridicule with searing effect. All of them had the knack of creating magnificent dilettantes who took no thought of the financial morrow, essentially worthless characters but always clever, elegant, and witty—never worthy but dull.

Moving in a narrow and restricted world, they were inevitably guilty of a kind of literary incest. Arlen's convention-flouting Iris March was based on Nancy Cunard, who in a racist age flouted convention well and truly by taking a black jazz musician, Henry Crowder, for a lover—but Nancy was equally the model for Lucy Tantamount in Aldous Huxley's *Point Counterpoint* and Myra Viveash in his *Antic Hay*, as well as Baby Bucktrout in Wyndham Lewis's *The Roaring Queen*. In Fitzgerald's *Tender Is The Night*, Dick and Nicole Diver were derived from his long-suffering hosts, the Murphys. The original of Lord Tarlyon in Arlen's *Piracy* was Napier Sturt, Tallulah's lover; Aram Melekian was Calouste Gulbenkian, "Mr. Five-Percent," who changed his teenage mistress every year until he reached the age of eighty. If the overweight Lord Castlerosse was Reginald, eleventh earl of Mount Wyroc in Arlen's *Young Men In Love* and Lord Markworth in Arnold Bennett's *Lilian*, he was also, because of his fearsome fights in public with his wife, the former Doris Delavigne, Elyot Chase in Coward's *Private Lives*.

Arlen himself became the Irishman, Michaelis, in D. H. Lawrence's *Lady Chatterley's Lover*—"he pined to be where he didn't belong . . . among the English upper classes"—and the beautiful if glacial Lady Diana Cooper was, by turns, Lady Queenie Paulle in Arnold Bennett's *The Pretty Lady*, Julia Stitch in Evelyn Waugh's *Scoop*, Lady Artemis Hooper in Lawrence's *Aaron's Rod*, Lady Leone in Nancy Mitford's *Don't Tell Alfred*, and Ruby Maclean in Enid Bagnold's *The Loved and Envied*.

Few, however, went to such lengths as did W. Somerset

Maugham, when rehearsals of his smart society comedy, *Our Betters,* fell due. For a memorable luncheon foursome, Maugham invited to his Bryanston Square flat the vulgarian millionaire storeowner, Gordon Selfridge, Lady Michelham, the gigolo-hunting former Geraldine Bradshaw, actress Constance Collier, and actor Alfred Drayton.

The play's first night at the Globe, in September 1923, was one that both Selfridge and Lady Michelham, indefatigable firstnighters, somehow contrived to miss, for, at the eleventh hour, intelligence reached them that Drayton and Miss Collier, all through luncheon, had been paying far more attention to their homework than their food. Behind the footlights the vain, pathetic Duchesse de Surennes and the coarse-grained tycoon, Arthur Fenwick, were them to the all-too-recognizable life.

* * *

For a tribe as free as the winds that blew, the Rainbow People's journeyings in the twenties were remarkably circumspect. No one chose to emulate Mrs. Eva Stotesbury, of Palm Beach, who embarked on a $500,000 African safari to equip herself with a matching set of crocodile luggage. Instead, their European round was a relentless pursuit of the right spot at the right time—to be sure of meeting the right people.

Easter, for example, was unthinkable except at Le Touquet, ten miles from Boulogne, "a piece of England dropped among the pine trees of the sea coast," where even the little villas had English names like "The Rookery." The attractions were the golf course, comparable to the best English links, and the Baccarat Club, as the gaming room in the Casino was known. David and Freda were always there, nodding and smiling to Lord and Lady Portarlington, Poppy Baring Thursby, and the golfing Sweeny brothers, Charles and Robert—people to whom they had nodded and smiled only twenty-four hours earlier at the first night of a Cochran revue. On at least one occasion, David, whose head for liquor was weak, entered the Casino falling-down drunk, in true Scott Fitzgerald tradition.

Equally, Whitsuntide, Pentecost, was the time to be seen at

Deauville, on the Normandy coastline, for a season that lasted, for some mystic reason, precisely nineteen days. This was the sorest of subjects with François André, the melancholy onetime undertaker's assistant who managed the Casino—"I don't want anyone to sneeze without it costing at least 100 sous."

It was at Deauville, in the huge, cream-colored main rooms of the Casino, that Rainbow royals like the Aga Khan and King Alfonso XIII of Spain plunged heavily at one of the forty chemin de fer tables; at Table Four, the minimum bet, even then, was £80, yet the Aga Khan would stake £1,600 on one turn of a card. In the private room at the back, the stakes were higher still, for here the Greek syndicate held sway, a formidable quartet of piranhas who reputedly cleaned up £1 billion at Deauville, Cannes, and Monte Carlo: Nico Zographos, son of a Greek professor of political economy, who knew up to 700 ways of winning at écarte; Eli Eliopulo, an elegant man who sported an eyeglass; Zagret Kouyoumdjian, a distant cousin of Arlen; and the tall, broad-shouldered Athanase Vagliano.

Teaming up in Deauville in 1922 to lure the rich suckers to the tables, they hit upon the insidious system of "Tout Va," meaning the sky was the limit, the syndicate would cover any wager of any size. To play baccarat with the Greeks, a thirty-million-franc float was called for, and punters like the motor-magnate, André Citroën, who often gambled to lose for publicity reasons—"It is only news if I lose and can obviously afford it"—might drop 13 million francs in one session. Another victim was bandleader Bert Ambrose, who once dropped £102,000 in four days; before he could return to the Embassy Club, Luigi Naintre had to cable him £100 fare money. Ambrose was one of many who never learned; in his lifetime his vendetta with the Greeks cost him £500,000.

By mid-May, many Rainbows had returned to England for the three-month London season, but late August and September offered a choice of resorts at which to be seen: perhaps the now-fashionable Cap d'Antibes, to nod and smile to Otto Kahn or the Princess Faucigny-Lucinge, in her white silk pantaloons and tight silk bodice, perhaps to Biarritz, to exchange the same salutations with Daisy Fellowes, Elsa Maxwell, or David himself—"Old battering-ram Elsa always gives the best parties," he acknowledged—or even to the Venice Lido, popularized by Elsa in 1920, where Noel Coward or Queen Marie of Romania might be found.

For some, Christmas was Christmas only in a suite at the Palace Hotel, St. Moritz, 6,000 feet up among the ski slopes of the Engadine valley, a caravanserai where the service under Hans Badrutt, grandson of the founder, was so streamlined that if a bulb glowing on a panel of 350 lights in his office did not go out in thirty seconds—showing a call for room service had been answered—Badrutt would know the reason why. Unlike the staid Suvretta House, the Palace, Badrutt would claim proudly, had always been for "the fast set," where Rainbows brought their mistresses rather than their wives. It was glittering and showy and cosmopolitan, with a guest list that included Gloria Swanson, (Marchioness de la Falaise), the first Hollywood star to marry into the French aristocracy; the Marchesa Casati, with her pet leopards on a leash; and Harold Dodge, the automobile heir, who ordered his first Planter's Punch at 5 P.M. and was still ordering them when the sun heralded the dawn.

After Christmas, there were only three acceptable places to be seen: on the Boulevard de la Croisette, at Cannes; on the Promenade des Anglais, at Nice; or in the Place du Casino, at Monte Carlo. Baron Maurice de Rothschild was one who never missed a Monte Carlo season; he arrived accompanied by a blood donor, in case his life was endangered, and his own chef. Since the kitchens at the Hôtel du Paris failed to please him, he hired a second, "eating apartment" with a huge kitchen, to which he retired at mealtimes. Always on the Monte Carlo scene were the Dolly Sisters, Rosie and Jennie (née Roszicka and Jancsi Deutsch, from New York), accomplished revue and cabaret artistes and equally accomplished coquettes, armored with diamond bracelets from their wrists to their elbows. In their wake trailed their own private sugar daddy, department store magnate Gordon Selfridge, whom Jennie mulcted of £2 million over an eight-year period.

Of all the casinos that lured the Rainbows, Monte Carlo, in the principality of Monaco, exerted the most potent spell; begun in 1856 as a thirty-year concession to two astute brothers, François and Louis Blanc, it had, as early as 1898, served as a magnet for forty-eight hotel proprietors and fifteen jewelers. By 1910, it had become the hub of the Rainbow world from December to March. "Everybody had money then," reminisced Paul Ketchiva, a croupier who spun his first wheel on February 25, 1912, "and knew how to lose it." But even in the twenties, the syndicate faced some plungers as reckless as Bendor, second Duke of Westminster, who played four of the eighteen roulette tables simultaneously to keep boredom at bay; for years, Bendor held the Monte Carlo record of backing black in maximums twenty-three times in succession.

Over the years, many Monte Carlo legends sprang up, some of them spun from whole cloth, like the spectacular suicide rate—which, in fact, averaged eleven a year among 350,000 visitors—but some wholly valid. Tradition *did* demand that the table be draped in black baize if the bank was broken. Two deaf-mutes, Costo and Rodolpho, indeed had charge of a storeroom where 100,000 names of those banned from the Casino were filed, a list including not only cheats but all domestic servants on principle. A professional physiognomist, M. Le Broq, who had memorized at least 60,000 of those faces, was on duty at the entrance to the Salles Privée for eight hours each day.

Yet the Casino had its own code of honor for those whose luck ran out. Up to 1939, they were scrupulous in repatriating all failed gamblers to their country of origin, even as far as Melbourne or Idaho—a system known as the *viatique* or fare home—and local residents who had gone to the wall sometimes received a monthly Casino "pension" to help them make ends meet.

As the twenties wore on, a new clan of chroniclers was arising to chart the foibles of society: men who knew, for the benefit of their readers, precisely what André Citroën had lost on any one Casino night, or the Dolly Sisters' bill of fare at Ciro's. These were the gossip columnists, whose origins were, inevitably, American; at the turn of the century, William Randolph

Hearst had led the field by decreeing that reverence was dead. In future, all socialites would be referred to by their first names: "Mamie" Fish, "Tessie" Oelrichs. The workaholic Irish proprietor of the London *Daily Mail*, Lord Northcliffe, was not slow to follow. "Get more names in the paper—the more aristocratic the better, if there is a news story around them," he counseled his editors. "Everyone likes reading about people in better circumstances than his or her own."

At a stroke, press barons like Hearst, James Gordon Bennett, and Northcliffe had virtually abolished privacy forever; all were tacticians of the new "gent's room" journalism, whose "gee-whiz" emotions were purveyed in headlines that could be read across a room. Their prevailing mood was so febrile that Hearst's managing editor, the elegant, monocled Samuel Chamberlain, if told there was no news, would yell at the reporters, "Get excited, damn it!"—but most often the piquant life-style of the Rainbows provided just that news that was otherwise lacking.

The mentor for all those who would follow was Maury Henry Biddle Paul, who, in 1919, in the New York *Journal*'s "Cholly Knickerbocker" column, had coined the phrase "Café Society." Hired by Hearst in this same year for $150 a week, "Mr. Bitch," a plump little exquisite who favored Mary Chess cologne and outsize lawn handkerchiefs, had soon built up a five-million-strong readership, working out of offices on Columbus Circle. He was the first Society editor to use photographs, and in the small select world bounded by the Upper East Side and the Waldorf his word was law; at the Colony Restaurant, on Madison Avenue, whose reputation he secured by claiming they were turning away custom, he picked up no checks, although tipping lavishly. A staunch supporter of the Old Guard, Fifth Avenue as opposed to Park, he felt a genuine pang when Society's leaders didn't live up to their duties. Though he duly chronicled their doings, for him Café Society was always "T-H-A-T Set." "To see oneself in print is as enticing to a parvenu as a Sargent portrait," one sage commented. And to keep in Paul's good books, socialites heaped gifts upon him, everything from Aubusson carpets to station wagons.

Like all the clan, Paul was an unabashed table-hopper; some

of his best newsbreaks stemmed from those suave intrusions. A typical "Cholly" beat came on May 10, 1922, when Paul, lunching at the Plaza Hotel, on Fifth Avenue, spotted the former debutante, Charlotte Demarest, in earnest conclave with Count Ed Zichy, from Budapest, a sometime flame of two years back at Southampton, Long Island. Signaling the waiter to bring his coffee to their table, Paul greeted them graciously, "My dears, what skulduggery are you up to?"

"Maury," the tall, romantic Count confided, "Charlotte and I love each other."

This was news indeed, for on May 11, as Paul knew from his clippings files, Charlotte was to marry George Burton, formerly Bernheimer, a young man-about-Manhattan, whose family had made a fortune out of brewing before prudently changing their name. Charitably, Paul reminded them of this fact.

"But that's just it, Maury," said Charlotte timidly. "I'm not *going* to marry George Burton. I'm going to marry Ed. I'm going to marry him today."

Cautioning them to sit tight, Paul hastened to a telephone and, in approved movie tradition, warned the *Journal*'s city desk to hold a sizeable chunk of tomorrow's front page. Then he returned to the star-crossed lovers to elicit details: Charlotte, going over the guest list one last time, had found Ed Zichy's name omitted and called him to request his attendance. When the Count, in return, invited her to lunch, it was suddenly a case of love at second sight.

Maury now lost no time in validating his scoop, bundling them into a taxi and downtown to the Municipal Building. Assured that the wedding was now accomplished fact, he returned to Columbus Circle to draft a page one story for his five million readers, one of whom was George Burton. Snug in the barber's chair at the Biltmore next morning, his face daubed with lather, Burton unfolded his *Journal* to read Maury's smug greeting: "George Burton will read here that his bride-to-be, Charlotte Demarest, whom he was to make Mrs. Burton this afternoon, is now the bride of another, having eloped yesterday with Count Ed Zichy. . . ."

It was reportedly with an outraged roar of "HELL'S BELLS!"

that Burton sprang from the chair like a man who had sat on a cactus and dashed the paper to the floor.

Such scoops were not uncommon in Rainbowland, and none was more adept at pulling them off than the wisecracking prophet of what he had christened "The Whoopee Era," the man calling himself "Mrs. Winchell's Little Boy, Walter." In 1924, when Paul was already firmly established, Winchell was a $100-a-week drama critic and Broadway columnist on Fulton Oursler's *Evening Graphic;* five years later, for $500 a week, he had switched to the New York *Mirror,* where his page ten column remained a fixture for thirty-four years. Soon more than 30 million Americans were following both Winchell's column and his broadcasts, delivered at a frenetic 215 words a minute over a 260-station hookup, using a dit-dah-dit telegraphic noisemaker to punctuate his items. With fans who ranged from President Franklin D. Roosevelt to Lord Louis Mountbatten, Winchell rose rapidly to the $500,000-a-year class.

He was a phenomenon who without the Rainbows would never have come to pass. For all his readers, the Broadwayites stood in for the nobility; with Winchell as their guide, they toured the night spots in the company of heiresses and playboys. A small, vulpine man, rarely seen without his gray snap-brim fedora, Winchell never once paid out a cent for information, yet his tipsters numbered everyone from bank presidents to office boys. "He wrote," said his fellow journalist Ben Hecht, "like a man honking in a traffic jam," a strident, staccato style, harsher than Paul's, yet cumulatively effective.

In the "Cholly" column, nobody ever fell in love; they "succumbed to the darts of that greatest of sharpshooters, Dan Cupid." Nobody, whether "sweetie sweets"—lovely people—or "sourie sours"—odious people—ever possessed money; they had "oodles of ducats." Was it a sunny day?—then "Old Sol reigned supreme." Winchell's lingo was entirely more succinct. A courting couple were "dueting," "that way," or "uh-huh." Marriage was "middle-aisling it" or to be "Lohengrined." The first birth was a "blessed event." "Phfft" was the inimitable sound of a marriage breaking up.

He awarded New Yorchids and Bokays of Okays to those he

esteemed; those he didn't—and there were many of those "Idyll Rich" along "Baloney Boulevard," as he called Broadway—were relegated to his "Drop Dead" list. Even a purist like H. L. Mencken saw Winchell's contribution to American slanguage as notably fertile: a Chicagorilla was a gangster, a Wildeman a homosexual, a debutante a debutramp, and giggle-water, hard liquor.

It was a hard act to follow, and the British, who came later to the scene, never really tried; given England's libel laws, they took refuge in discreet innuendo. Columnists like Charles Graves, the 6′ 3″ ex-public schoolboy, whom the *Daily Mail* paid £3,500 a year plus expenses, and the sixth Marquess of Donegall (the *Sunday News,* the *Sunday Dispatch*) followed the Rainbows on their annual pilgrimage, dutifully reporting that King Alfonso XIII was seen drinking a cocktail (gin, dubonnet, a dash of angostura) named in his honor by Émile, the bartender at the Hôtel de Paris, that bandleaders won favor with David if they featured *La Vie en Rose* or that a fashionable wedding at St. Margaret's, Westminster, now cost a trifle over £60.

This penchant for hiring the wellborn to report on their own kind originated in a whim of Lord Beaverbrook's, in April 1926, to assign "The Londoner's Log" column of his *Sunday Express* to Valentine Charles Browne, Viscount Castlerosse, the heir to the Earldom of Kenmare. But though Castlerosse knew everybody and went everywhere on the international circuit, no escapades he ever reported stood comparison with his own.

At Stornoway House, Beaverbrook's London mansion, and Cherkley, his country seat, Castlerosse, with his moon-faced grin and humpty-dumpty body, was essentially Beaverbrook's court jester, a perfect complement to his master. Beaverbrook was a small, puckish, sardonic Canadian; Castlerosse was noisy and expansive. Beaverbrook was a frugal eater, to whom a slice of chicken and a pear were an adequate lunch; Castlerosse, whose weight veered between seventeen and twenty-two stone, was a glutton in the "Diamond Jim" mold. Offered a portion of game pie at his club, he instructed the waiter, "Bring the whole pie, you fool"; at various times he was seen to devour four chump chops followed by a whole ham and six lobsters at a sitting.

Beaverbrook was a notably conservative dresser; Castlerosse was famed for his sable-collared, mink-lined topcoats, and his black silk slippers, embossed with scarlet "C's." At the Savoy Grill, the waiters took bets on which of his three dozen fancy waistcoats he would wear that day.

Beaverbrook's Scottish ancestry decreed prudence over money; Castlerosse's life was one long tradesman's writ. He bought eau de cologne by the flagon, cigars by the thousand, shirts three dozen at a time. In any one year, he ran up debts of more than £4,000—and Beaverbrook settled them, as Castlerosse knew he would. At Walton Heath Golf Club, questioned as to his handicap, Castlerosse could truthfully answer, "Drink and debauchery."

"Congratulations, my Lord," scribbled David on an Embassy Club menu, on hearing of Castlerosse's marriage to Doris Delavigne in May 1928, but his good wishes were misplaced. Within a year, Castlerosse had returned to his bachelor quarters at the International Sportsman's Club in Upper Grosvenor Street; the furious no-holds-barred slinging matches that he and Doris staged in public places, when blows were freely traded, had become notorious. In private, they belabored one another with shoes and ornaments, and on one notable occasion Doris, dropping to her hands and knees, bit Castlerosse in the thigh. For this, her husband did, in time, forgive her, magnanimously sending her £200 worth of orchids, charged to Beaverbrook's account, but by March 1933 they had separated for good and all.

To the very end, though—he died in 1943, aged fifty-two—Castlerosse remained the unrepentant sybarite, conscious that he was Britain's most widely read gossip columnist; at least eight copies of the *Sunday Express* would be ordered for the average weekend house party. "What's the good of being a viscount if you don't get something out of it?" he would demand rhetorically. "Tradespeople should be honored by my patronage."

* * *

It was not only the French Riviera, in the twenties, that saw the history of the Rainbow People equated with a saga of rocketing real estate. Sun worship was also a crucial cult with the American Rainbows; Baroness Orczy's "bloated bullfrog" shrank to insignificance beside the excesses that contemporaries called "the Florida Frenzy."

In truth, Florida had for years been simmering on the architectural back burner. It had sprung initially from Rockefeller money, as far back as 1878, when Henry Morrison Flagler, then a senior partner in Standard Oil, first chanced upon Jacksonville as a semi-tropical retreat for his ailing first wife, Mary. But the primitive facilities staggered him. No railroad then ran beyond Jacksonville. Miami was still a fishing village; Palm Beach as yet innocent of palms. When Alice died in 1881, Flagler, then a hale fifty-one-year-old, decided to pull out of the oil business and devote his interests to that tempting 500-mile finger of land thrusting toward the Caribbean.

Two years later after he had married his first wife's nurse, Ida Alice Shourds, they honeymooned at St. Augustine, the oldest town in the United States, thirty-seven miles southeast of Jacksonville, and the Old World charm and the balmy climate captivated them both. On a whim Flagler decided to build the finest resort hotel in the world: the $1,250,000, 540-room Ponce de Léon, each room lit by electricity, with $1,000 worth of furnishings. Like all his kind, Flagler thought Rainbow: to attract the right kind of guest, the hotel, at first, must operate at a loss. When a new manager, unaware of this policy, wired for permission to fire the overpaid French chef and the equally overpaid dance band, Flagler wired back: HIRE ANOTHER COOK AND TWO MORE OF THE BEST ORCHESTRAS.

This was just the opening round. By 1894, Flagler, after buying the tropical spit of land called Palm Beach, separated from the mainland by a dreamy lagoon, for $75,000, had built what was then the world's largest hotel: the six-story Royal Poinciana, with thirty-two acres of grounds and accommodation for 1,750 guests. The more prudent among them, sited in the remoter wings, allowed two hours each evening for the business of dining: an hour to dress, half an hour to reach the dining room, and half an hour to return.

Next came West Palm Beach, as "a city for my help," and the

extension of Flagler's Florida East Coast Railway all the way from St. Augustine to Palm Beach, where Flagler's mighty mansion, the $2,500,000 Whitehall, sometimes called "the Taj Mahal of North America," would one day in its turn become a luxury hotel. The stage was set for "the Florida Frenzy."

There were many contributory factors: a climate comparable to that of the French Riviera, easy accessibility from the populous northeast, the rise of a new generation of automobile owners, the euphoria of what was called "Coolidge Prosperity" (after the taciturn thirtieth U.S. president, Calvin Coolidge), and above all, the delicious propinquity of hostesses like Mrs. Harrison Williams, Mrs. William B. Leeds, and Mrs. Eva Stotesbury, who normally hit Palm Beach in the season—from mid-December often until mid-March—with eighty retainers, then proceeded to hire thirty more.

As Harry Reichenbach, publicist to the architect Addison Mizner, who was to Florida what Barry Dierks was to the French Riviera, put it, "Get the big snobs and the little snobs will follow."

By 1925, land over the entire peninsula was changing hands like pieces in a game of Monopoly. Travelers on the eighteen-foot-wide Dixie Highway counted the license plates of eighteen separate states among the logjam of traffic; in Miami alone there were soon to be 2,000 real estate offices and 25,000 agents marketing house-lots or acreage. Lots were sold and resold five or six times in one week; latecomers to a line outside a real estate office would offer early birds $100 for their places. To ensure first chance of a lot next morning, one man padlocked himself to an agent's door overnight.

This was Miami, where a lot worth $800 in the early days sold for $150,000 in 1924, and Palm Beach saw Miami as Newport, Rhode Island, would have viewed Coney Island. But in time the boom extended to Palm Beach, too, with a sudden influx of land-hungry Rainbows: the Duc de Richelieu, Elizabeth Arden, Lady Diana Cooper, and the Duchess of Sutherland. The seventy-two-mile strip between Miami and Palm Beach had become the new "Gold Coast."

A few miles south of Palm Beach, at Boca Raton—"Beaucoup Rotten" to his rivals—Addison Mizner and his brother Wilson were having a field day; on the first day of trading they sold $11 million worth of lots. Not only was Addison promoting the area, with its built-in ocean to carry electrically driven gondolas to one's door; he was designing the properties and furnishing them besides. His repertoire was limited. What a Mizner client got, whether he wanted it or not, was a Spanish medieval castle, complete with notched battlements for crossbowmen, parapets for pouring down flaming pitch, and ancient portal knockers sited at horseback height. To complete the illusion, armies of workmen in hobnailed shoes waded through the setting cement of the stairways to counterfeit the imprint of knightly spurs.

A fine Mizner house in Palm Beach, like Playa Reinte, the vast showplace he designed in 1923 for Joshua Cosden, the oil millionaire and onetime Baltimore streetcar conductor, was, in fact, the sure road to social eminence; hadn't the Cosdens netted David and the Mountbattens as their house guests in 1924? True, Mizner furnishings, which were shipped to Palm Beach from three cluttered warehouses in Madrid, were no Macy's basement bargains; a two-dollar Oriental rug sold for $2,000, and the going rate for a seventy-dollar refectory table was $4,000. A ready accomplice of Addison's in cornering the Spanish market was, he claimed, King Alfonso—"That little son of a bitch will do anything for me." Another Mizner "must" was organs—priced from $25,000 to $45,000—of which he got 10 percent from the Wurlitzer Corporation on every one he unloaded. "Of course you have to have an organ," Addison would reprove doubtful clients. "You're going to entertain on a large scale and you can't do without one."

Truly, it seemed, the boom could never end. Stock in the Mizner Corporation jumped from $100 to $1,000 a share. On Flagler Street, Miami, one lot was priced at $70,000 per foot frontage—a figure preposterous even in New York. By late 1925, 5,917 real-estate operators were in business in this one city; in that year, they sold $7 billion worth of lots. That shrewd assessor of the gullible, Texas Guinan, opened up a night spot, charging $2.50 for a glass of cracked ice.

For it was, as Wilson Mizner truly said, "a platinum sucker trap."

Palm Beach had become a parvenu's paradise, where old clothes bins, parked on street corners for the deserving poor, were crammed with discarded ball gowns, old tuxedos, and outmoded suits of tails. It was in keeping that one man attended a costume ball at the Everglades Club dressed as a social climber; the four-rung ladder on the back of his outfit was labeled, from bottom to top, "Common People," "People," "Nice People," "Right People." Palm Beach, said its old-timers, had its own definition of a gentleman: "a man who for three generations has pronounced 'to-may-to' 'to-mah-to'."

It was a world to which there was one passport: solvency. Each night in the season of 1926, 1,000 Pullman sleeping cars, many of them privately owned, were heading south for Palm Beach or returning north. Many of the yachts, like C.K.G. Billings's 240-foot *Venadis*, were too large for the inner harbor to accommodate; anchored three miles out to sea, on the edge of the Gulf Stream, *Venadis*'s houseguests were ferried to and from the shore by a fleet of brass-bound, mahogany-finished small boats, running on the hour and half hour. In the nonstop games of stud poker on the private trains, stakes were sky-high. George Loft, the New York candy magnate, intent on buying into a game already in progress, produced a roll of $1,000 bills as his bona fide. Obligingly, Joshua Cosden passed over one single white chip.

That shrewd observer of the social scene, Joseph Hergesheimer, cast an eye over Palm Beach and was uneasy at what he saw. He found the women "brilliant and hard and definite; cruel rather than not." Mizner's mansions were, for him, like "amazing rococo theaters," peopled by "women arrogant in emeralds, in frosty diamonds, and pearls." At Palm Beach, "the tragedies . . . were light and thin, like champagne, with problems barely deeper than the deliberations at backgammon." The women "saw themselves, brilliantly colored and roped in pearls, in the continuous mirrors of their startled and pleased consciousness."

Hergesheimer had, in fact, hit on a phenomenon instantly recognizable to any anthropologist: Palm Beach Woman, a species infinitely grander than her New York, Newport, or Bar Harbor counterparts. The perennially "best-dressed" Mrs. Mona Harrison Williams was archetypal, with her lambent Persian-cat eyes, her so-English accent, her so-French clothes, and her penchant for stark black-and-white decor. "Mrs. Williams," Hergesheimer once teased her at one of her dinner parties, "are you satisfied with your life?" Mrs. Williams smiled back wanly. "Mr. Hergesheimer," she answered, "is anyone ever satisfied?"

Certainly Palm Beach Woman never was, or would be—not even Mrs. William B. Leeds, heiress to the great tinplate fortune, with her $40,000-a-year dress allowance and her $8 million collection of diamonds, so dazzling as to defeat the photographer's lens—"Try it at one five-thousandth of a second," she would advise cameramen on their shutter opening. Of course, there were temporary satisfactions to be gained in stealing a march on one's neighbors. Mrs. Marjorie Merriweather Post—who at this time was Mrs. Edward Hutton—knew just such a brief satisfaction when she called in Joseph Urban, stage designer for the showman Florenz Ziegfeld, to create a residence that would eclipse all others in Palm Beach and Florida besides. Given his head, Urban duly obliged by building the house, Mar-a-lago, around a $1 million marble dining table seating thirty-six, inlaid with eighteen-carat-gold tracery. There was, one house guest noted, gold almost everywhere but on the front door, but this was swiftly put to rights; on the night he departed a pair of magnificent gold-plated griffons, with gold battle lanterns pendant from their beaks, lit him on his way.

Palm Beach Woman might not have been born to the purple, but given the wherewithal she was swift to adapt. Lucretia "Eva" Roberts Cromwell was forty-three when, in 1912, she married Edward T. "Little Sunshine" Stotesbury; although the widow of a well-to-do lawyer, she was still a stranger to affluence. Her wedding settlement from her bridegroom—some said $3 million, some said $4 million—changed all that. ("The best and most profitable financial transaction I ever made," she joked once, "was marrying Mr. Stotesbury.") On her Palm Beach honeymoon she was so laden with jewelry that a detective had to dog her everywhere except the bridal chamber.

It was as well that E. T., after long years as a Pierpont Morgan partner, decided that it was time to be "a sport"—a resolution reinforced by the purchase of 150 fancy dress costumes. A sporting spirit was at all times helpful in keeping up with Eva's Marie Antoinette life-style—certainly at their 147-room Philadelphia home, Whitemarsh Hall, but most especially at El Mirasol, a $1 million Mizner mausoleum with a forty-car garage and quarters for a staff of eighty, working in shifts on twenty-four-hour call.

Eva would have amply testified to Alva Belmont's plaint concerning the hard lot of a Society hostess. She was the one Palm Beach Woman whose staff included not only a full-time personal fashion designer but a costume secretary, whose job was to sketch Eva down to the last diamond clip, revealing exactly how she would look in advance. When Eva received at El Mirasol, tall and stately with her piled hair and pearl collar, even her jewelry had been planned like a dinner party. A special dressing room next to her private apartments held a collection of life-size mannequins decked out with pearls, diamond clips, and bracelets; she had sixty-five mannequins, and, like a Cartier display stand, each item was tagged with a typed memo as to when it had last been worn.

Boasting perhaps more outfits than Grace Wilson Vanderbilt, Eva saw the need to be highly organized. Each morning her personal maid brought a clutch of dress books, so that Eva, at a glance, could decide, "I will wear costumes 170, 162, and 82 today." She was likewise the only Palm Beach Woman to employ a part-time tiara attendant, Mrs. Edward J. MacMullan, a Philadelphia socialite. When the top-heavy diamond and emerald tiara to which Eva was addicted began to list to one side at parties, Mrs. MacMullan was always on tap to tilt it back into place.

All this E. T. could take in his stride; the one subject on which he and his wife differed markedly was architects. Men like Mizner were the bane of E. T.'s life, though, to be fair, hostesses as demanding as Eva were equally the bane of men like Mizner. Soon after World War I, E. T. had bought Wingwood House, the Bar Harbor, Maine, house of Alexander Cassatt, of the Pennsylvania Railroad, for use as a summer residence. To Eva, its fifteen servants' rooms were ludicrously inadequate; she needed forty at least. Wingwood House was to be torn down and rebuilt, to be ready and furnished, Eva instructed, when she returned next summer. One year later, after a silent survey of the premises, Eva shook her head. "It won't do," she told the architect. "Tear it down and build it over again; and this time I'll stay here and see that it's done properly."

It was little wonder that when Marjorie Hutton confided in E. T. that she was planning an extension to surprise her husband, the little man turned pale. "Don't," he begged her. "Don't do it. Husbands don't like surprises."

Yet on his eightieth birthday in August 1929, which was celebrated not, of course, at Palm Beach but at the Bar Harbor Club, E. T. had only the best of news for his hosts at the small select dinner party in his honor, news that seemed to indicate that the spending need never stop.

"I have today achieved my life's ambition," he told the suitably impressed assembly. "I have just received a letter from my financial adviser telling me I am worth one hundred million dollars."

Who ever could have wished for more?

* * *

All through 1928, when David toured East Africa and hunted at Melton Mowbray and drifted away from Freda into a brief affair with another married woman, Lady Furness, the former Thelma Morgan, daughter of an American career diplomat, the air had been heady with euphoria. "It has been a twelvemonth of unprecedented advance, of wonderful prosperity—in this country at least," noted *The New York Times,* on January 1, 1929. "If there is any way of judging the future by the past, this new year may well be one of felicitation and hopefulness."

For all the pointers were there. Since 1920, the increase in the national income in terms of physical goods was 93 percent. On that New Year's Day, both weekly cash wages and real wages were at their highest point in American economic history. Since 1914, real wages had more than doubled.

Coolidge's successor as president, an engineer named Herbert Hoover, fully shared the *Times*'s optimism. In his 1928 election campaign he had told the American people roundly that things had never looked better. Two chickens in every pot, two cars in every garage, would become part of their normal standard of living.

And Wall Street, with every upward surge of the Dow-Jones index, echoed these sentiments. Hoover's election in 1928—by 21 million votes to Al Smith's 15 million—saw blue chips like U.S. Steel, American Telephone, and Eastman Kodak reach all-time highs. By August, Dow-Jones industrials had hit 380. Madison Avenue even had a song for it: "Now's the time to buy, so let's have another cup of coffee, and let's have another piece of pie."

Speculation had become the national sport. People bought shares on margin, margins that were soon to be exhausted, and a gigantic edifice of prices, undermined by shaky credit, began to crumble under its own weight. Then came Black Tuesday, October 29. Buy and sell orders flooded the Stock Exchange faster than any human being could handle them. Long after trading closed, the ticker chattered on; an all-time high of 16,410,000 shares changed hands. Two million investors were virtually wiped out, together with the brokers who financed them and the banks from whom they had borrowed, and many Rainbows, even the canniest among them, suffered. The wily Sir Joseph Duveen dropped $10 million. In the brokerage office of the liner *Berengaria*, 500 miles from New York, Helena Rubinstein watched impassively as the board registered her $1 million loss in the electrical manufacturer, Westinghouse. Confessed the great steel executive "Smilling Charlie" Schwab, "I'm afraid, every man is afraid." Both Stotesburys dropped heavily; Eva by $1,250,000, E. T. by far more. He was worth no more than $10 million when he died in 1938.

By November 13, even the luster of the great names was tarnished: General Motors had slumped from 72¾ to 36, U.S. Steel from 261¾ to 150, and American Telephone from 304 to 197¼. The Dow-Jones average had dropped to 198.7; the Big Bull Market was dead, and, so, too, was Coolidge-Hoover Prosperity.

On the worst night of all, Black Thursday, October 31, in the restaurant of New York's Pennsylvania Hotel at Thirty-second Street and Seventh Avenue, orchestra leader George Olsen was handing out to the band parts of a new number that at the eleventh hour had been dropped from a forthcoming musical. Casting a dubious glance over the lyric and over the Pennsylvania's stunned and silent diners, Olsen could see why. He stage-whispered to vocalist Fran Frey, "Sing it for the corpses."

As the first brassy notes of the refrain came home to them, an incredulous look crossed the faces of many of the diners. In this blackest of hours, they could scarcely believe their ears:

> *Happy days are here again!*
> *The skies above are clear again!*
> *Let's all sing a song of cheer again—*
> *Happy days are here again!*

Slowly, by degrees, uneasy smiles, at first of disbelief, then of growing conviction, dawned on many countenances. For, in the long run, mightn't it just be true?

> *All together, shout it now!*
> *There is no one here can doubt it now . . .*
> *Happy days are here again!*

No philosophy could have been more Rainbow than that.

6 / THE WORLD OF BABS AND "QUEEN WALLY":
"Your Life's a Wild Typhoon"

On a sunny afternoon in May 1931, Noel Coward, lunching at the London Ritz with the writer Beverly Nichols, was intrigued by the sight of a plump, pleasant girl with wavy hair seated at the next table, her fingernails, tipped with mother-of-pearl, "waving about in front of a dish of quails." Who was she? Coward wanted to know.

Nichols, most savvy on Rainbows, put him in the picture. This was the eighteen-year-old heiress, Barbara Woolworth Hutton, who this week was to make her curtsy as a debutante before King George V and Queen Mary. In approximately two years' time, when she came of age, she was to inherit an incredible $45 million, tax-free—the bulk of the fortune left by her grandfather, Frank Winfield Woolworth, who had died in 1919 leaving a 1,000-strong chain of five-and-ten-cent stores.

"Good God," Coward muttered, "and yet she still has the face of a child," to which Nichols responded obligingly, "Cue for song. 'Children of the Ritz'."

Like the trouper that he was, Coward picked up his cue. At London's Adelphi Theatre, the revue *Words and Music* in due time featured Nichols's suggested song:

> *Children of the Ritz*
> *Sleek and civilized*
> *Frightfully surprised,*

*We know just how we want our quails done
And then we go and have our nails done . . .*

In that year, Barbara Hutton—Babs to her friends and to the press—was briefly a fugitive from a world that bitterly resented her incipient wealth: a world of grinding depression, of breadlines, and "Brother, Can You Spare A Dime?" in which 8,700,000 Americans vainly sought work, a world where the jobless sold apples on the sidewalks of New York and eked out their rootless days in grim collections of shacks called "Hoovervilles." It was against this background, one year earlier, that Barbara's father, Franklyn Laws Hutton, had crassly staged his daughter's coming-out with a $60,000 party at New York's Ritz, when Rudy Vallee's orchestra played, along with three others, amid bowers of silver birches and pink and white roses. "The press picked up on it," Barbara would relate bitterly later, "and made me a sitting duck."

In London, it was possible for her, briefly, to forget all this. In her heavy, shimmering white satin dress, the three Prince of Wales feathers in her hair supported by a diamond diadem, she had curtsied gracefully before the monarchs at Buckingham Palace; at the dance that followed, David had sought her as a partner and they had gone through the motions of "Tea For Two," while the Prince confessed to having seen her at Biarritz two years back at one of Elsa Maxwell's parties. Despite the presence in London of Frank, her stockbroker father, and Irene, her stepmother, both of whom she detested, this sojourn away from a hostile New York was a welcome escape. It was one of the rare occasions when she did not ask herself, "Why am I so alone?"

No one was ever alone for long on the London debutante scene of the thirties; often the debs of the day attended four dances in one night, squatting on the stairs between numbers, annotating their programs with pink and blue pencils. Every hostess kept a list of eligible males, often called The Stagline, and dowagers like Lady Clancarty, known irreverently as "Lady Blank Cartridge," and Lady St. John of Bletso, could net up to £1,000 for any debutante they presented. It was a field in which many specialists thrived nicely. The large red vans of Tom Kingston's Mayfair Catering Company laid on a ball supper for nine shillings a head and breakfast for ninepence, with fixed charges for all those dancing attendance: £2 10s for each detective, 10s 6d a head for the linkman and the cloakroom lady, 15s 6d for the headwaiter. Even Miss Betty Vacani's dancing academy got in on the act, teaching debutantes to curtsy at 1s 6d per minute.

The debs themselves approached the season with cheerful cynicism. "Society was conducted on a strictly cutlet-for-cutlet basis," noted Daphne Vivian, who came out nine years before Barbara; she herself found the young men "a spotty weedy crew," and Mary Pakenham, another deb, wondered, "How was it possible for mortal men to be so *ugly*?" Most were more than aware that their mothers saw it as a marriage mart, and Irene Hutton hoped devoutly, on the strength of one dance, that David could be persuaded to propose to Barbara.

In truth, Barbara Hutton was symbolic of a new generation of Rainbows: one who, for all her wealth and freedom, would be manipulated rather than the reverse. After her mother, Edna, had committed suicide in mysterious circumstances when Barbara was five years old, she had lived a lonely life, confiding only in governesses and nannies, sometimes visiting Grandpa Woolworth's gloomy ornate mansion at 990 Fifth Avenue, where piped organ music filtered through every corner of the house, emerging even from closets and hollow bedposts.

Given wealth like Barbara's, one would never lack company for long. The world of what columnists like Winchell dubbed The Poor Little Rich Girls teemed with fortune-hunters, and this was far from being a repeat of the Dollar Princess scenario. Pigeons like Consuelo Vanderbilt and Anna Gould had been plucked unmercifully, but by genuine if unscrupulous aristocrats, with lands of their own and an entrée into all the right circles. Barbara's generation were the victims of a new breed: phony aristocrats with phonier titles, like "Count" José René Holstein Dorelis, of Romania, a country possessing no counts, yet who nonethelesss left behind two contented ex-Romanian countesses in Palm Beach. By 1936, after years of these imposters, Baron Suriani formed the Noblemen's Club in New York, to weed out 400 authentic titles from 8,000 spurious ones circulating in the United States.

Millicent Rogers, the Standard Oil heiress, was a case in point. Touring Europe with a marriage-minded Mama, she met up in Vienna with Count Ludwig Salm von Hoogstraten, an Austrian from a country that no longer had an emperor. When Mrs. Rogers decided that Ludi was not the son-in-law she had envisaged, she hastened Millicent back to New York—followed hotfoot by Ludi, once he had borrowed the fare. When they eloped, Colonel Rogers cut Millicent off with $50,000—exactly enough, though he didn't know it, to settle Ludi's outstanding debts. Hearing that his daughter, in Paris, was pregnant, the Colonel hurried thither, offering Ludi $12,000 a year to stay in Europe. But Ludi, conscious of his own nuisance value, hung out for three years, to receive a final settlement of $325,000. In the meantime, Millicent, in Paris, had met up with an Argentine "aristocrat," Arturo Peralta Ramos, who sufficiently impressed the Colonel to stump up a $500,000 marriage settlement.

By the time Arturo was revealed for what he was—a gigolo with no title and, indeed, no *estancias*—the Colonel had parted with a further $300,000 to see the marriage wound up.

All these sums were paltry compared with those that Barbara, a born loser in the matrimonial stakes, would be forced to disgorge over the years. At Biarritz, in the late summer of 1931, Elsa Maxwell, who counted on a commission for arranging such matches, steered Barbara in the direction of the most decadent of the "marrying Mdivanis," twenty-five-year-old Alexis, who along with his brothers claimed to be a prince from Russian Georgia, where there were, again, no princes. This had not deterred the movie stars Mae Murray and Pola Negri from marrying "Prince" Serge and "Prince" David; nor had it deterred Louise Van Alen, of Newport, Rhode Island, a title-hunter who was a match for any fortune-hunter, from marrying Alexis.

All three male Mdivanis, along with their sisters, Nina and Isabel Roussadana (Roussie), were the children of an obscure Russian infantry colonel from Tiflis; apart from their lucrative marriages, their main claim to fame was that they had learned the two-step from the British assistant military attaché, Archibald Wavell, the future desert commander of World War II.

On the Biarritz polo field, the muscular Alexis cut a dashing figure, and Barbara, the most susceptible of innocents, was titillated by Elsa's bland pronouncement, "The Mdivani brothers are absolutely wicked and corrupt, and they're very dangerous to young, impressionable girls."

The outcome was predictable. That night, at a party given by the couturier Jean Patou, Alexis, despite the presence of Louise, led Barbara on to a moonlit terrace, kissed her fervently, and promised, "To Paris, this fall." The hunt for the $45 million pot-of-gold was on. To the entire Mdivani family, from this moment on, Barbara's code name was "the Prize."

At the Paris Ritz that autumn, Franklyn and Irene Hutton were increasingly disturbed by the all-too-blatant attentions of "that cheap fortune-hunting Russian guy," who sneaked Barbara off for champagne cocktails or for spins in his maroon-and-silver Rolls-Royce. It was a siege that he was to pursue assiduously for more than a year—the more so after Louise, tiring of his infidelities, got a divorce at The Hague on December 1, 1932. By early in 1933, Alexis, ensconced at New York's Savoy Plaza, was a constant and unwelcome visitor to the Huttons' lavish duplex at 1020 Fifth Avenue. When Franklyn Hutton asked him coldly what he wanted, Alexis answered candidly, "Your daughter."

Confused and unhappy, Barbara took off on a world cruise—but in Bangkok the remorseless Alexis caught up with her and won her consent. That evening he cabled his sister, Roussie: "Have won the Prize."

His price came high: a $1 million marriage settlement, in advance of the June 1933 wedding in Paris's Russian Orthodox Cathedral, plus a string of polo ponies to replace those he had sold to finance his courtship. For their honeymoon on Lake Como and at St. Moritz, Chanel and Molyneux had worked on a trousseau that filled twenty suitcases: a true case of love's labor's lost. That night, Alexis, the gallant charmer, the so-solicitous suitor, gave place to the true Alexis: the spoiled, callous, fortune-grabbing fake. "Goddamn it, Barbara Mdivani," he told her cruelly, "you're too damn fat!"

It was again Noel Coward, eight years earlier, in a revue called *On With The Dance,* who had so accurately charted the destiny of Barbara and all those like her:

> *Poor little rich girl,*
> *You're a bewitched girl*
> *—Better take care.*
> *Laughing at danger,*
> *Virtue a stranger,*
> *Better beware.*
> *The life you lead sets all your nerves a-jangle*
> *Your love affairs are in a hopeless tangle,*
> *Though you're a child, dear,*
> *Your life's a wild typhoon.*
> *In lives of leisure, the craze for pleasure,*
> *Steadily grows.*
> *Cocktails and laughter, but what comes after?*
> *Nobody knows.*

* * *

Nobody knew less than David, Prince of Wales. His life, too, as early as 1930, resembled the "wild typhoon" of Coward's fancy. The urban manners that had so delighted Barbara Hutton were less and less in evidence with his entourage. What ailed him was a malady afflicting many a film star of that period: David was beginning to believe his own publicity.

His Empire tours had made him the darling of the media, and the more he realized it the more stubbornly arrogant he became. From the daily press he learned that he had become a fashion plate, famous for his large, floppy neckties—the Windsor knot—for his multicolored Fair Isle sweaters and his baggy plus fours—"more like plus sixteens," was one invidious comment. More and more his manner was rude and overbearing, especially with servants; he would rouse a valet from sleep at midnight for some trivial whim, and kept secretaries standing for hours while he paced the room dictating. (Unless royalty is seated, no one else can sit.) Increasingly, he shirked his public duties, arriving late or in a savage temper; at Edinburgh's Royal Infirmary, planting a commemoration tree, he kicked out savagely at the superintendent's playful fox terrier when it jumped up for a caress.

From 1929 onward, he had withdrawn increasingly from Society at large; the Embassy's Peter Pan was now a country boy at heart. It was then that Fort Belvedere, a grace-and-flavor house on the edge of Windsor Great Park, twenty-five miles from London, had fallen vacant. Built in the eighteenth century for William, Duke of Cumberland, it was, in the words of Sir John Aird, David's equerry, "an unstately ruin," but for David, much to his father's mystification, it would be "My Get-Away-From-People-House." "Why do you want the queer old place?" King George demanded. "Those damn weekends, I suppose! Well, if you want it, it's yours."

The renovations began in the summer of 1930, following a long, wearisome official tour of Africa from Cairo to Capetown, helped at times by Freda Dudley Ward, more often by David's new inamorata, Thelma Furness. Even old friends like "Burghie" Westmorland and "Fruity" Metcalfe and his wife, Lady Alexandra, were unwelcome unless they weighed in as unpaid gardeners with billhooks and sickles; Prince George was forbidden to visit unless he would wield a scythe. It was some time in this year—the exact date was never clear—that Thelma introduced David to a couple who had settled in London in 1928: the shipbroker Ernest Simpson, son of an English father and an American mother, and his Baltimore-born wife, Wallis.

Bessie Wallis Warfield Spencer Simpson, Ernest's bride of two years, was then thirty-four years old. Such position as she had in London Society she owed largely to Thelma and to her sister-in-law, Maud Kerr-Smiley, but first impressions of her were rarely more than halfhearted. To the star debutante of 1930, Margaret Whigham, "she was not outstanding in any way, nor well dressed. Her hair was parted down the middle, arranged in 'earphones,' and her voice was harsh . . . quite a plain woman, with a noticeably square jaw." For Henry "Chips" Channon, Tory M. P. for Southend, the greatest snob ever to inflict himself on London Society, she was "a neat, quiet, wellbred mouse with startled eyes and a huge mole." Cecil Beaton found her "loud and brash, terribly so"; Harold Nicolson dismissed her as "slightly second-rate." Only Emerald Cunard, for somewhat partisan reasons, sprang to her defense: "Little Mrs. Simpson knows her Balzac."

"Little Mrs. Simpson" knew rather more than that; she knew where she was going. On the weekend of January 30, 1932, when the Simpsons, for the first time, became David's guests at Fort Belvedere, Wallis, from unpromising beginnings, had come a long, long way. The daughter of a country auctioneer, who had died when she was five months old, it was said of her, unkindly, that her first words were not "ma-ma" but "me-me." She spent so much time riveted to her mirror as to prompt the nickname "Wallis-Through-The-Looking-Glass"; her dolls were named "Mrs. Astor" and "Mrs. Vanderbilt." As a child, until her mother took in paying guests, she was much beholden to charity: from her grandmother, the starchy Mrs. Henry Mactier Warfield, and from the aunt who became her lifelong confidante, Bessie Merryman. Security would thus become the dominant obsession of Wallis's life.

Her first marriage, in 1916, to a handsome but alcoholic naval lieutenant, Earl Winfield Spencer, foundered ignominiously; her second was, judging by appearances, relatively stable. At the socially ambitious Simpsons' flat, No. 5 Bryanston Court, such guests as Anne, Lady Sackville, "Chips" Channon, Diana Cooper, and Emerald Cunard came to relish Wallis's speciality, hot hors d'oeuvres, and to admire the William and Mary walnut chest and the eighteenth-century Dutch secretary, pieces for which she had foraged in the little Chelsea antique shops.

More and more, as 1932 wore on, the Simpsons became part of David's circle—marked by two more visits to Fort Belvedere that autumn and four that winter. David the homebody, they noted, was fast supplanting David the man-about-town; the maid who brought them their breakfast in bed would inform them that his Royal Highness was already at work in the garden, clearing away undergrowth with a machete, and few weekends were complete without a guided tour of the closets where he kept his shoes and suits, his central heating system, and his own private steam bath. He was proud, too, of the little-known flag that flew from the mast of the topmost tower: an inverted pyramid of fifteen golden balls on a black background—"That's the flag of the Duchy of Cornwall. I fly it to show that this is to be recognized as a private house, not as a royal residence." Thelma was always there, too, along with the Simpsons, and often Lord Louis Mountbatten, Perry Brownlow, David's lord-in-waiting, with his wife, Kitty, and his equerries, John Aird and Colin Buist.

Yet with Wallis's arrival, some, the Metcalfes in particular, were conscious of exclusion. It was as if Wallis were subtly determined to erect a stockade round the Prince, hemming him in with her own intimate friends. "Some of the ancien régime stayed on and made the adjustment," Lady Alexandra would recount later. "We didn't try to." Thelma, for her part, only encouraged the association. It was she who drew the Simpsons into her little supper parties for David at the Embassy and the Café de Paris; on June 19, 1933, Wallis's thirty-seventh birthday, it was seemingly at Thelma's prompting that David hosted a birthday party for her at Quaglino's.

He had, he confided, invested in a "prezzy" for her—David was prone to baby talk—but since it was an orchid it would not bloom for a year. Wallis, who knew full well that any objet d'art of which David tired ended up in the Fort Belvedere cottage of Osborne, his butler, replied: "A year? By that time, sir, I'll be in Osborne's cottage!"

Wallis was destined for no such relegation. Perhaps indeed she knew it. But neither did Thelma have any premonition. In the autumn of 1933, Thelma's precarious marriage to Marmaduke, Viscount Furness, had finally collapsed, and David had greeted this news with relief. "Oh, my darling," he told her. "I am sure you have made the right decision. I am so very, very happy." Accordingly, Thelma, with a light heart, began packing for a trip to America, where her twin sister, Gloria Morgan Vanderbilt, was preparing to dispute the guardianship of her ten-year-old daughter, also named Gloria: the most sensational custody trial in United States history.

Three days before her departure, she and Wallis lunched at the London Ritz. "Oh, Thelma," Wallis said concernedly, "the Little Man is going to be lonely."

"Well, dear," Thelma replied, "you look after him while I'm away. See that he does not get into any mischief."

Midway through January 1934, just before sailing time, in the bar of the liner *Aquitania,* Cecil Beaton chanced on Thelma sipping a glass of champagne. The one thing on her mind was David's devotion. "Come out on deck," she told the photographer. "I'll show you something." Overhead a small plane was circling Southampton; back in the twenties, David had learned to pilot his own aircraft.

"There he is now!" she called excitedly. "He's telling me goodbye."

Thelma never spoke a truer word.

* * *

At 3:32 P.M. (Mountain Time) on Tuesday, December 5, 1933, one solitary item of news drove all other topics from the front pages of America: Utah had become the thirty-sixth state to ratify the Twenty-first Amendment, and Prohibition was at an end. For the Rainbows, who for almost fourteen years had rejoiced in the illegality, the cocktail bar and the licit nightclub reluctantly became their new way of life.

In London and on the Riviera, the smarter cocktail bars had been Rainbow havens since the aftermath of World War I. Their advent had been marked by the day in 1920 when Cleveland-born Harry Craddock, a quiet, silver-haired man with the saintly mien of a bishop, forsook New York's Hoffman House to preside over the new American Bar at London's Savoy—so called because it was the first in Europe to chill the Martinis. For if Edward's had been the age of the Dedicated Dish, the age of Babs and David was that of the Dedicated Drink, and for nineteen years thereafter Craddock was to invent a new cocktail every week of the year.

There was his Barney Barnato (angostura, curaçao, a South

African aperitif called Capertif, and brandy) and his Caruso (dry gin, dry vermouth, green crème de menthe), his Fairbanks No. 1, for Douglas, Sr. (lemon juice, grenadine, apricot brandy, dry vermouth, and dry gin) and his Gene Tunney (orange juice, lemon juice, dry vermouth, and gin). There were Craddock cocktails to celebrate crazes, like the Mah-jongg (Cointreau, Bacardi, and dry gin) and events, like his Strike's Off, marking the end of the 1926 General Strike. All over Europe, bartenders were putting on their thinking caps to honor the chosen few; at the Paris Ritz, Frank Meier dreamed up The Green Hat for Michael Arlen, The Seapea for Cole Porter, and the Prince of Wales, as a tribute to David.

Appropriately, Craddock's successor, Eddie Clarke, perfected a cocktail called The Rainbow, which in the thirties was highly priced at 12s 6d (62p): a 100 percent liqueur drink, containing crème de caçao, crème de violette, yellow and green chartreuse, maraschino, benedictine, and brandy. The making of it took many minutes, for, as Clarke explained, "It had to give the right rainbow effect when the glass was held up to the light."

All these men were masters of their craft, and in 1934 the formation of the United Kingdom Bartenders Guild, to act as a kind of unofficial employment agency, with affiliates throughout the world, ensured that standards remained resolutely high: no bartender was eligible to join until he had served a five-and-a-half-year apprenticeship. Out of the 8,000 recipes registered with the Guild by 1939—including such long-forgotten follies as the Bunny Hug, Corpse Reviver, the Glad Eye, and the Pooh Bah— men like Craddock, high priests of the Boston Shaker (for drinks containing egg) and the Hawthorn Strainer (for wine drinks) would carry up to 500 recipes in their heads; their infallible advice on how to drink a cocktail was, "*Quickly*—while it's laughing at you!" Some head bartenders, like Eric Forrester, who oversaw the main bars at Deauville and Cannes casinos, received no salary whatsoever—yet Forrester contrived to retire a wealthy man on 3,000 franc tips.

In the United States, the system was much the same; all those presiding over "the glitter scene" at all times walked a potential tightrope of insolvency. At 154 East Fifty-fourth Street, New York, Fred Carino, headwaiter of the up-and-coming night spot, El Morocco, displayed what Frederic Morton was to call "an exercise in velvet ferocity," deciding not only who would glitter, but where; Carino could dress a room with the famous the way Molyneux would dress a woman. His secret was not hard to fathom. As maître d', Carino was on only token salary—but since customers would slip him $200 for a table of their approximate choice, Carino died worth $450,000.

For with the passing of Prohibition, New York was now subject to a new pecking order, whose rulers were even more radically self-made than most. At the zebra-striped El Morocco, the proprietor, Italian-born John Perona, was a onetime busboy and associate of the Club Sportiva, a Mafia hangout of the twenties. In the dim blue dusk of the Stork Club, on East Fifty-third Street, "the New Yorkiest place in town," according to the nightly occupant of table fifty, Walter Winchell, the boss man, Sherman Billingsley, a onetime druggist from Enid, Oklahoma, had served a three-month stretch in Leavenworth for bootlegging. At "21," on West Fifty-second Street, as subdued as an English chophouse, with its red-and-white checkered tablecloths, proprietor Jack Kreindler, a former Viennese bartender with the dignified air of a Prussian officer, was another survivor from speakeasy days.

Yet in one year alone—1937—these three establishments among them turned away 60,000 would-be patrons. Only faces as well known as Barbara Hutton's and Elsa Maxwell's were automatically swept past the velvet rope.

The concept of all three men—to get rich off the rich—coincided with a need. Despite the Depression, most Rainbows still had money, some of it old, some of it new, some of it borrowed, and not too much of it blue-blooded, and all of them craved places where they could not only be seen but have the reassurance of being noticed and fussed over. Thus all three owners employed a basic formula: exclusiveness and effusiveness. All three were unacknowledged Rainbow dictators, and most, with their basic insecurity, welcomed such leadership and authority. To be admitted into the inner sanctuary of the Stork Club's upstairs Club Room—as were Tallulah Bankhead and Cornelius Vanderbilt, Jr.—was to be established. In the world of Billingsley, Perona, and Kreindler, the $64,000 question was, "Have you a reservation?"

Once you were accepted, all three made things as nice as could be. Regulars like Barbara soon learned "Sherm's" coded hand-signals and chuckled knowingly when the Coke-drinking, table-hopping host tugged at his ear. That meant that he was bored with a customer; a watching waiter should call him to a phone. A pull at his nose meant, "These are unimportant people—don't cash any checks for them." But favored guests were lavished with everything from orchid corsages—which cost Billingsley $7,000 a year—to automobiles (he gave away more than two dozen over the years).

Being there was fine, but only part of the battle: you went to "21" not only to eat and drink but to be mentioned in the same breath as, say, Cole Porter and Gertie Lawrence, who were also in on the scene. And here John Perona stole a march on his rivals; learning that Jerome Zerbe, a young Society photographer, was taking pictures at The Rainbow Room, in Rockefeller Center, Perona lured him to El Morocco for $150 a week to snap candid shots of the fashionable. Not only did Maury Paul use four sets of photographs a week; magazines all over the world, like the London *Bystander,* were in the market for Zerbe pictures. Soon Perona was grossing $400,000 a year from Rainbows who flocked to El Morocco to mug for Zerbe, often sending word in advance: "The Duchess of Sutherland has arrived and would love to have her photograph taken."

An integral feature of the night spots on both sides of the Atlantic was the great name bands. From 1929 on, the vibrato sax section of Guy Lombardo's Royal Canadians was the main lure of the Grill Room at New York's Roosevelt Hotel, and until she fled the New York scene, Barbara always commanded a ringside table right by the saxes, drinking in the rhythm of "You're Driving Me Crazy" and "Little White Lies." In London she soon became a devotee of the whispering cornet of the elegant, Denver-born Roy Fox at the Monseigneur and the Café de Paris.

Maestros of this caliber—Gus Arnhem, at the Coconut Grove in the Hotel Ambassador, Los Angeles, Ted Fio Rito, at the Beverly Wilshire, Leo Reisman, in the Waldorf-Astoria's Wedgwood Room—called their own tune. For thirty-three years, Lombardo's Royal Canadians commanded a flat 25 percent of every Roosevelt dinner check; bandleaders like Bert Ambrose could ask—and get—£42,000 a year from a hotel or nightclub, paying out, perhaps, £30,000 in wages—£13 being the minimum wage, £24 the maximum. And wages could further be supplemented by two weekly three-hour recording sessions at £3 a time. Recalls Sonia Roy, whose husband, Harry, was a star favorite at the Café de Paris and the Mayfair Hotel, "They were like gods."

Their day, beginning at 11 P.M., rarely ended before 4 A.M., after which Harry Roy would arrive home ravenous for cheese-and-onion sandwiches. Most, sleeping until late afternoon, rarely saw the daylight for weeks on end. Perched on their throne, nine inches above the dance floor, their speciality—except on broadcast nights, when a printed card on each table gave the customers due warning—was music as discreet as a Ritz table lamp, as unobtrusive as a Rolls-Royce engine turning over; in the words of Sid Colin, Ambrose's guitarist, "the brass tightly bottled up, the rhythm section dainty and discreet, the saxophones polite, and delivering an unbroken daisy chain of choruses in two tempi, quickstep and foxtrot."

In essence, this was what U.S. music critics dubbed "The Lombardo Sound"; whereas one band would make a tune last thirty seconds, Lombardo would prolong it to sixty. It was what Colin, who like most of his fellow musicians preferred straight jazz, disparaged as "oom ching" music.

Pop music of the kind heard at New York's Roseland Ballroom or London's Hammersmith Palais found no favor with the Rainbows. It was as if a small exclusive coterie of composers existed, like court minstrels, to write for them alone: Coward, George Gershwin, and above all, Cole Porter.

A neat, dapper little man, with a face like a marmoset, Cole was thirty-nine years old in 1930, and even then what a pediatrician would term "a late developer." A product of Worcester Academy in Massachusetts and Yale, Cole, through his maternal grandfather, James Omar Cole, a self-made millionaire, was rich from the very first—though not, as he liked to stress, *rich*-rich, like his wife, Linda Lee Thomas, who had accepted a divorce settlement of $1 million in 1912.

Thus for years, cushioned by Linda's money and his own, Cole led a self-indulgent, dilettante life, in which parties at their Paris home, 13, rue Monsieur, or their rented Venetian palazzo loomed larger than the urge to work. Unlike the hard-pressed Coward or Gershwin, Cole had no need to sell himself in the marketplace, beating at the music publishers' doors; in the twenties his songs, tricky and sophisticated, seemed in advance of their time and were swiftly forgotten.

At times there *were* intimations of a chic and sassy talent awaiting its full development. Cole's clever pastiche of Duveen's sale of Gainsborough's *The Blue Boy* to Henry E. Huntington in the 1922 revue *Mayfair and Montmartre*—"We've Got Those Blue Boy Blues"—struck a chord with the Rainbows, as did his spoof of "Jazz Age" disillusion, in "Two Little Babes In The Wood," which the Dolly Sisters put over in *The Greenwich Village Follies of 1924:*

> *They had found that the fountain of youth,*
> *Was a mixture of gin and vermouth.*

Then, in 1928, in the revue *Paris,* Cole hit the note unerringly with his catchy, witty "Let's Do It, Let's Fall In Love," sung by Irene Bordoni and Arthur Margetson. Overnight this zoological concatenation of the love lives of bluebirds, oysters, jellyfish, katydids, pigs, bees, fleas, and guinea pigs established Cole as one of a new elite: composers who had broken out of the thirty-two-bar prison to use restless modern harmonies, such as flattened fifths and thirteenths, men who knew their way round a thesaurus and could joke in French for sophisticated audiences:

The most select schools of cod do it,
Though it shocks 'em, I fear.
Sturgeon, thank God, do it—
Have some caviar, dear.

A year after Margaret Whigham (now Margaret, Duchess of Argyll) had married the golfer, Charles Sweeny, in 1933, Cole celebrated this, too, in "You're the Top," the hit song from his new musical, *Anything Goes,* which exalted the talents of a loved one with contemporary superlatives:

You're the nimble tread of the feet of Fred Astaire,
You're Mussolini,
You're Mrs. Sweeny,
You're camembert.

Hastily excised from the show after a tryout in Toronto was a refrain revealing a hidden facet of Cole that Linda, for the most part, tolerated: the composer who at times was into hard drugs like hashish, the homosexual stud who lusted after beautiful gondoliers and Hollywood masseurs:

You're the burning heat of a bridal suite in use,
You're the breasts of Venus,
You're King Kong's penis,
You're self-abuse.

Thus Porter numbers—"Night and Day," "Begin the Beguine," "It's De-Lovely"—were increasingly a part of the nightclub scene all through the thirties; for the Chicago-born Marion Harris, then starring at the Café de Paris, Cole, over one weekend in 1934, wrote a number, dedicated to Elsa Maxwell, "Miss Otis Regrets (She's Unable to Lunch Today, Madam)," later absorbed into the show *Hi Diddle Diddle.* To feature it for just one week, the Café paid Miss Harris £200, for this was a crucial fact of Depression economics: a nameband or a name cabaret artiste could make or lose a night spot £1,000 a week. Thus stars like Beatrice Lillie ultimately commanded £400 a week, Josephine Baker, £375, while a veteran like Douglas Byng could count on a steady £7,000 a year.

A trouper with a natural gift for devastating mimicry, Byng was an international talent who, as early as 1931, as the "highest paid English cabaret star," was paid $1,000 a week at New York's Central Park Casino, attired, at their own request, by Hawes and Curtis. Designing all his own costumes, writing his own palpably risqué lyrics, Byng's appearances at the Café de Paris or the Monseigneur on Jermyn Street always saw Margaret Sweeny and Barbara at front-rank tables.

Sometimes, in a flaming red wig, Byng emerged as Flora MacDonald:

> *Flora MacDonald, Flora MacDonald,*
> *Healthy with haggis and dripping with dew,*
> *Many's the time she's been out in the heather,*
> *Bending the bracken with young Charlie Stu.*

On other occasions, suitably gnarled, he "arranged his roots" and was metamorphosed into a tree, albeit

> *A tree with fallen branches, all my children*
> *   now are faggots,*
> *You must admit it's lousy to be full of wind*
> *   and maggots,*
> *Gawd knows why I'm a tree.*

Or suitably garnished with sheaves, he might appear as

> *Ceres, the goddess of plenty,*
> *And plenty I've had in my day,*
> *Oh, many a god with a good-looking bod*
> *Singed his wings when he flew my way.*

Despite this carnival gaiety, those dependent on the Rainbows for their livelihood found the thirties increasingly a gamble. Renaissance-style patrons, like Barbara Hutton, who maintained a three-room suite at the Paris Ritz, for £300 a week plus service and taxes, whether she was in residence or not, could literally do no wrong; the London Ritz was similarly beholden to the Aga Khan, who had an identical arrangement. (Though he settled his bill only once a year, it was normally for £5,000.) For the hotel trade was in the doldrums, and for Savoy shareholders, in particular, there was bitter medicine to swallow: a £99,000 profit in 1930 had slumped in two years to a bare £10,000. In 1930, the London Ritz was bolstered only by a hefty £130,000 debenture from the Carlton, whose own shares soon slumped to 27p; one year later, Ritz staff wages were reduced and the directors took a 25 percent cut in fees.

These unpalatable economics sharply pointed up an unique phenomenon: hotel porters, commissionaires, and cloakroom attendants were literally paying their employers to dance attendance on the wealthy, in the hope of ultimately recouping.

There was precedent for this. Back in 1908, Jerry Pelton, the cloakroom attendant at George Rector's restaurant on Broadway, was paying $5,000 for the concession. By the thirties, this custom had swiftly spread. Arnold Schmid, the head porter at the London Ritz, paid the hotel £200 a year for this privilege; each carriage attendant paid fifteen shillings a week to work; the restaurant cloakroom attendants paid £15. At Quaglino's, Victor Legg, then a cloakroom attendant, paid £5 a week to keep his job; Tom Markwick, commissionaire at the Kit Kat Club off the Haymarket, paid £25 a week, which scaled down to £10 when he moved to the Café de Paris. Yet all of this made hard economic sense. Since most Rainbows worthy of the name each paid out £18 a year in tips, an attendant's weekly tips averaged between £50 and £100 by retrieving silk hats and mink, chinchilla, and ermine wraps from cloakrooms. It was the same at every level. One head porter, due to retire in 1932, put his job up for auction with a reserve of £4,000, and this was a conservative estimate.

These men were part of an inimitable brotherhood of fixers, for whom even the impossible took only just a little longer: the 1,900-strong organization of the Golden Keys, concierges from seventeen European countries, instantly recognizable from the symbol of the crossed keys on their lapels. A man like Robert Pazeller, one of Barbara's favorite concierges at the Palace, St. Moritz, could, given time, fix almost anything for his clients, as could Cosimo de Giorgio of Rome's Excelsior, whose *buona maniera* would, if necessary, secure any Rainbow an audience with the pope. Of Luigi Tortorella, at Venice's Bauer-Grunwald, it was said, "In Venice there are three Ts—Titian, Tintoretto, and Tortorella." When Robert Lehman, the banker and art collector, wanted three first-class sleeper tickets to Paris, Tortorella fixed it where no travel agent could—by buying an entire twenty-two-berth car and selling off the extra berths to the first takers. On another occasion, when the actor Eduardo de Filippo, returning from a tour of Russia, lost the goods wagons bearing his scenery for a season in Venice, Tortorella took over, talking for two days and nights on the telephone in French, English, and German: all Golden Keys have to know at least four languages and have at least five years' service behind the counter.

Finally, after running up £200 in telephone bills, Tortorella triumphantly ran the wagons to earth—marooned in an obscure siding on the Russo-Hungarian border.

Of all tips given, with $16 as a good average, hall porters like the Waldorf-Astoria's Dennis Coleman retained 40 percent, and there were fixed commissions from travel bureaus, car hire firms, and leading shops to further augment their bank balance. Few hall porters died in penury; when Nicholas Mockett retired after forty years at London's Savoy, the directors voted him a generous pension to free his last years from want. To the astonishment of all, the "needy" Mockett, not many years later, left £40,000.

A maître d'hôtel had a similarly exalted status—whether, as in New York, he paid £20 a week to secure his job, or, as in London, paid no danegeld but received no salary, merely an annual guarantee of £3,000 or upward from the *tronc,* a collection box, in which all tips, wrapped in tissue paper with the waiter's name appended, were securely locked. Whatever the arrangement, theirs was a golden harvest; as early as 1908, Rector's headwaiter, Paul Perret, gleaned tips of $2,000 in Christmas week alone, and in the thirties, Luigi Santarelli, the Savoy's restaurant manager, grossed an average £5,000 a year.

Waiters were, in general, the Cinderellas of the trade, working, to be sure, but too close to the breadline for comfort. Frank Stockman, a *commis* waiter at the Savoy and Claridge's throughout this time, averaged a little over £2, with no share of the *tronc*, for a six-day week of assisting the chef waiter at a "station" of seven tables; at the Savoy, the *tronc* was the exclusive province of the headwaiters, the chef waiter, and the sommelier. At New York's Plaza, Tony Soma, later a restaurateur in his own right, earned a dollar for each sixteen-hour day, faring even worse than Dave Marlowe, a Londoner, who got no more than a shilling an hour for a six-and-a-half-day week. The secret, Marlowe discovered, was to try one's luck in a New World night spot; at bandleader Rudy Vallee's Villa Vallee, from 1933 on, he pulled down $70 a month, plus tips. With a $5-a-head cover charge, night spots not only did better but paid better.

Yet recruiting standards and regulations, Frank Stockman recalls, were almost as rigorous as the Brigade of Guards. No waiter was permitted to wear a ring, or a watch, or spectacles; false teeth disqualified a man as much as a cast in the eye or a speech impediment like a stutter or a lisp. At Claridge's, where they must at all times carry a waiter's cloth—the Savoy permitted napkins—the waiters took up their stances precisely two yards apart, forbidden, on pain of dismissal, to cough, sneeze, or blow their noses. The best among them, men who would rise in the trade, developed what Charles Ritz, son of César, would later call "table radar": an inbuilt instinct as to when a coffee cup needed refilling or an ashtray must be emptied, without any signal from the host.

Many, in this age before jet travel, preferred to chance their arms as stewards on the great transatlantic liners, sixty-nine of them in all, for in the thirties the war among the shipping lines for the Rainbows' custom was as intense as that among the grand hotels. Each voyage was, in fact, a calculated risk, for liners like Cunard-White Star's *Queen Mary,* launched in 1934, had to be more than two-thirds full to make the voyage a paying proposition. Every streamer of brown billowing smoke that poured from her funnels each minute represented one ton of oil, 220 gallons; with oil at $22 a gallon, a voyage cost $200,000 for fuel alone. Only when booked to capacity could the *Mary* gross $500,000 on a one-way trip, for which her 704 first-class passengers would pay $254,000 in fares.

Canny stewards worked hard—sometimes thirteen hours a day—but found it a paying game. A first-class bedroom steward's greatest pride was to store cabin color combinations in his memory, so that when Rainbows like the Marquis and Marchioness de la Falaise crossed, the entire suite looked exactly the same as when they had last occupied it. To get the best food and the quickest service for passengers dining in their suites, the stewards would tip the pantryman, who in turn would tip the chef. To save time and give better service they often ate their own food standing up in their pantries. To dry-clean the clothes of favored passengers they would shamelessly remove fluid from the fire extinguishers.

Their training, as laid down by Cunard-White Star, was rigorous. No dining room steward graduated to first class, where he waited on no more than five passengers but must know, like a good butler, the exact timing of every dish, until he had served ten diners for many months in tourist class and eight diners in cabin class. But for first-class bedroom stewards, paid £20 a month for valeting seven to ten suites, one three-day, one-way trip might net £100 in tips.

The rivalry among the lines grew keener as the thirties wore on. Barbara Hutton's favorite liner, the *Ile de France,* which from 1927 made the Atlantic crossing at twenty-four knots, offered such enticements as a twenty-nine-foot bar to banish the sorrows of Prohibition, the first seagoing Roman Catholic chapel, a mailplane on deck, designed to reach New York one day earlier, lampposts and hydrants for Rainbow dogs, and no fewer than 130 chefs. The *Mary,* not to be outdone, was paneled in twenty-eight contrasting woods, from avodire to zebrano, and boasted that entry into Oldrich Kerb's Verandah Grill, where unreserved tables were less common than diamond bracelets, was akin to getting into Eton—"you had to be put down at birth." Huge sums were spent on decoration and gimmickry; from 1932 on, the French Line's *Normandie* advertised their dining room as longer than the Versailles Hall of Mirrors. In 1938, Cunard-White Star surpassed all this with their brand-new *Queen Elizabeth,* for if the size of the *Queen Mary* was overwhelming, the size of the *Queen Elizabeth* was stupefying. Against the *Queen Mary*'s twelve decks, the *Elizabeth* boasted fourteen. She had thirty-six elevators against the *Mary*'s twenty-one, and three anchors to the *Mary*'s two. Even her passenger capacity, 2,314, outclassed the *Mary*'s by 320.

This was an era when every third name on the first-class passenger list was followed by ". . . and valet" or ". . . and maid," when pursers like the *Ile de France*'s Henri Villar judged the elegance of a crossing by the number of dogs in the kennels: dogs indicated hotel suites, and thus rented estates, and thus travel by automobile. Specialists like the *Normandie*'s chef des cuisines, Gaston Magrin, were single-minded to a fault; Magrin saw the liner as no more than a set of engines propelling him from Le Havre, where he could buy *langoustes,* to New York, where he could obtain bluepoint oysters. In Magrin's personal atlas, ports were marked by the names of the comestibles he could buy in them.

For the liners had long ceased to function as mere ocean carriers; they were pleasure palaces, bejeweled ferryboats for the very rich, where twenty pieces of hold luggage were minimal. (A passenger, after all, changed his or her clothes four times a day.) From Manhattan's West Side Highway, the piers above the Hudson River were at all times a bright, colorful sea of house flags: the somber red and black of the French Line, the red, white, and blue of the United States Lines, the renowned "Cunard red." At sailing times, the pierside teemed with longshoremen manhandling Vuitton luggage, cabins were choked with bon voyage gifts, boxes of red long-stemmed Baccara roses from Constance Spry, lavender tins of chocolates from Louis Sherry—and no liner worthy of the name ever sailed before midnight, to a ritual accompaniment of popping champagne corks hitting the cabin lights, rolls of colored streamers drifting like tumbleweed toward the docks, and a pierside band playing "Anchors Aweigh," almost drowning the stewards' stentorian cries of "All ashore who are going ashore!"

Soon, though few perceived it, all this would be part of history.

* * *

At York House, no less than at Fort Belvedere, there were signs of imminent change—none of them, thought the old faithfuls of David's entourage, for the better.

The rot, as they saw it, had set in on Tuesday, January 30, 1934, when the Simpsons attended a dinner party of David's at the new Dorchester Hotel, the first London hotel to be constructed in reinforced concrete, a pioneer concept of the civil engineers, McAlpine, to provide jobs for their work force in the Depression. Wallis, seated on David's left, had posed probing and intelligent questions on David's efforts to provide better housing for the poor. "I know about the poor," she remarked meaningfully. "I was one of them."

"Wallis," David told her gravely, as the evening ended, "you're the only woman who has ever been interested in my job."

The very next afternoon, dropping into Bryanston Court for cocktails, David stayed on for dinner—and he followed the same routine on the Thursday and Friday. On the Saturday, the Simpsons were guests at Fort Belvedere; on Wednesday, February 7, after dinner at Bryanston Court, David took the Simpsons to a night club. On the Friday, he and Wallis dined alone at Quaglino's; next day, she and Ernest were again weekend guests at the Fort. By March 22, when Thelma Furness returned to London, Wallis and David had met on at least six more occasions.

Both at York House and Fort Belvedere, Osborne, the butler, and the other servants were bitterly resentful. This American woman was not only advising their master on new color schemes but was planning his menus at both establishments; when they complained to him, as complain they did, they were told to take their orders from Mrs. Simpson. On Thelma's return, David presented himself at her house, "cold and aloof," to broach rumors that on her return voyage, Prince Aly Khan, the Aga's hellion son, had been "unduly attentive" to her. Thelma, rightly, made light of the episode. Something was clearly wrong, but just what she could not fathom.

On her first weekend at Fort Belvedere—again with the Simpsons—the pieces fell neatly into place. New furniture arrangements had replaced her own; it was Wallis, not David, who was issuing orders to the servants. Moreover, it was Wallis, at the dinner table, seeing David pick up a piece of salad from his side-plate, who playfully slapped his hand as if taking a refractory child to task. Thelma, shocked, shot her a glance of outrage. Wallis only stared right back at her—"that one cold defiant glance had told me the entire story," Thelma recounted later. The next day she packed and left the Fort; nor would she return.

In the words of Sir Alan Lascelles, then Assistant Private Secretary to King George V, David was now revealed as "the meanest royalty that has ever been." The next to receive this shabby treatment was his mistress of seventeen years, Freda Dudley Ward, who, despite her knowledge of Thelma, had been in the habit of telephoning York House almost daily. In May 1934, Freda called for the last time. An embarrassed switchboard operator broke the news: David had instructed that her calls would no longer be accepted.

Wallis, meanwhile, more and more openly flaunted her power. On one occasion, London Society was aghast when she dropped her handkerchief and waited imperiously for David to pick it up—which he dutifully did. She would reach out in public and straighten his necktie; in Lady Cunard's box at the Royal Opera House, Covent Garden, after telling him to hurry away or he would keep Queen Mary waiting at the London County Council ball, she firmly plucked a cigar from his breast pocket. "It doesn't look very pretty," she admonished him.

In Biarritz, that autumn, at the rented Villa Morotmont, Wallis's aunt, Bessie Merryman, on a visit to Europe, was alarmed by the attentions and jewelry David was lavishing on her niece; to make matters worse, Ernest was absent on a business trip in the United States. Aunt Bessie ventured a word of caution. "You don't have to worry about me," Wallis replied curtly. "I know what I'm doing."

In that same autumn, Wallis was presented for the first—and last—time to King George V and Queen Mary at a Buckingham Palace reception. To some, the Queen's attitude seemed restrained, even frosty—perhaps because, as rumor had it, a Palace servant had spread the story of how Wallis, surveying Queen Mary's famous flower beds of prize petunias, had commented, "Of course when I live here, this will all be tennis courts."

"He's either mad," King George commented bitterly of his son's infatuation, "or the biggest rake in Europe."

The gulf between David and his own family was now well-nigh unbridgeable. With his pursuit of Wallis, he had forfeited all his mother's sympathy. His father was unapproachable. His brothers Bertie and Harry rarely visited the Fort; their wives wanted no part of Wallis. Only the Mountbattens and Prince George, Duke of Kent, who had recently married Princess Marina of Greece, were still companions, though George was less than sympathetic to his brother's obsession. "He is besotted with women," he declared angrily. "One can't get a word of sense out of him."

This was the shape of things when, on January 17, 1936, King George V, at Sandringham, scrawled a barely legible last entry in his diary: "I feel rotten." Three days later, as his physician and friend, Lord Dawson of Penn, noted gracefully, "his life moved peacefully to its close." Just before midnight came the moment David had dreaded all his life. With his father's passing, Queen Mary stopped before her eldest son, took his hand, and kissed it; the Duke of Kent followed suit. But a lady-in-waiting, noting the new King's anguish, thought it "frantic and unreasonable," far exceeding that of other members of the family.

The Sandringham carpenter constructed a simple coffin, and as it was borne through the gardens to the altar of the village church, Forsyth, the King's piper, wailed a last lament. Then, on the morning of January 23, the coffin was loaded onto a gun carriage and driven three miles to Wolferton Station, en route to King's Cross Station, London, for the lying-in-state at Westminster Great Hall.

Soon after leaving King's Cross, a symbolic incident, which few were to notice, occurred. The imperial crown, brought hastily from the Tower of London's Jewel House, had been affixed to the lid of the coffin, which another gun carriage, black-draped and hauled by man power, was to bear to the Great Hall. The Maltese cross, topping the crown, became loosened by the jolting, and abruptly a cluster of 200 diamonds and a large square-cut sapphire fell sparkling into the gutter. Without missing a step, a quick-witted Grenadier Guards sergeant, pacing beside the carriage, scooped up the cross and stuffed it into his pocket.

From the corner of his eye, David had spotted the incident. "Christ!" he muttered. "What's going to happen next?"

It was the new King's Minister for Agriculture, Walter Elliott, overhearing him, who commented most appropriately. "That," he remarked to a companion, "will be the motto of the new reign!"

7/ THE WORLD OF BABS AND "QUEEN WALLY":
"Don't Abdicate, You Fool!"

The headlines resounded with Depression: "That Man," President Franklin D. Roosevelt, lambasting America's men of wealth as "economic royalists," was a traitor to his class. In Britain, too, it was becoming increasingly hard, even for Rainbows, to ignore 3 million unemployed and 250,000 living below the poverty line. The headlines charged aggression: Adolf Hitler, Führer and Chancellor of the Third Reich, had, in March 1936, flouted the League of Nations by marching German troops into the demilitarized Rhineland. Five months earlier, his fellow dictator, Italy's Benito Mussolini, had displayed the same contempt for human rights in invading Ethiopia.

Such topics were still of scant interest to columnists like Castlerosse and Maury Paul. When it came to human interest, they at all times accorded priority to Barbara Hutton.

Barbara had been seen in London, at the Café de Paris, where "Prince" Alexis had angrily forbidden Albert Swaebe, the British equivalent of Jerome Zerbe, to take her picture. Barbara had been seen at the Venice Lido, where she always had the blue-and-white striped cabana no. 2; Barbara had bought a palazzo on the Grand Canal. Living on black coffee and RyKrisp, in response to her husband's criticisms, Barbara had shed sixty pounds in weight; she had taken to chain-smoking Marlboro cigarettes. At the Palace, St. Moritz, to which she always brought her own blue cashmere blankets, she was seen wearing black lipstick and black nail varnish. At other times she changed her nail varnish from scarlet to blue to gold to match the colors of her Molyneux day clothes.

Her only rival in the world of Poor Little Rich Girls, Doris Duke, the tobacco heiress, said to be worth $4 million a year tax-free, was less feted by the press. Not only had she married an all-American boy, Jimmie Cromwell, Mrs. Eva Stotesbury's son by her first marriage; she was known to be a penny pincher, who used toilet paper for her hair curlers. As headline material, "Dee-Dee" was not in Barbara's league.

That the Mdivanis were splitting up was known to the press and to all international Society. At the London Ritz, head porter Arnold Schmid noted that Alexis, carelessly swinging a polo mallet and resplendent in silk shirt and jodhpurs, departed for the polo grounds at Ranelagh as early as 8 A.M., rarely returning to dress for dinner before 7 P.M. Overnight, in consequence, Alexis's stock slumped dramatically.

Thus, when Barbara and Elsa Maxwell lunched at Claridge's with Bendor, second Duke of Westminster, Charles Malandra, the haughty restaurant manager, seated them in the main dining room—while Alexis, arriving later with a German girl on his arm, was seated well to the rear, an area known to Society as Slobovia. True, Alexis would be present at Babs's twenty-second birthday party at the Paris Ritz on November 15, 1934—where their extravagance in flying in Jack Harris's band from London for $10,000 brought a storm of unwelcome publicity—but the end was not far off.

Mdivani had no regrets. In eighteen months of marriage he had mulcted Babs of $3 million in securities, plus furniture, jewelry, polo ponies, automobiles, and the fifteenth-century Venetian palazzo, which Barbara had bought and put in his name. It was time to move on to fresh stamping grounds.

It was, of course, Elsa Maxwell who, on that November evening, steered Barbara's second husband in her direction: the tall, good-looking, forty-year-old Count Kurt Haugwitz-Reventlow. Kurt was indeed a genuine Danish aristocrat, but a predator like Mdivani, willing to split his share of the take with Elsa in return for that much-prized introduction. That evening, observers were quick to note, he danced with Barbara no fewer than seven times.

Thus, in Reno, Nevada, on May 13, 1935, Barbara shed the Mdivani name in exchange for a new title, and the tabloids bannered the news across America:

> PRINCESS BABS BECOMES COUNTESS BABS
> WOOLWORTH HEIRESS TAKES ON NEW TITLE
> COUNT REVENTLOW BECOMES BARBARA'S
> NEW MILLION-DOLLAR BABY

"Alexis cared far more for his polo ponies than for me," Barbara was quoted as saying. "I didn't know that Alexis had planned to marry me when I came of age."

Less than three months later, she was once more in the headlines:

> COUNTESS REVENTLOW HEARS OF DEATH OF
> FORMER HUSBAND AND GOES INTO SECLUSION IN
> LONDON

Alexis's final settlement had availed him little. On August 1, gunning his Rolls-Royce at 100 miles an hour over Spanish roads, he hit a stone wall between Palamos and Figuéras head-on; the car turned over five times and Alexis was decapitated. A few weeks later, "Prince" Serge, who had kept things in the family by exchanging Pola Negri for the Mdivani-oriented Louise Van Alen, was killed before her eyes at a polo match when a pony kicked him in the head. Barbara was finally free of "the marrying Mdivanis."

Yet by 1936 she knew that her second marriage was equally a mistake.

The reason was not hard to fathom: total incompatibility. Barbara liked to read best-sellers; Kurt never opened a book. A man's man, he liked to spend most of his time in Pall Mall clubrooms. Apart from the Duke and Duchess of Kent, whom he welcomed—Kurt loved the monarchy and the trappings of protocol—he found her other friends, like her homosexual cousin,

Jimmy Woolworth Donahue, and Elsie de Wolfe (Lady Mendl), distasteful. He was irritated by her eternal RyKrisp diet, which she stuck to even in fashionable restaurants; Kurt tackled his food with animal gusto. Yet, despite her reservations, Barbara knew that this was no time for the marriage to crack up. She was six months pregnant.

Her pregnancy, like everything else concerning her, would echo round the world. Even *The New York Times* saw it as rating a headline when Lord Horder, physician-in-ordinary to King Edward, as David had become, paid her an emergency visit: BARBARA HUTTON, COUNTESS HAUGWITZ, SERIOUSLY ILL. Frail and weak, Barbara was suffering from anorexia nervosa, a legacy from the Mdivani days; on February 18, 1936, when her son, Lance Hutton, a 7½-pound baby, was delivered by a caesarian operation, Barbara herself weighed less than 100 pounds.

Lance Hutton was to grow up in a gilded cage: a fifty-room Regency mansion near London's Regent's Park, the site of the former St. Dunstan's Home for the Blind, set in 12½ acres of grounds. This Barbara planned as a £500,000 dream house, complete with fourteen-carat-gold shower handles and towel racks, an oaken double staircase modeled after an old French château, £2,000 worth of ivory-pine paneling to line every wall, and, for Lance, a six-room nursery suite, its walls padded with soft pink kid.

In due celebration of the Old Money, Barbara insisted that this sumptuous habitation must be called Winfield House, after her grandfather's middle name. In justice, he was a deity she often invoked. Whether buying a ribbed gold Cartier cigarette case, pavéed with sapphires, for Jimmy Donahue, or presenting Elsa Maxwell with a Fabergé case that had belonged to the Emperor Franz Josef, her reaction was always the same: "Don't thank me—thank Grandpa Woolworth."

Try as she might to escape the limelight, the headlines continued to dog her. It was news when, under pressure from Kurt, she renounced her United States citizenship and became subject to Danish law. It was news when several hundred angry hunger strikers in the Brooklyn and Manhattan branches of Woolworth sought her intervention to procure a living wage—although she had long ago sold the bulk of her Woolworth stock. MISS HUTTON COUNTS MILLIONS WHILE FIVE AND TEN GIRLS COUNT TEN AND TWELVE DOLLAR SALARIES, read the placards of the picketers.

But midway through 1936, the Rainbows of the international set were engaged by a more urgent topic than Barbara's matrimonial problems. David was facing the biggest crisis of his life.

* * *

It was a tragedy, thought Harold Nicolson, that "that silly little man . . . should destroy a great monarchy by giggling into a flirtation with a third-rate American." It was equally a tragedy, Nicolson knew, in which heads had already rolled—almost as if the country was being ruled not from York House but from Bryanston Court.

For what now seemed increasingly apparent was that David would be crowned King only on his own terms, with Wallis—super-efficient, Molyneux-gowned Wallis, the impeccable hostess—at his side. As Bernard Rickatson-Hatt, a journalist and later the Bank of England's first public relations officer, was to tell it, Ernest Simpson, in February 1936, asked him to come to York House for a private supper with the King. To the journalist's embarrassment, as David entered the room, Ernest, having cleverly secured himself a witness, staged a confrontation. Wallis, he said, would have to choose between them, and what did David intend to do about it?

"Are you sincere?" Ernest asked rhetorically. "Do you intend to marry her?" Rising from his chair, David replied roundly, "Do you really think I would be crowned without Wallis by my side?"

Plainly David saw Wallis not as a latter-day Alice Keppel but as his Queen Consort or nothing.

Two men who were loath to connive at this were dismissed out of hand within weeks: Admiral Sir Lionel Halsey, David's comptroller, and Brigadier Gerald Trotter, then his groom-in-waiting. When Halsey protested at the levies on royal funds to finance Wallis's spending sprees, David told him tersely, "I'm sorry, but I no longer want your services." Trotter's peccadillo was to be seen dining in the Savoy Grill with Thelma Furness. "I am through with Thelma and very keen on Wallis, so please cut Thelma," David instructed him.

"Sir, I made friends with Thelma at your request," was Trotter's courageous response. "I don't sack my friends." Since royalty carries no money, it had always been Trotter's function to pay David's bills at the Embassy and Quaglino's, expecting reimbursement in due course, but whereas King Edward had always settled up with his equerries, David never had. When Trotter was dismissed, his resources were almost exhausted; the one job he could secure was as a department store floorwalker. He was bankrupt when he died in 1949.

Now the only people who were admitted to York House or Fort Belvedere were those who had nailed their colors to Wallis's mast. This was thus a time when ambitious hostesses came into their own.

Chief among them was Emerald, Lady Cunard, born Maud Burke in San Francisco, who had settled in England after marrying Sir Bache Cunard, of the shipping family, in 1895. By 1911, Maud had tired both of her country seat, Nevill Holt, near Corby, in Leicestershire, and of her bucolic, fox-hunting husband, whose hobby was decorative ironwork; Sir Bache had labored for hours at his forge to build her an ornamental gate, with the words "Come into the garden, Maud" picked out in miniature horseshoes. Understandably, Maud had decamped to London with her daughter, Nancy, in 1911. In 1926, when she moved to her celebrated rendezvous, 7 Grosvenor Square, she had rechristened herself Emerald—"Maud is too Tennysonian"—after her favorite precious stone.

David and Wallis were always welcome at Emerald's lapis lazuli dinner table, which seated up to thirty, for Emerald, as Peter Quennell put it, "delighted in mixing her guests like cocktails": Winston Churchill as well as Somerset Maugham, and her lover, the conductor Sir Thomas Beecham, Diana Cooper along with "Chips" Channon, Barbara Hutton as well as Cecil Beaton and Alice Astor Obolensky.

Her guests' recollections of her allowed for no half measures.

"Chips" Channon was intrigued by her "pretty wrinkled Watteau face," though to Harold Nicolson she resembled "a third-dynasty mummy painted pink by amateurs." The explorer Roderick Cameron credited her with "a mind as nimble as a Figaro aria," but Virginia Woolf found her "a ridiculous little parakeet-faced woman." Most of the similes describing Emerald were avian: "a brilliant humming bird," "a canary of prey."

Her introductions were all in a nutshell: "This is Michael Arlen, the only Armenian who hasn't been massacred," "This is Gerald Berners—he's a musician and a saucy fellow." At least one guest, Prince Youssoupoff, introduced as "the man who murdered Rasputin," seized up his hat and departed. She was perky and at times mordantly witty. When Somerset Maugham, a renowned homosexual, prepared to leave a dinner party early— "I have to keep my youth"—Emerald murmured, "Why didn't you bring him with you?"

Only once did a guest get the better of her, in 1922, when George Bernard Shaw brought his self-effacing wife, Charlotte, to a luncheon party of Hazel Lavery's. Emerald, who had a spiteful streak, harped repeatedly on the love letters of Shaw and Mrs. Patrick Campbell, which the actress, defying Shaw's absolute veto, had recently published. "You must read them," Emerald persisted more than once, in the face of Mrs. Shaw's stony silence. "As love letters they are unsurpassed. Promise me you will read them."

"I shall certainly read them," Charlotte Shaw replied deliberately. "And when I have read them I'll tell you what I think of *them* and what I think of *you*."

Thereafter, recalled Christabel, Lady Aberconway, Emerald was silent for all of ten minutes.

Such an interchange would have been unlikely in the salon of Sibyl, Lady Colefax, at Argyll House, King's Road, Chelsea, where malice was rarely indulged in. Sibyl's preference, in the scornful words of Virginia Woolf, was "to listen to clever talk and to buy it with a lunch of four courses and good wine." A small, neat, dark-haired woman with a slight stoop, "Coalbox" was the latter-day equivalent of Dickens's Mrs. Leo Hunter: an indefatigable seeker-out of celebrities, whatever their field. Novelists, poets, politicians, royalty like David were all equally welcome at Argyll House; like an ardent lepidopterist, the thrill for Sibyl was as much in the chase as in the entrapment.

Once they were in the bag, some noted ruefully, her attention was prone to wander while she sought out fresh prizes, and the Broadway star, Alfred Lunt, who once escorted her to the theater, swiftly tired of her habit of bobbing up and down in the stalls to see who was escorting whom. "Sibyl," Lunt declared, "you have been taken to the first night of a very interesting play by one of the greatest living actors. You will sit down, talk to me, and listen to the play, or I shall leave."

Yet such was Sibyl's insatiable appetite for celebrities that the satirist Osbert Sitwell, after declining one invitation to a party, stationed himself on a nearby roof with a powerful megaphone, greeting the arrival of each notability like a zealous toastmaster; an editor of pronounced pacifist convictions was hailed as "Signor Mussolini," a rising politician as the "ex-Kaiser Wilhelm of Germany," and a has-been actress as "Miss Mary Pickford."

This hunger to tiptoe in the corridors of power involved Sibyl in the crisis of David and Wallis even more closely than it did Emerald Cunard. Following the death of her husband, Sir Arthur, in February 1936, Sibyl set up as an interior decorator, in rivalry to Somerset Maugham's estranged wife, Syrie, who had launched a "whiteness" vogue with an all-white ball: girls in white dresses, men with white carnations, lilies banked against white screens, carpets of clipped sheepskin. Sibyl, who favored pale almond-greens and grays, with touches of yellow and rose, set up shop in one room of the Bruton Street house of Lady Islington, netting a £2,000 profit in her first year—and this tasteful salon became a discreet rendezvous for Wallis and David.

As Sibyl Colefax was to relate it, Wallis was in a quandary. The possibility of David's abdication had not then occurred to her. He had, she said, threatened to commit suicide if she left him, yet she never thought he could be serious about marriage, nor had he proposed to her. Her one fear was that if she left England to avert scandal, David would follow her and provoke more scandal yet.

That summer, the world was resolutely divided into two camps:

the Wallis-David camp, which numbered not only Emerald and Sibyl, Winston Churchill, Lord Beaverbrook, and Lord Rothermere, but, incredibly, William Randolph Hearst, who dispatched a star journalist, Adela Rogers St. Johns, to London, with the blanket instructions, "Let us see if we can't make her Queen of England."

In opposite camps, convinced that David's duty to the throne came above all other considerations, were Mrs. Ronnie Greville, who espoused the case of Bertie, Duke of York, and Mrs. Laura Corrigan, a onetime waitress from Stevens Point, Wisconsin, who was faithful to the interests of George, Duke of Kent.

Like Grace Wilson Vanderbilt, Mrs. Ronnie prized only pedigree: although she had entertained David back in 1922, the Yorks had spent their honeymoon at her country house near Dorking, Polesden Lacey. Born Margaret Anderson, the illegitimate daughter of the Scottish brewer William McEwan, she had brought a £1,500,000 nest egg to her marriage with the deathly dull Ronald Greville, a courtier of King Edward VII's, who had esteemed Greville as much as he disliked Greville's wife. But despite the venom of her tongue and her squat, misshapen figure of a snowman on the point of melting, Maggie's money—"I'd rather be a beeress than a peeress," she went on record—enabled her to cultivate royalty to the exclusion of most other breeds: King Fuad I of Egypt, the Queen of Spain, King Faisal of Iraq. "One uses up *so* many red carpets in a season," was her much-quoted lament.

This closeness to the British Royal Family gave her an unique opportunity to spite her hated rival, Emerald Cunard, so deeply enmeshed with David and Wallis. "You mustn't think that I dislike little Lady Cunard," she purred. "I'm always telling Queen Mary that she isn't half as bad as she is painted."

Laura Corrigan, the widow of a Cleveland, Ohio, steel millionaire, had also used her money to bulldoze her way into Society; unable to storm the starchy echelons of "The 400," she had descended on London in April 1922 to take over Alice Keppel's old house, 16 Grosvenor Street, for £500 a week and—for a further consideration—Alice Keppel's guest list. But where

Maggie was viperish, Laura was entirely devoid of malice. Her pleasure was to give, and give freely, particularly to friends like the Kents. Her wedding present to Marina had been a £5,000 mink coat, but anyone attending one of her £6,000 tombola parties—"Tom Bowler" to Laura—could expect their share of the goodies: dukes could count on coroneted sock suspenders, brides on pink monogrammed sheets and, in due time, rattles with gold bells for their firstborn.

A kindly soul, Laura was as renowned for her five auburn wigs, designed for every occasion from breakfast to bed to swimming, as for her malapropisms. She referred cheerfully to a cathedral's "flying buttocks" and to the growing fashion for "confused lighting." She liked Mrs. Keppel's Chippendale chairs, but thought them spoiled by the "petits pois." Once, on meeting the Aga Khan, she beamed, "I know your brother, Otto." Perhaps because Wallis was determined to distance herself from another and more obvious parvenu, David resolutely gave Laura a wide berth. On the one occasion that they met, at Emerald Cunard's, he ignored her the entire evening; later he agreed to attend a function only if Laura was not invited.

On August 10, 1936, David, his instinct for public relations increasingly blunted by crass conceit, embarked on his most tasteless blunder yet. With his father's funeral a seven-month memory, and the nation still in its year-long period of mourning, he announced that he was chartering Lady Yules's yacht, the *Nahlin*, for an extended cruise of the Mediterranean with his friends. The guest list was predictable: the Coopers, the Brownlows, Emerald, Wallis's friends, Herman and Kathleen Rogers, and, of course, Wallis herself. David was also taking along 3,000 golf balls, to practice driving from the deck into the sea, and gutting the library to make room for the cargo of liquor.

All through the month-long cruise, the tensions mounted. Of necessity, British press coverage was restrained, but the American press, in pursuit of "the biggest story since the resurrection, 'Queen Wally,'" knew no such inhibitions. David and Wallis were openly ensconced in the best suite at one end of the yacht; the remaining guests were segregated at the other. As the *Nahlin* plowed on—from Sibenik, in Yugoslavia, to Athens, thence to Istanbul—David's flouting of established convention became increasingly apparent; even meeting up with consuls and mayors, he went naked save for straw sandals and gray flannel shorts. He apologized constantly for everything: the food, the company, the accommodation. "Wallis is wearing very badly," Diana Cooper wrote home to a friend. "Her commonness and Becky Sharpishness irritate."

Events were now moving toward a crisis point; timing was of the essence, for the coronation was fixed for May 1937. In London, Ernest Simpson was openly joking, "My only regret is that I have but one wife to lay down for my King." Angered by some of the stories appearing in the American press, Wallis wrote urgently to Aunt Bessie, "Please send my family papers. People are saying that I'm a plumber's daughter." Promptly, Aunt Bessie replied, "Your family papers are on the way. They are very fine. Just don't behave like a plumber's daughter."

Meanwhile, Ernest Simpson had done what was then, for an Englishman, "the decent thing," furnishing evidence of his adultery at a Thames-side hotel with a professional corespondent, Miss "Buttercup" Kennedy. Accordingly, on October 27, in a nineteen-minute hearing at Ipswich Assizes, Wallis petitioned for and obtained a divorce, which one American headline summarized gleefully: KING'S MOLL RENO'D IN WOLSEY'S HOME TOWN.

Just prior to this, alarmed by the adverse publicity, the Prime Minister, Stanley Baldwin, had attempted to take a hand. At a Fort Belvedere interview, which Baldwin himself requested, he begged, "Couldn't you have this coming divorce put off?" David at once replied, "Mr. Baldwin, that is the lady's private business. I have no right to interfere with the affairs of an individual." Baldwin was somber: "I don't believe that you can go on like this and get away with it."

David, of course, always believed that he could, ignoring the fact that though the Royal Marriages Act did not apply to him, the powers of the Crown were so circumscribed that no monarch could consider matrimony without his government's consent. "We are faced with an impasse," "Chips" Channon noted in his diary. "The country, or much of it, would not accept Queen Wallis, with two live husbands scattered about." When Winston Churchill asked him, "Why shouldn't the King marry his cutie?" Noel Coward spoke for many when he retorted, "Because England does not want a Queen Cutie."

On Sunday, November 15, David summoned his old friend, Walter Monckton, who was to act as a mediator between monarch and cabinet from this time on, to Windsor Castle. If the government was against his marriage to Wallis, he was prepared to go. "He [Baldwin] will not like that," Monckton hazarded. "I shall not find it easy to say," David assured him.

Yet, the following day, at 6:30 P.M., he said it, nonetheless—a decision he also communicated to Queen Mary over dinner that evening and to his brothers the next day. There was but one reaction: consternation. "Well, Prime Minister," the Queen greeted Baldwin, "here's a pretty kettle of fish." The Duke of York, who was automatically next in line for the succession, was appalled. "This is absolutely terrible," he was to tell his cousin, Lord Louis Mountbatten. "I never wanted this to happen; I'm quite unprepared for it. David has been trained for this all his life. I've never even seen a State Paper."

On Thursday, December 3, Wallis's nerve broke abruptly. At first she had welcomed the proposal of Esmond Harmsworth, Lord Rothermere's son, of a morganatic marriage, a device used by continental royalty when a lowborn wife did not rank as consort. But though David had reluctantly put it to Baldwin, the Cabinet rejected it out of hand—and now, outraged Britons, indignant at the prospect of a Rainbow queen, had smashed every windowpane at Wallis's rented apartment at 16 Cumberland Terrace. It was high time to be gone.

Along with David's friend and lord-in-waiting, Perry Brownlow, his chauffeur, Ladbroke, and his personal detective, Inspector Evans of Scotland Yard, Wallis set off on a three-day journey to the home of her friends, the Herman Rogerses, the Villa Lou Vieie, at Cannes—pursued every inch of the way, like a heroine in a melodrama, by the baying bloodhounds of the press. Somehow, at every stop on the journey, she contrived to phone David, while berating Inspector Evans as "a stupid Scotland Yard flatfoot" for failing to give the reporters the slip.

It was reportedly from Lyons that she terminated her call with the desperate advice, "*Don't* abdicate, you *fool!*"

Already the rats were leaving the sinking ship of state. At a cocktail party, Emerald Cunard, running into Mrs. Ronnie Greville, sought a favor. "Maggie, darling," she begged, "do tell me about this Mrs. Simpson. I have only just met her."

David was now so befuddled by liquor as to be scarcely responsible for his actions. On December 4, one day after Wallis's departure, he was so far gone in brandy he tore a Buckingham Palace telephone from the wall in a drunken rage; his alarmed equerry, Colonel Piers Legh, at once sent for Lord Horder, who applied the stomach pump. "The man is mad. MAD," Baldwin told Harold Nicolson, gripping him by the arm in a House of Commons corridor, though at one Fort Belvedere meeting around this time, Baldwin made a noble attempt to rise above personalities. Raising his glass of whisky-and-soda, he announced, "Well, sir, whatever happens, my Mrs. and I wish you happiness from the depths of our souls." To his lifelong embarrassment, David burst into a flood of tears, and a moment later Baldwin himself was weeping.

For Baldwin, a pragmatic Worcestershire pig-breeder, it was an unique insight into the essential immaturity of a Rainbow persona. "It was almost uncanny: like talking to a child of ten years old," he wrote to his niece, Monica, "He kept repeating over and over again: 'I can't do my job without her—I am going to marry her and I will *go*.' There was simply no moral struggle. . . ."

On the evening of December 11, introduced by Sir John Reith, Director-General of the B.B.C., as "His Royal Highness Prince Edward," David gave his last broadcast to the nation, in a room in the Augusta Tower, Windsor Castle—a speech that Americans, too, would hear in hotel lobbies and radio shops and on rainy New York street corners. "You must believe me when I tell you that I have found it impossible to carry out the heavy burden of responsibility and to discharge my duties as King as I would wish to do without the help and support of the woman I love."

Inevitably, the Rainbows' verdicts were tempered by their own vantage points. In the dining room of the London Ritz, Alice Keppel, now an erect white-haired, sixty-seven-year-old, spoke her mind forthrightly. "The King has shown neither decency, nor wisdom, nor regard for tradition," she maintained. "Things were managed better in my day."

At a cocktail party in New York, by contrast, Harold Ross, the tough, abrasive editor of *The New Yorker,* was splitting his sides with laughter, and Noel Coward, then starring in *Tonight at 8:30* at the National Theatre, was profoundly shocked. "In England we're all terriby *terribly* distressed," he rebuked him. "It is absolutely no occasion for levity."

Ross, being Ross, had the last word. "You mean," he spluttered incredulously, "the King of England runs away with an old American hooker and *that* ain't funny?"

* * *

It was not a departure much mourned by English Society. On December 11, the day that the Duke of Windsor, as David would henceforth be known, departed from Portsmouth in the destroyer H.M.S. *Fury,* shares rocketed on the London Stock Exchange; it was as if the Depression, rather than a 325-day reign, had finally ended. It was now that the souvenir merchants came into their own. New York department stores featured silk scarves reproducing the abdication speech. On Baltimore's East Biddle Street, Wallis's former home opened as a tourist attraction, "A Shrine to Love," charging a one-dollar entry fee and a further twenty-five cents for the privilege of lying down in her bath tub. In the *Bradford Telegraph and Argus,* a canny preserves manufacturer took space to announce, "The King may abdicate, but with the love for Dixon's jams and pickles, the family sticks together like the Empire."

For the two main participants, the six months before Wallis's divorce was made absolute were for Wallis a time of diversion, for David a time of black frustration. Wallis was now in the element that would be hers for the rest of her days: the employment of no fewer than four couturiers to assemble her sixty-six-item trousseau. Older talents like Captain Molyneux and Jean Paquin were well to the fore, but so were two rising stars in the firmament of haute couture: the Roman-born Elsa Schiaparelli, creator of the padded shoulder, the $750 cocktail jacket, and the hot Italian pink called "shocking," and Main Rousseau Bocher, a forty-five-year-old Paris-based Chicagoan, whose wedding dress in "Wallis Blue," a hard, electric shade, brought him fame overnight. Such patronage ensured that Mainbocher could eschew all department store deals; no would-be client viewed his collection without first an introduction and then—after her credit rating had been discreetly checked—an invitation.

At the Schloss Enzesfeld, outside Vienna, home of the Baron Eugene de Rothschild and his wife, the former Kitty Wolff of Philadelphia, David was behaving as badly as could be. Since British divorce laws were strict regarding collusion, he and Wallis had put frontiers between them; only two days before the abdication, a coded cable, tantamount to a royal command, had asked Rothschild whether David could rest up at the Schloss. Out of courtesy, Rothschild had little option but to agree. In fact, the castle had lain empty for several years, maintained only by a skeleton staff; it became Kitty's lot, working long distance from her Paris home, to engage a household staff, order floors to be polished, rugs unrolled, and paintings, silver, and porcelain to be brought from store.

Two days after David settled in with an eleven-strong retinue, Kitty de Rothschild arrived from Paris to check that all was well. To her surprise, David's attitude was cool and remote, as if she, the chatelaine, were no more than an uninvited guest. The Rothschild cellar, she found to her dismay, had been replaced by David's own private stock. At length, David's dinner was announced—but Kitty was not invited to share it.

At this time David was much preoccupied with finances—his own, rather than the Rothschilds'. He telephoned his financial advisers in London several times a day, wrangling over the annual income to be paid to him by King George VI, as the Duke of York had become: a sum estimated at £60,000 a year. But he also telephoned Wallis daily in Cannes; the first telephone bills caused Baron de Rothschild, despite his wealth, no little concern.

There were other boorish instances. To assuage the pangs of being parted from Wallis over Christmas, Kitty redecorated an entire salon for a party, with a vast Christmas tree, and brought in musicians and entertainers from Paris. At the last moment, advancing no reason, David sent word he could not attend. In Vienna, where he was known as a stingy shopper, he billed all purchases to the British Minister, Sir Walford Selby, who promptly forwarded them to the Baron. This was far from what the Baron had had in mind; David could by all means live rent-free, provided he settled the household expenses. But plainly he had no such intention. On the telephone to a friend in London, Kitty announced, "As far as I'm concerned, anyone can have him any time!"

By March, the Rothschilds were growing desperate; David was still a fixture, and still the bills were mounting. It was then that the Baron took up the matter with his legal experts, who hit upon a brainstorm. The city fathers of Vienna would enact a little ceremony to play on David's vanity; he would be proclaimed "Master of Schloss Enzesfeld," and thereafter all bills would be directed to him. David at once panicked; in no short order he and his entourage moved out and into the Pension Appersbach, on the Wolfgangsee, near Salzburg, for an all-in, out-of-season rate of ten dollars a day.

After all the traumas of 1936, the Windsor wedding, on June 3, 1937, at the Château de Candé, near Tours, owned by a French-born naturalized American efficiency expert, Charles Bedaux, was something of an anticlimax. No member of the British Royal Family, since they did not recognize divorce, could attend. The clergyman who performed the ceremony, the Reverend R. A. Jardine, a Darlington vicar, was a volunteer, willing to break the laws of his church for the publicity value; he later toured the United States as a "celebrity." The "chapel" that housed the thirty-two guests—among them "Fruity" Metcalfe and his wife, Wallis's Aunt Bessie, the Herman Rogerses—was a hastily converted music room, lacking even an altar; in the confusion of seeking out a suitable table someone knocked over and cracked an Italian lamp. At once, as if he had been the local electrician, David put everything aside to try and mend it.

Finally, an ornate rococo chest was chosen, but still an altar cloth was lacking; a tea cloth would do perfectly, Wallis decided, but when Mr. Allen, David's solicitor, produced two heavy candlesticks as a final touch, she remonstrated, "Hey, you can't put those out; we want them for the dinner table tonight."

Her cockney maid, Mary Burke, fazed at having to unpack an entire linen trunk to secure the tea cloth, grumbled, "If it's as much trouble as this getting married, I'm sure I'll never go through with it myself."

It was Wallis, that matrimonial veteran, who felt duty-bound to reassure her, "Oh, it isn't always as bad as this—only if you're marrying the ex-King of England!"

By the summer of 1938, Barbara Hutton was still, as consistently as ever, a headline writer's dream. At 3 P.M. on the hot afternoon of June 20, she walked briskly up the steps of London's Bow Street Police Station to seek an interview with one of the magistrates, accompanied by the eminent barrister, Sir Patrick Hastings, K.C.

That same evening, in his third-floor suite at the Paris Ritz, Kurt Haugwitz-Reventlow heard the ominous news that Barbara had accused him of using threats toward her, fearing that she stood in danger of her life, and that in London a warrant had been issued for his arrest. Indignantly, Kurt at once returned, surrendering himself on £2,000 bail, but a few days later Barbara withdrew all charges.

Once again the Reventlows were living out their lives in public:

> SPLIT FOR COUNT AND COUNTESS, TOO MANY DIFFERENCES, SAYS BABS
> COUNT PLANNING TO GIVE BABS FIVE YEARS OF HELL.

For Barbara had sued for, and was granted, a judicial separation, claiming sole custody of Lance Hutton, though Kurt won the right for the boy to spend half the summer holidays with his father. All this was grist to the mercenary mill of Elsa Maxwell, who brashly claimed that she could bring about a reconciliation, a service for which Kurt, who had removed himself from Winfield House to Claridge's, had agreed to pay her $50,000. Otherwise, as the tabloids had predicted, he would give her "five years of hell in the headlines." Thus when Barbara, that November, also announced her intention of quitting Winfield House, Elsa warned her, "You'd better stay here—or you'll lose your son."

This was precisely what Barbara feared, for in the summer of 1939, at the Excelsior Beach Hotel, on the Venice Lido, Kurt offered a flat ultimatum: a $5 million payoff or Lance would mysteriously disappear. That September, as the war clouds darkened, he was as good as his word. Weeks later, in the Hôtel du Palais, Biarritz, when Barbara once more took possession of Lance, bound for the United States for the duration of the war; this concession on Kurt's part cost her $500,000. His price for a divorce came higher, though three years later she was to pay it: a further $1,500,000.

Outside New York's Hotel Pierre, at Fifth Avenue and Sixty-first Street, the placards of the omnipresent picketers that greeted her return were as familiar to her as the headlines:

BARBARA HUTTON! IS EIGHTEEN DOLLARS A WEEK TOO MUCH?
BABS HUTTON FLEES EUROPE'S WAR, SEEKS PEACE. BUT HOW ABOUT PEACE WITH THE UNION?

After all the years away, nothing had been forgotten or forgiven.

* * *

All through the long hot summer of 1939, the gaiety of the Rainbows was undiminished. Few believed in the prospect of war, for most were inclined to give the dictators the benefit of the doubt. Hadn't David and Wallis, through the good offices of their Nazi-oriented friend, Charles Bedaux, visited Germany in October 1937, to take tea with Göring and confer with Himmler, Hess, Göbbels, and the Führer himself? The German Ambassador to the Court of St. James's, Joachim von Ribbentrop, was entirely persona grata with Emerald Cunard and Mrs. Ronnie Greville; after all, hadn't Hitler pledged himself to abolish vivisection and hadn't Mussolini declared Capri to be a bird sanctuary? Ribbentrop's Italian counterpart, Count Dino Grandi, once told this author of how, during a weekend at Cliveden, he ventured some remarks mildly critical of *Il Duce*. When the guests departed to dress for dinner, he was taken aside by his hostess, Lady Astor.

"Young man," she told him severely. "Please remember that in this house nothing is *ever* said against Signor Mussolini."

On the Riviera, the Rainbow royals were out in force. Prince Aly Khan was at Cannes on a spending spree, tipping his caddy a two-seater car after a round of golf at Mougins, dropping £15,000 at a time to the Syndicate at Monte Carlo, yet more worried, at twenty-eight, by his ebbing virility. A man utterly given up to fornication, who had once made love for five hours before reaching a climax, Aly was lately troubled by premature ejaculation; a doctor had suggested keeping one hand dipped in a tumbler of cold water throughout and Aly was discussing this strange panacea with all those who would listen.

Ex-King Alfonso XIII of Spain was also much in evidence; deposed in 1931, he never tired of talking of how that had come about. Given a scant half-hour to pack he had first, as a man of honor, had to destroy 250 compromising "girlie" photographs and had thus arrived in Marseilles with no more than one suitcase. But a man who had foiled seven assassins, including one whom he had ridden down—"Polo came in handy that time"—he was a philosopher at heart. A hotelier manqué, Alfonso had whiled away the time helping design the Moorish-style Grill Room at the Dorchester, driving his $30,000 Bugatti at a fearsome eighty m.p.h. along the Grand Corniche, trying unsuccessfully to buy Marion Davies for a night and playing endless games of bridge.

"If there is a war," Alfonso opined, "I predict that it will be finished when next June comes around."

By the following June, Paris had fallen and Alfonso had but one more year to live.

At the rented Villa La Croë, Cap d'Antibes, David and Wallis likewise had no thoughts of war. At times, in their Paris home, 24, boulevard Suchet, David had seemed restless and irascible and was drinking heavily; a large flask, ostensibly of cologne, on his dressing table was known to contain neat brandy. Time lay heavy on his hands, and Wallis was apt to dispatch him on errands all over Paris, collecting finished orders from dressmakers' showrooms. She would confide in her friends, sotto voce: "No one will ever know how hard I work to make the little man feel busy!"

But at La Croë, with their three well-loved cairn terriers, Pookie and Detto and Prisie, David could more easily banish his boredom, plunging violently into the pool, playing whirlwind rounds of golf, and parading for hours on the flat gun-turreted roof of the villa, which was fitted out like the deck of a ship, skirling monotonously on the bagpipes.

For the staff of the villa, even this melancholy mood-music was preferable to Wallis's eternal fussing. Ernest King, who served out his time as butler for the sake of £900 a year in tips, which he split down the middle with the footmen, was outraged that Wallis had even installed a telephone in his private lavatory: Wallis was swift to share all suggestions that occurred to her. "She thought of everything for her guests' enjoyment," King was to recall. "The trouble was she thought too much, she tried too hard." Bells, which had to be answered on the dot, were installed behind every shutter on the villa's terrace. When guests were expected, placements at the dinner table were sometimes laid and relaid three times—first in the dining room, then on the terrace, then back in the dining room again. All through the service of the meal, Wallis would scribble notes on a little gold writing tablet, like an umpire at a culinary contest: "Too hot," "Too cold," "Cigars handed at the wrong time."

Thus the Rainbow rituals continued to the end.

On the night of August 31, 1939, one day before Germany invaded Poland, Elsa Maxwell threw a party—this time at the expense of Major Eric Loder, onetime Master of the Pytchley Hunt, at the Villa Lou Paradou. For "old battering-ram Elsa" was not departing from her perennial philosophy: "When in doubt, give a party. When in grave doubt, give a bigger party." Two hundred guests were invited; two hundred guests arrived. The driveway to the villa was jammed with cars. Waiters prized the corks from champagne bottles. The party grew to its strident peak.

Suddenly the guests beheld a strange sight. Chatting on the terrace they watched the lights sparkling on the Croisette at Cannes wink out one by one. Then the lights of Juan-les-Pins vanished; in the distance the pink glow that was Nice also faded. The French Government were readying for war with a practice dimout.

Characteristically, the Rainbows were also ready, champagne glasses in hand, at the most chic and glittering party of them all, to herald the crack of doom.

8 / "SHOW ME A MILLIONAIRE...":
The World of Daddy-O

On Monday, September 4, 1939, John Hansen, the tall, imposing head porter at London's Savoy Hotel, could scarcely believe his eyes. The glass panels of the front hall's swing doors had been coated with dark blue paint. The board that showed the departures and arrivals of the great luxury liners had vanished from above his desk. For the first time in history, incredulous reception clerks watched Sir George Reeves-Smith, the hotel's chairman and managing director, pass through the hall clad not in a tall silk hat and frock coat but in a bowler hat and lounge suit. World War II had come with a vengeance to Rainbowland.

Then, following Hitler's ruthless twenty-six-day conquest of Poland, the British knew an acute sense of anticlimax. Geared for Armageddon, they faced only a winter that had brought them rationing, 25° of frost, and a blackout that had plunged the United Kingdom into the pitch-darkness of the seventeenth century. As January 1940 dawned, the blackout, with its thirty-three deaths a day, was taking a greater toll than the war.

For the Rainbows, their staffs awaiting the call-up, life now centered around the great London hotels. Along with her maid, Mary Gordon, Emerald Cunard had transferred her quarters to the Ritz. Mrs. Ronnie Greville was at the Dorchester, on Park Lane; with its reinforced concrete structure and its luxurious air raid shelters with pink and blue silk curtains, it was popular with cabinet ministers, too. In that long winter and false spring of the Phony War, the Dorchester, with orchestra leader Jack Jackson's silver-toned trumpet enlivening the ballroom and Harry Craddock dispensing the cocktails, was the hub of the Rainbow scene.

To this cushioned and tranquil world, where the blackout remained the biggest inconvenience, the Dunkirk evacuation of the British Expeditionary Force, followed by the fall of France on June 17, 1940, was a shock as devastating as a cherished servant giving notice to quit.

The white dusty roads of France were all at once teeming with Rainbow refugees. From a small Indian tramp steamer, built to carry 180 people, 1,500 refugees, among them Baron and Baroness Robert de Rothschild, at length reached England. A grimy little 4,000-ton collier from Cannes, the *Saltersgate,* finally disgorged Somerset Maugham, who headed thankfully for Suite 420 at the Dorchester. Across the Franco-Spanish border hurried the Grand Duchess Charlotte of Luxembourg and Her Highness the Maharanee of Kapurthala, the former Spanish dancer, Anita Delgrado. Also seeking refuge in Spain was the jeweler, Pierre Cartier, and hot in his wake, heading first for Barcelona then for Lisbon, came David and Wallis. Ironically, David's erstwhile hosts at Schloss Enzesfeld, Eugene and Kitty de Rothschild, had already arrived in Lisbon.

On June 10, when Mussolini, too, declared war on France, Alice Keppel made a headlong dash from the Villa dell'Ombrellino, outside Florence, a property she had bought through shrewdly investing in Sir Ernest Cassel's tips; her account of her journey was so highly charged that Maggie Greville scoffed: "To hear Alice talk . . . one would think she had swum the Channel with her maid between her teeth."

In this strange new world of danger and discomfort, the most anachronistic refugee was perhaps Archduke Otto—"Otto the Last"—returning to Lisbon with his mother, the Empress Zita, to plot the restoration of the Hapsburg Empire. The richest was most likely the former King Zog of Albania, who on June 24, 1940, arrived at the London Ritz with his half-American wife,

Queen Geraldine, an entourage of twenty-three, and a mountain of luggage so heavy it took a team of porters to lift it. Did it contain anything of great value? asked the new head porter, George Criticos.

"Yes," said the King succinctly. "Gold."

It was swiftly transferred to the Bank of England, whence Zog's secretary, Mr. Martini, withdrew a thousand-pound banknote every week.

To some, clinging resolutely to older standards, the mood of London in the breathless summer of 1940 seemed distressingly egalitarian. Many women now went hatless and wore slacks—"Horrible!" lamented the couturier Victor Stiebel. "Women seemed to think that now at last they could forget about fashion and go about as they liked." On July 26, one playgoer noted the hitherto unacceptable: in the stalls of the Piccadilly Theatre, lounge suits had replaced dinner jackets. Even at the Ritz, august dowagers dined with portable radios on the table, keeping up with the war news. Clothes, style, and wealth abruptly seemed to matter less. "In the England of the future," conceded Somerset Maugham, "evening dress will be less important than it has been in the past."

Under the circumstances, a friend's assurance to Lady Cunard—"Don't worry, Emerald, within three weeks of the declaration of peace, all the classes will be back in their proper places"—seemed less than prophetic.

Britain's Minister of Food, Lord Woolton, was just as concerned to see equity established. A spot check had revealed no fewer than eighty items on the menu at London's smart Grosvenor House Hotel—too large a choice by far in a Britain at war. "My mail shows that the working class is concerned that rich and poor should be treated alike," he informed Prime Minister Winston Churchill, and with this in view Woolton rationed Rainbow diners-out to one main course, with a total limitation of three courses and a maximum five-shilling charge. To offset the cost of such grace notes as snowy table linen and rolls and butter, hotels like the Dorchester imposed an additional six-shilling cover charge for dinner and a fixed rate of 2s

6d a head for dancing, yet, even so, chefs like the Dorchester's Eugene Kaufeler and the Savoy's Abel Alban faced intractable problems. Men who in St. Moritz and Lausanne had acquired a lavish hand with the best butter, dairy cream, and truffles must now for the first time cope with unpalatably ersatz ingredients like dried egg and synthetic cream.

Despite the blitz, when, between September 1940 and May 1941, more than 18,000 tons of bombs rained on London, the city's morale remained intact. As early as February 1941, the Savoy was bombarded with requests for tables on "Victory Night"—whenever that might be—giving precise details of the number of *couverts*, the menu, and the position of the table. Even the bomb that on March 8, 1941, plummeted onto the edge of the balcony at the Café de Paris, killing eighty-four, including the proprietor, Martin Poulsen, and wounding at least seventy others, did not diminish the optimism. Fully a score of survivors from the carnage, singing a pop hit of the day, "Oh, Johnny, how you can love!" moved on bloody but unbowed to dance at the Mayfair or the Embassy.

In one small and privileged area—Palm Beach and all of resort Florida—Rainbow values remained stubbornly unchanged: the sinuous arm of land embracing Biscayne Bay was in full hothouse bloom, enjoying the giddiest, gaudiest season since the Depression. Lots on Lincoln Road, Miami Beach's swanky main shopping street, were selling for up to $50,000; the yachts and cruisers in the harbor included William Kissam Vanderbilt's *Alva* and the *Virago*, lately chartered by J. P. Morgan, Jr. Rainbows like Mrs. Byron Foy, the milliner Lilly Daché, and the couturière Hattie Carnegie were in town, along with Walter Winchell, who was surveying the scene from the garish $75-a-day Roney Plaza. Columnists noted that a new arrival was the Philadelphia socialite, Alfred Ilko Barton, who taught the new-rich how to be lavish with their money.

Many Rainbows, cut off from the way of life they knew, were temporarily at a loss. King Carol of Romania, who fled from his country in September 1940 along with his mistress, Helena Lupescu, three bulletproof limousines, four Rembrandts, $2.5

million worth of jewels, and a million-dollar haul of gold coins, was now condemned to permanent exile in Spain, Mexico, and Portugal. For nine years he and Helena had treated Romania as a cash register, to be ransacked at will, with regal rake-offs from both the state railroad and the state textile mills; now they must subsist, like Albania's Zog, on the money stashed in their suitcases. Things were not much better for the Aga Khan, holed up in the Palace, St. Moritz, and fretting how to siphon sufficient funds into Switzerland to settle his bills.

Some adapted admirably to changing circumstances. Captain Edward Molyneux who, like Maugham, had escaped from France on a collier, had, by 1941, established an export beachhead in America; he passed his nights fire-watching on the roof of Claridge's and traveled everywhere by bicycle—a far cry from his famed Hispano-Suiza. From her suite in the Paris Ritz, Laura Corrigan had generously adopted an entire French regiment, a gesture for which the Vichy Government's Marshal Henri-Philippe Pétain awarded her the Croix de Guerre. In another Ritz apartment, "Coco" Chanel, who had closed down her business in 1939, sat out the war with her German lover, *Brigadeführer* Walter Schellenberg, of the S.S.

Barbara Hutton had gravitated to Beverly Hills, California, along with her third husband, the film star Cary Grant, whom she had married in July 1942—an alliance the Rainbows dubbed "Cash and Cary." Eventually, within three years, this marriage, too, would fall apart; three attempts to produce a child resulted in three miscarriages, and with Cary tied up by a full day's shooting schedule, Barbara was thrown back on the company of fellow-exiles from Europe, Elsie de Wolfe (Lady Mendl), Baron Eric de Rothschild, and the inevitable Elsa Maxwell. "Barbara," commented one of her last lovers, Philip Van Rensselaer, shrewdly, ". . . was only happy with a man she could buy, and she couldn't buy a number-one box-office attraction who was making $500,000 a year."

For David, who in August 1940 took over as Governor and Commander-in-Chief of the Bahamas—the only member of the Royal Family ever to govern a Crown Colony—this chance to redeem his past errors completely eluded him. From the first he waged a running feud with Etienne Dupuch, the Associated Press correspondent for Bahamian affairs. His racist prejudice was quite blatant: no colored personnel were permitted to enter Government House, Nassau, by the front door. Nor did Wallis prove helpful. The repainting of a public room in soft pink, to match her face-powder, was bitterly resented by the locals—and so, too, was the flying in, at taxpayers' expense, of a hairdresser from the Saks Fifth Avenue branch of Antoine, armed with two bottles of rum and five eggs for a shampoo.

Their sojourn in New York, in the autumn of 1941, was an unmitigated public relations disaster. Along with a Windsor aide, Adela Rogers St. Johns, of Hearst's staff, had laid down guidelines designed to guarantee them, as representatives of beleaguered Britain, the friendliest possible reception. (Two months before Pearl Harbor, America was still on the sidelines of World War II.) The Windsors were cautioned to check in to a medium-grade hotel, with as few servants and as little luggage as possible, to avoid nightclubs, and to enter into no social engagements until President Roosevelt had made the first move. They were advised to lean heavily on press barons like Hearst and Roy Howard for friendly counsel.

The memo might never have been drafted. Although Roosevelt received David for a brief, half-hour colloquy, Wallis, on the advice of Secretary of State Cordell Hull, was not invited to the White House. But in New York itself, which they reached via Baltimore and Chicago, the Windsors ignored every precept laid down. At the Waldorf-Astoria, where they checked in, they commandeered an entire floor. Their luggage was so extensive that the customs officials at Miami, their first port of call, gave up counting. Along with the Duke's valet came two maids for Wallis, two secretaries, four Cairn terriers, and all of Wallis's jewelry. They made no approach to the press chiefs, content with the syndicated gush of Maury Paul and Elsa Maxwell, who chronicled their nightly jaunts to the Stork Club and El Morocco.

No plaudits were forthcoming from the acerbic Walter Winchell, whose *Journal* column, which had dubbed them "The Dook and Dookess," likewise bade them a sour farewell: "Good riddance to them both—the snobs."

On March 16, 1945, when David tendered his resignation as Governor, most Bahamians felt exactly the same way. Not for the first time—or indeed the last—Prince Charming had outstayed his welcome.

* * *

On August 6, 1945, with a flash "brighter than a thousand suns," the Atomic Age dawned above the Japanese city of Hiroshima. The guns grew silent. After almost six years of war, the world was at peace—or what would pass for peace in the second half of the twentieth century. Once more the Rainbows prepared to take up the threads of the life they had known. All would be as it had been before; it *had* to be.

But would it? A new acronym, born of war, had entered the language: DPs, meaning "displaced persons." Were there 20 million uprooted Europeans, or 25 million? Nobody knew, but their existence could scarcely be denied, any more than the deaths of six million Jews. It was an unpromising climate for "the pursuit of pleasure," for fun and frivolity.

Yet the Rainbows would not easily be gainsaid. In June 1946, two weeks after the world's press had gathered at Bikini Atoll, the northernmost in the Pacific chain of Marshall Islands, to witness the first public atomic bomb explosion, a Paris swimsuit designer first gave this name to an abbreviated two-piece—and within days it had been highlighted in the columns of *Nice-Matin*. Soon bikinis were familiar sights along the Croisette and the Promenade des Anglais, and so, too, were the old familiar faces: Rosie Dolly returned to her favorite seat at the Monte Carlo Casino, where she had once trimmed Nick Zographos of 10 million francs. Somerset Maugham came back to his Villa Mauresque, to find that it had been pillaged by Italian troops, and his spleen was more than ever in evidence—"Willie's been true to himself," admitted his American publisher, George Doran. "He's always had a bad word for everybody." Prince Aly Khan flew down to buy the Château de l'Horizon, for Maxine Elliott had died in 1940, leaving £326,000. The tiny airport at Nice was crowded out, as Doris Duke Cromwell, Elsa, and the Aga Khan all returned.

At St. Moritz, the Cresta Run was rebuilt and old-timers like Barbara, the shipowner Stavros Niarchos, and Count Theo Rossi took up the morning ritual of coffee with croissants and cherry jam, then headed for the funicular with packed lunches, returning for tea at Hanselmann's before the nightly ritual of après-ski.

There were still undeniable moments of pure magic, and at least one of them can be pinpointed precisely: at 10:30 A.M. on Wednesday, February 12, 1947 at 30, avenue Montaigne, Paris. Yet no one among the fashion editors massed in the newly opened salon of the shy, forty-five-year-old Christian Dior, whose backer was the textile king, Marcel Boussac, was expecting great revelations; thus far, the Paris collections had been dull. "This," muttered Carmel Snow of *Harper's Bazaar*, New York, "had better be good."

It was much more than good; it was a watershed. Just as fashion, following World War I, had awaited "Coco" Chanel, this bleak, rationed, and desperately weary era had waited for the palpable femininity of Dior. The skirts were vast—one had fully eighty yards of fabric—and full and billowing, swaying from tiny wasp's waists of whalebone and grosgrain; the shoulders were soft and the bodices tight, with padded, stiffened double linings of muslin and taffeta; the hats were tiny, bound on by veils under the chin. As the models swept almost arrogantly through the salon, bowling over the ashtray stands, the sound of swishing petticoats was heard for the first time since 1939; cheers broke out and some spectators were weeping. "It was like a new love affair, the first sight of Venice," wrote fashion expert Janey Ironside. ". . . in fact, a new look at life."

On that day, in truly Rainbow style, the New Look was born, for as Dior himself admitted, with gowns priced at between £250 and £1,200, only 2,500 women in all the world could afford him. But beauty and taste—one side of the Rainbow coin, the other being vulgarity—were once more in evidence, and Paris was back in the mainstream of fashion. The way was clear for all the great names who would dominate the fashionable fifties: Pierre Balmain, Jacques Fath, Pierre Cardin, Yves Saint Laurent.

For one coterie of Rainbows, the year 1947 loomed as a gigantic question mark: the Maharajahs of India, although showered with honors, including twenty-one-gun salutes, and privileges by the British, now that India was achieving independence, were faced with a bleak future if Jawaharlal Nehru and the socialists of congress had their way. All in a sense were quasi-Rainbows, for all were characterized by one besetting passion to the exclusion of all others.

With the Maharajah of Baroda, it was gold; only one family in his state was allowed to weave the threads of his spun gold court tunics, and their fingernails were grown to mandarin length, then cut and notched like the teeth of a comb, the better to coax the threads into perpendicular symmetry. The Maharajah of Mysore was bemused by aphrodisiacs, most especially crushed diamonds; every year, hundreds of precious stones were pulverized in the mills of Mysore for the benefit of his dancing girls, who were paraded through the state on elephants, whose trunks were studded with rubies.

The obsession of the Maharajah of Gwalior was toy electric trains; in his banqueting hall a 250-foot track of solid silver rails connected the dining table with the royal kitchens. Seated at his control panel, Gwalior could thus dispatch vegetables or gravy to individual guests or shuttle an express to the kitchens for a second helping; at one formal banquet, in honor of the viceroy, the panel short-circuited and the trains went berserk, spraying gravy, roast beef, and a green pea puree over the heads and faces of the unhappy guests. Even this eccentricity paled beside that of the dog-loving Maharajah of Junagadh, north of Bombay; his pets, assigned apartments with telephones, electricity, and personal servants, were, at the end of their allotted life spans, borne off to marble mausoleums to the strains of Chopin's "Funeral March." When his favorite bitch, Roshana, married a Labrador called Bobby, Junagadh far outdid Mamie Fish, with a dogs' dinner that cost £60,000.

All these exotic rulers would—some with more misgivings than others—by July sign the Act of Accession, joining their states to either India or Pakistan, losing their sovereignty forever, while retaining the honors and titles the King-Emperor had bestowed on them.

If the Maharajahs knew full well that their time was up, other Rainbows seemed to nourish the same suspicion. The fifties, more than ever before, witnessed the grander-than-grand gesture, the *faux-naif* statements, reminiscent of "let them eat cake," that seemed as much designed for posterity as for contemporary consumption. This was the time when Nubar Gulbenkian, showing off a Vauxhall car custom-built to permit his wearing a silk top hat, announced, "It will turn on a sixpence—whatever that may be." It was the time when Gloria Swanson, on a rare visit to the Caprice Restaurant, told the proprietor, Mario Gallati, "I only come to London nowadays to have the dents removed from my Rolls-Royce."

In this period, a Maharajah with an entourage of five, after settling a two-week bill for $11,000 at the Palace, St. Moritz, turned back to ask the reception clerk, "Now may I pay for the rooms of my friends?" It was also the time when the haughty Princess Fawzia, sister of King Farouk of Egypt, ordering a banquet for 211 guests at St. Moritz's Suvretta House, insisted on Dover sole flown in from London, vin rosé flown in from Provence, white roses flown in from Rome, and the entire repainting of the oval room off the bar.

That was in 1951; one year later, in July 1952, an army coup drove Farouk into permanent exile.

The changing face of the great department stores mirrored this new almost "camp" approach to wealth and privilege. From middle-class beginnings, mostly in the nineteenth century, they had come by degrees to cater not only to Rainbows who had everything and naturally wanted more still; increasingly they existed to foster fresh whims as much as to gratify existing ones. On New York's Madison Avenue, Abercrombie and Fitch, "the greatest sporting goods store in the world," had from 1892 onward supplied split-cane rods and niblicks to conventional sportsmen like Woodrow Wilson and Herbert Hoover, but by the fifties their 350,000-strong mail-order list offered such bizarre items as falconry gear, indoor treadmills for exercising dogs, and explorers' chain mail suits, guaranteed to deflect poison arrows. Harrods, on London's Brompton Road, which began as a modest grocery store in 1849, had expanded by degrees to become the largest department store in Europe; its telegraphic address (from 1895), "Everything, London," was ultimately reflected in 13½ acres of selling space.

Known to the French as *"le magasin le plus snob du monde,"* Harrods, with its 150,000 account customers, had always taken pride in the store's notable "firsts": the first escalator, installed in 1898, with sal volatile and cognac on offer for passengers unnerved by the ride, the first free delivery, shopping by telephone, and an all-night answering service. They were one of the first recognized rendezvous for Edwardian Society women, when the Royal Red Orchestra played for afternoon tea, a store that stubbornly insisted on cash-down transactions until Lillie Langtry was rated credit-worthy in 1884.

But from the 1950s onward, Harrods lived up to their slogan, "Enter A Different World," with a vengeance. Only at Harrods could a fretful Rainbow invest in a £10,000 set of emerald worry beads. No other bakery department could produce a birthday cake 3' 9" high by 2' 6" wide, weighing 1½ hundredweight and costing £425; no wine department could match their Nebuchadnezzar, the world's largest bottle of vintage port, a Taylor 1963 holding the equivalent of forty-eight bottles and priced at £6,000. Haberdashery likewise held the record, with a £1,000 necktie, a patterned number in navy blue Italian silk with a matching diamond brooch, bought by a Middle Eastern potentate; the jewelry department could boast the largest-ever cash-over-the-counter sale, a £82,000 tiara.

When Crown Prince Leka, son of King Zog, the pretender to the Albanian throne, sought to express his admiration for Ronald Reagan, then governor of California, he knew just the present he wanted—a baby elephant, as a symbol of the Republican Party—and just where to order it: Harrods Pet Shop. A fifteen-month-old female Indian elephant weighing five hundredweight was accordingly dispatched to Sacramento, where the bewildered Reagan donated her to the zoo.

Much the same transformation was undergone by Bloomingdale's, on Lexington Avenue, New York, which even in the twenties had been an unadventurous middle-of-the-road department store. But in the fifties and sixties, "Bloomie's" became the mecca of the hip "Saturday Generation," "with more groupies than any other store"; their specialty became "country French" furniture, turned out by small continental factories, then "distressed" with hammers, chains, and files to make it look properly fly-specked and antique. Only Bloomingdale's 7,000-item Delicacies Department would feature such way-out Rainbow delicacies as "Killer Bee Honey"; only Bloomingdale's would model a restaurant on that old Riviera veteran, Le Train Bleu, where diners waiting to be seated heard an announcer intoning softly over and over, "En voiture, attention, passagers pour Lyon, Marseille, et Monte Carlo."

At Neiman-Marcus, Dallas, Texas, founded as a quiet country store in 1907, the name of the game, by the fifties, was togetherness: His and Hers Beechcraft airplanes, His and Hers Submarines, His and Hers Chinese junks (for $11,500). "We're not against conspicuous consumption," Stanley Marcus said once, "as long as it doesn't show." And over the years the store developed a finely tuned anticipation of gifts their customers had never realized they wanted—until now. Gold-plated brandy kegs for public-spirited St. Bernards were one novel concept, as were mink-swathed hip flasks, a telephone stand relaying music to any caller forced to hang on, a clock that ran backward, and a live Black Angus steer (for $1,925) along with a solid silver trolley from which to serve him when roasted. But gifts were only one facet of the services offered to charge accounts in thirty-nine countries by Neiman-Marcus's eighty-seven departments; they were also in the travel business, with the choice of a $30,000 safari to Utah (dinosaurs guaranteed) or a $35,000 cruise with 598 intimate friends (perhaps oriented to Elsa Maxwell). Sartorially, they were all set to put hesitant Rainbows to rights, with a "Neiman-Marcus Opera Libretto," detailing exactly what husband and wife should wear (at $1,455 per head) for the three-day visit of the Metropolitan Opera to Dallas.

Even then, one critic pointed out, it was dubious whether the husband could squire his wife to either of the two Sunday performances. By a regrettable oversight, Neiman-Marcus had forgotten to tell him what to wear.

* * *

Throughout the forties and fifties, and even the sixties, the world of the Wayfaring Windsors was the Rainbow world in miniature. Although in 1952 they acquired their first actual home, La Moulin de la Tuilerie, at Gif-sur-Yvette, a forty-five-minute drive from their Parisian apartment at 85, rue de la Faisanderie, they were most often on the move—as restless and driven by inner promptings as they had ever been. Increasingly, the tensions between them were becoming public property. At Palm Beach, in the season of February 1947, Wallis's irritation that David still clung to the white dinner jacket in tropical climates—a fashion she considered passé—finally boiled over. Seizing a tray of hors d'oeuvres from a passing waiter and thrusting it into David's hands, she railed, "Here! If you're going to dress like a waiter, you might as well act like one!"

The hint was taken. David never again wore a white dinner jacket.

Ironically, after all the years that he had caviled against "the tyranny of starch," David was adamant that the courtesies applicable to English royalty should be accorded to him and Wallis—at Palm Beach and everywhere else in the world. At the Robert R. Youngs, for example, it was David and Wallis, not Mr. and Mrs. Young, who sat at the head of the table—following the ancient tradition that every English home, at least technically, was the property of the King. David, who was always addressed as "Sir," was entitled to curtsies and expected them; Wallis, who was not, was addressed as "Your Grace."

Much of the tension between the two arose from a conflict of wills; David's lifelong parsimony warring with Wallis's ingrained extravagance. (In the thirties, it had taken Cartier of

London fourteen months to recover the £150,000 that David, after lavishing jewelry on Wallis, owed them when he left the United Kingdom.) But even in the fifties, Wallis's annual outlay on clothes and accessories totaled $100,000—on jewelry from Van Cleef and Arpels, on handbags (fifteen at a time) from Louis Coblentz of New York, on hats from Mr. John ($100 apiece), on furs from Maximilian, on gowns from Mainbocher, Hattie Carnegie, Fath, Dior, and the Spaniard, Cristóbal Balenciaga—the one couturier whom neither she, nor any client, met face to face. "A distinguished lady always has a disagreeable air," was the maestro's firm ruling.

For four brief years, from 1950, the tension was eased, for Wallis at least, by the presence of thirty-four-year-old Jimmy Donahue, Barbara Hutton's homosexual cousin, who in this year inherited $15 million from the estate of Grandpa Woolworth. Soon he and the Windsors had become inseparable, though at first David had bitterly resented his presence; he refused to associate with what he called "fairies," "those fellers who fly in over the transom." To this, Wallis would rejoin heatedly, "Where am I going to find stray men in Paris? If you want to fill out the table, you've got to invite the pansies." But soon enough David began to see the advantage of Donahue's always tagging along; when a restaurant presented the bill at the end of a dinner party, he was wont to finger it suspiciously, easing it away from him, hoping that this was one tab someone else would pick up. That was all the hint Jimmy needed. It was *his* treat—that night and every night.

"He was a man who destroyed everything he touched," was the socialite photographer Jerome Zerbe's verdict on Donahue, and it was plain that whatever understanding still existed between David and Wallis was eroded by Donahue's eternal presence as court jester. For despite Jimmy's gay orientation, the affinity between him and Wallis grew until they held hands at the dinner table or scribbled each other billets-doux; at one of the Parisian boîtes de nuit they favored, a Spanish marquesa, seeing the glances they exchanged, exclaimed breathlessly, "Why they're in *love!*" It was noticeable that Wallis and Jimmy often seemed to conspire, wittingly or no, to cause David public humiliation. After a night on the town in New York, at El Morocco or the Stork Club, staff at the Waldorf Towers remarked how Wallis would pin deterrent notes on her bedroom door: STAY OUT or DON'T COME IN HERE. If David ventured to touch her in public, Wallis quite conspicuously froze.

Two separate incidents at the Monseigneur, near the place Pigalle, in Paris, only served to point this up. As the Windsors' party, including Charlie de Bestigui, the South American millionaire, the Duff Coopers, and the Henry Fords entered to the strains of a tzigane orchestra, Donahue, calling over the flower girl, presented Wallis with four dozen red roses, Lady Diana with three dozen, and Mrs. Ford with two dozen. At once Wallis called for the largest vase on the premises, thrusting her white ostrich fan into it along with the roses.

"Look, everybody!" she called jubilantly. "The Prince of Wales's plumes and Jimmy Donahue's roses!"

At least one woman guest noticed David's eyes fill with tears.

On another occasion, before leaving Monseigneur early, David bought Wallis a gardenia from the flower tray. Not to be outdone, Jimmy followed suit. No sooner had David gone than Wallis tore David's flower from her corsage, crushing it into the ice bucket with the base of the champagne bottle, before replacing it with Jimmy's flower.

It was less than surprising that a caller at the Paris townhouse once heard David respond to a tirade from Wallis, "Darling, are you going to send me to bed in tears again tonight?"

In 1954, following a blazing row at a private supper party in the Badischer Hof Hotel, Baden-Baden, in which Jimmy kicked Wallis on the shin and drew blood, David belatedly reached the breaking point. "We've had enough of you, Jimmy," he said tightly. "Get out!"

In keeping, their final interchange was suitably Rainbow. A few minutes after Jimmy had left their suite, the phone rang. It was Jimmy. "Sorry, sir," he told David, "I'm trying to leave on the early plane, but I can't find my valet to pack for me."

It was a predicament to enlist all David's sympathy; in sixty years he himself had never learned to pack a suitcase.

"Very well," he said, "goodbye."

* * *

It was fitting that Jimmy Donahue should now seek a reunion with an old friend who stood in no need of his subsidies: his favorite cousin, Barbara.

Like many an American matron, Barbara Hutton had developed a passion for shopping—not only for furs and jewels and lingerie, but for husbands, besides. On February 28, 1947, at Chur, near St. Moritz, she had married for the fourth time, thirty-eight-year-old Prince Igor Troubetzkoy, another Russian, onetime amateur cycling champion of France. By August 1950, this, too, had soured; Barbara drifted off to Tangier, where she had bought a twenty-room palace, and the hapless Troubetzkoy—"I've been taken for the greatest ride I ever saw"—received no settlement but was saddled with the costs of the Paris divorce.

By 1954, when Jimmy Donahue came back into Barbara's life, she had already parted from her fifth husband: a lusty Dominican Republic diplomat named Porfirio Rubirosa, a man so virile he was nicknamed "Ethelred the Ever Ready," who had briefly been married to Barbara's rival, Doris Duke Cromwell. As marriages go, Barbara's union with "Rubi" was both brief—seventy-three days—and expensive. It was to cost her a $200,000 B-25 transport plane, five polo ponies, a cocoa plantation, $1 million worth of assorted gifts, and $3 million for the final divorce.

Between marriages, she worked assiduously at the strenuous task of being Barbara Hutton. Most of the morning she spent in bed, either telephoning or hiding from life beneath the crepe de chine sheets; her afternoons were spent shopping or preparing for the evening ahead. Every day, her hair took two hours to fix in elaborate coils; every three days, color had to be applied so that the roots were not visible. The object of all this grooming was, of course, no secret: to attract a husband who would love her for herself alone.

One likely contender was Baron Gottfried von Cramm, the tennis ace, for by now Barbara, on a perpetual high of champagne and Seconal, could believe exactly what she wished to believe. After their marriage at Versailles in 1957, her illusions were short-lived; following a settlement of $2 million, von Cramm promptly besought another $1 million. In Germany, the roofs of several von Cramm castles were leaking badly.

That divorce came in 1961.

There were other men in her life—Jimmy Douglas, Lloyd Franklin, a brawny twenty-four-year-old Englishman—but only one more husband: Prince Doan Vinh Na Champassak, a Vietnamese eking out a living as an artist in the Casbah of Tangier. When they separated in 1966, the Prince went on record for the press: "She gave me more than $4 million. She gave me love."

In May 1979, she was to die as a sixty-six-year-old recluse in a penthouse at Hollywood's Beverly Wilshire Hotel. By then, her teeth and gums had given out; her eyesight had become so troublesome that the lampshades in her suite were draped in pink Kleenex to spare her pain. Living on a diet of Coca-Cola, Metrecal, and cigarettes, she weighed no more than five stone eight pounds.

At Harry's Bar, on Venice's calle Vallaresso, the most Rainbow watering hole in all Europe, the proprietor, Arrigo Cipriani, remembered her with sorrow and affection—"usually with a party of thirty or so, and some bronzed husband, drowning her beautiful sadness in alcohol." She had been so nervous of predators, Cipriani recalled, even among her close friends and family, that Cipriani was always called upon to sign her bills.

* * *

Around 1954, Cipriani first set eyes on another customer who impressed him less favorably—"intelligent, mean, perfidious, crafty, who always knew from where the wind blew." For though he came often to Harry's Bar, Aristotle Socrates Onassis left little behind him "save a tincture of Gulf-oil and Coca-Cola."

In that year, Onassis—whom *Women's Wear Daily* of New York christened "Daddy-O"—was much in the world's headlines. The ambitious, expansive, forty-eight-year-old Greek shipping magnate was seen to be branching out; what he called his "hobby enterprises" now included a 40 percent stake in the Société des

Bains de Mer, which controlled a sizeable chunk of Monte Carlo real estate, including five hotels and the Casino, and a twenty-year lease of Olympic Airways from the Greek Government. In this year, too, the columnists noted, a north German shipyard completed the conversion of a Canadian frigate, the *Stormont*, into the 1,600-ton yacht, *Christina*, named after his daughter.

It was a craft from which gossip writers extracted maximum mileage, and with reason; everything about *Christina* was guaranteed to provoke raised eyebrows. It boasted its own yellow twin-prop, five-seater amphibian plane, the *Piaggio*. Onassis's private quarters, a three-room apartment, featured not only El Greco's *Ascension*, but swords in gleaming golden scabbards, a gift from the Arabian King Saud, Russian icons, and a master bedroom with gold-plated combs and brushes. The owner's greatest pride was his bathroom, a faithful replica in sienna marble of King Minos's bath in the lost Cretan Palace of Knossos, but any conducted tour dwelt boastfully on other exotic trappings: the hand-carved lapis lazuli fireplace in the smoking room—"cost me $4 a square inch"—and the bar stools covered in white whaleskin—"made from a whale's testicles." There were nine double guest cabins and forty-two telephones, and things ran smoothly thanks to a crew of fifty under Captain Costa Anastasiades.

Not that Onassis was the richest Greek in the world of tankers. Despite his wealth—a conservative $400 million—he was far eclipsed by "Bodo" Bodossakis, who kept a low profile in his native Athens, and his own father-in-law, Stavros Livanos, whose daughter Athina (Tina) Onassis had married in 1946. Yet of all the Greeks, Onassis was the one who unashamedly courted publicity; of the twelve-man retinue who always surrounded him, the most important was Johnny Meyer, whose job was to see that "Daddy-O" never lacked press coverage for long.

The *Christina* made Meyer's task that much easier. The yacht was a magnet, designed to attract international Society, and Society duly took the bait: Prince Aly Khan, Diana Cooper, Elsa Maxwell, Greta Garbo, Prince Rainier and his wife, the former Grace Kelly, even the senile Winston Churchill, whom Onassis reverently spoon-fed caviar.

Although Onassis liked to stress his peasant origins, this was merely to foster a rags-to-riches legend; since he had a peasant's tastes and a peasant's manners, many journalists fell for it. His favorite food was sliced raw onions drenched in olive oil; his idea of a joyous night on the town was to smash up to $700 worth of crockery in a bouzouki tavern. Aboard *Christina* his favorite ploy was to drain the swimming pool, throw a luncheon party on its bottom—then flood it again, halfway through the main course.

The truth about his origins was more prosaic. The son of a prosperous tobacco merchant from Smyrna (now Izmir), he had emigrated to the Argentine as a teenager, dabbling first in tobacco, then in freighters, first switching to tankers in 1936. By degrees he evolved the secret of his phenomenal success; the wise move was to secure long-term charters for 60 percent of his seventy-strong fleet, and keep 40 percent free. Though tonnage rates could fluctuate wildly, the canny Onassis saw to it that his ships always earned their average £3 a ton.

As a self-made man, he was notably free with advice. "Show me a millionaire," he liked to say, "and I'll show you a heavy borrower." His formula for success had elements of con man wisdom: "Keep looking tanned, live in an elegant building (even if you're in the cellar), be seen in smart restaurants (even if you nurse one drink), and if you borrow, borrow big."

From the summer of 1959 on, Onassis was to receive more publicity than even he deemed desirable.

It had begun on December 19 of the previous year, when the thirty-five-year-old diva, Maria Callas, whom the Italian press dubbed "The Tigress," made her Parisian debut at a charity gala concert at L'Opéra. Around breakfast time, somewhat to her surprise, a huge bunch of red roses arrived at her hotel, with a card signed Aristotle Onassis—a man she had met only once in her life. At lunchtime, there was a second bouquet—with good wishes in Greek and the signature, Aristotle. By evening there was a third bunch—now with no signature, merely the good wishes.

In three short years, Maria Callas had proved fully as headline-worthy as Onassis himself. Born Maria Kalogeropoulos, of

Greek parents in Manhattan, she had nine years earlier married Giovanni Battista Meneghini, an Italian construction tycoon twenty-eight years her senior, who had sold his business, dieted her to reduce her ample 200-pound frame, and became her manager. Maria was now launched not only as one of the twentieth century's greatest talents but as a woman for whom the term "prima donna" might have been invented. After breaking with the Lyric Opera, Chicago, she moved on to New York's Metropolitan—forcing the reluctant management to fire the baritone, Enzo Sordello, for holding out a high note while hers cracked. In quick succession she split with the Vienna State Opera, the San Francisco Opera, and the Met; she feuded with Milan's La Scala and walked out after the first act of *Norma* at the Rome Opera House, despite the presence of the Italian president. A packed house had booed her lustily.

This was the woman for whom Onassis, ruthless in his pursuit of everything he wanted, was prepared to sacrifice a stable marriage of twelve years' standing.

For on June 19, 1959, when Maria sang *Medea* at London's Covent Garden, Onassis, who normally snored heavily through an evening of opera, was again there to applaud her, with a bewildered Tina in tow. In the ballroom of the Dorchester Hotel, after the show, even seasoned party-goers like Cecil Beaton were stunned by the lavishness of a room redone entirely in pink for this one night, and massed with pink roses. This was Daddy-O's party for Maria, and he proved an entirely solicitous host. What was her favorite dance? The tango? A £50 bank note to the bandleader ensured that nothing but tangos would be played all night. It was 3 A.M. before Maria left the Dorchester—and for posterity the photographers recorded her being embraced in the foyer by both Meneghini and Onassis.

And Onassis was skillful in his blandishments. Even the stormy, smoky-voiced Callas could scarcely resist the honor of being asked to cruise the Aegean in such distinguished company as that of Winston Churchill and the motor magnate, Gianni Agnelli—and since Meneghini and Tina Onassis would be there, too, where could be the harm? And hadn't Elsa Maxwell let slip that Maria had been chosen to replace Greta Garbo, who no longer cared for cruising? But on July 23, when the *Christina* left Monte Carlo, bound for Portofino, Capri, and the Gulf of Corinth, Meneghini, for one, was conscious of a decadent atmosphere that was alien to him. "Many of the couples split up and found other partners," he recorded. "I had the impression of finding myself in the middle of a pigpen."

On August 7—following landfalls at Izmir and Istanbul—Meneghini saw the danger signs. The *Christina* had anchored at the foot of Mount Athos, and on that day the Patriarch Athenagoras came aboard, happy to meet two such illustrious compatriots. Speaking in Greek, he blessed them together, almost, noted Meneghini prophetically, "as if he were performing a marriage rite."

As, in a sense, he was. Two days later, after Maria had danced nonstop for two nights in Onassis's arms, the *Christina* reached Athens. Haggard with fatigue, after an onshore party that lasted until 4 A.M., Meneghini retired to bed. But Maria did not return to their cabin until 9:30 A.M.

His casual query provoked only a violent tantrum. "You act like my jailer," Maria raged. "You never leave me alone. You control me in everything. You're like some hateful guardian, and you've kept me hemmed in all these years. I'm suffocating!"

Around 2 A.M. next day, Meneghini, lying sleepless on his bed, heard the cabin door open as a woman slipped into the room. She flung herself on the bed beside him, and the alarmed Meneghini realized she was sobbing. It was Tina Onassis. "Battista," she told him, "we are both miserable. Your Maria is downstairs in the lounge in my husband's arms. Now there is nothing more that can be done. He has taken her away from you."

At 2 P.M. on August 13, the *Christina* returned to Monte Carlo. Three hours later, the Meneghinis reached their home in Milan's Via Buonarotti. In all that time only a frigid silence had prevailed between them. Two days later, Maria came to her decision: "It's all over between us. I have decided to stay with Onassis."

It was a choice she would ultimately regret. On September 10, with her poodle, Toy, she flew to Venice to join Onassis aboard *Christina*, for an idyllic two-week away-from-it-all cruise, the first of many such, when the hi-fi blared into the small hours and swooping lights transmuted the pool from scarlet to emerald to blazing white. There were parties like the one in Majorca when Elsa Maxwell took over the orchestra's piano in the local club and Jerome Zerbe put on Mrs. Robert Considine's wig and whirled Princess Grace into a dance; others like the one at Monaco, when "Daddy-O," a small, swarthy Pied Piper, led a conga-line of local musicians back to *Christina*, with Maria warbling on a saxophone.

But Maria's star was already on the wane. In 1960, she gave only seven performances of two operas; in 1961, five performances, all of *Medea*. In 1962, she twice sang *Medea* at La Scala. In 1963, she gave no stage performances at all.

The first warning signs had come as early as November 6, 1959. In Dallas, Texas, singing the penultimate *Lucia* of her career, she missed her high E flat for the first time in her life. Her battle to salvage something of her voice was just beginning.

There was one cruise, in the summer of 1963, from which she was carefully excluded. That was when Princess Lee Caroline Radziwill broke the news to Onassis that her sister, Jacqueline Bouvier Kennedy, wife of the U.S. president, was heartbroken with grief at the death of her infant son, and Onassis, jubilant at the prospect of netting yet another celebrity, suggested that an Aegean cruise might help assuage Jackie's grief.

With Maria, Onassis was gradually revealing himself for the despot that he was. He liked her in black, and though Maria's chosen colors were red and turquoise, increasingly, black was what she wore. He criticized her hairstyle; Alexandre of Paris was instructed to lop her flowing tresses and create a shorter, younger look. Though he had prodded her to go on singing, mainly as a showcase for his own ego, he had scant sympathy once her voice began to give out. "What are you?" he jeered at her. "Nothing. You just have a whistle in your throat that no longer works."

Maria, in fact, was fast discovering what the crew of *Christina* had always known: that Onassis was a man who took exquisite pleasure in crushing those too weak to withstand him. Taking the advice of a fellow yachtsman, Perry Embiricos, he had once made a surprise raid on the crew's quarters, yanking the lids off the garbage cans to check on wasted food. To the crew from that time on, he was *skilapsaro*—the shark—and Captain Anastasiades put it more bluntly still. When Meneghini, on the August 1959 cruise, noting the black, fetid waters of the port of Istanbul, commented, "We're in shit," the captain retorted, "The real shit, my dear sir, is that which lives on board."

Although both their divorces were validated in 1959, neither Onassis nor Maria ever contemplated marriage. Their final split came in the summer of 1968, when Onassis flew back from the United States to find Maria where he had left her, on the *Christina* at Monte Carlo. "I want you to go back to Paris and wait for me there," he told her flatly.

"Go to Paris in August?" Maria echoed, aghast. "Are you mad?" But Onassis was adamant; Maria must go. "I'm having company," he told her evasively, "and you can't be aboard."

"Who?" Maria persisted. "Why can't I be aboard?" But, of course, she knew. Almost five years after an assassin's bullets had struck down President John F. Kennedy in Dallas, Texas, a mad gunman in Los Angeles's Ambassador Hotel had cut down his brother Bobby. In both instances, Jacqueline Bouvier Kennedy had been incoherent with grief, and it was to comfort her on this second occasion that Onassis had flown to Hyannis Port, Massachusetts. The *Christina* was soon to acquire a new hostess, and Maria sensed it.

"Then I'm leaving you," she told Onassis, who replied impatiently, "I'll see you in September after the cruise."

"No, you don't understand. I'm leaving you. You're never going to see me again—ever."

So Maria left the *Christina*—nor did she ever return. She was somewhere in the United States, roaming between Denver, Colorado, and Las Vegas when the news broke on October 20, 1968, that in a ritual prescribed by Greek Orthodox tradition the sixty-two-year-old Onassis had married thirty-nine-year-old Jacqueline Bouvier Kennedy in the tiny neoclassic chapel of Panayitsa on Skorpiós, the 500-acre island that had cost him the best part of $3 million in 1962.

It was a marriage that never ceased to bewilder their fellow Rainbows—then or later. Reaction ranged from dismay to a kind of shocked ribaldry. "She's gone from Prince Charming to Caliban," commented one Kennedy aide. JACKIE, HOW COULD YOU? lamented Stockholm's *Expressen*. Even *Women's Wear Daily*, for whom Jackie had always been "Her Elegance," demoted her to "Jackie-O," on a level with the despised "Daddy-O."

Yet the wedding made sense—of a sort. In childhood, Jacqueline Bouvier, like Wallis Windsor, had known only a surrogate security. When her father, John Vernou "Black Jack" Bouvier II, registered a $7,500,000 loss in the Wall Street crash of 1929, all his hopes devolved on his father-in-law, James T. Lee, a crabby Irishman who despised his son-in-law for his Sulka shirts and his "high sassiety" ways. Though Lee refused to part with as much as a dime, "Black Jack," his wife Janet, and the six-month-old Jackie were permitted to live rent-free in a large duplex apartment building that Lee owned at 740 Park Avenue.

Thus all Jackie's childhood privileges—her English nanny, her education at Miss Porter's School for Girls, at Farmington, Connecticut, her time at Vassar and the Sorbonne—were dependent on money that was hers only by chance: initially from Grandpa Lee, later from the wealthy Hughdie Auchincloss whom Janet, after splitting with "Black Jack," married in 1942.

Increasingly a prey to alcoholism, "Black Jack" was too drunk to give his daughter away when she married young Jack Kennedy at Newport on September 12, 1953; Hughdie had to stand in. The need for security and a father-figure would henceforth loom large in Jackie's life.

By inclination she was a jet-setter and a free-spender, much beloved by Bloomingdale's, New York. If reports of her $50,000-a-year couturiers' bills were exaggerated—"if so, I would be wearing sable underwear," Jackie countered—her huge bills when her husband reached the White House still gave him cause for grave concern. "She's driving me crazy, absolutely crazy, I tell you," he anguished to Senator George Smathers, instancing how he had queried just one item in her budget, "Department Store—$40,000."

"What the hell does this mean?" he had asked, to which Jackie had responded vaguely, "Oh heck, I don't remember."

Since Kennedy's income as president was only $100,000 a year, and Jackie's total personal expenses for her first White House year were $145,446.14, plainly money would figure largely in her life. And if Onassis, as one ex-employee alleged, lavished $20 million worth of gifts on her in one year, Jackie could feel secure indeed.

The couple, most Rainbows felt, had almost nothing in common. Jackie had a gourmet's taste in food; Onassis liked his raw onions. Jackie drank sparingly; Onassis could kill a bottle of Scotch in an evening. Jackie loved Givenchy originals; Onassis had about 400 suits, all of which looked as if they had been cut for another man altogether. Onassis continued to woo publicity—"it's like rain; when you're soaking wet, what difference do a few drops more make?" Jackie hated it so intensely that she took Ron Galella, a member of the New York paparazzi, to court for invading her privacy and that of her children.

Onassis was a dedicated desk-man, whose lifeline was a telephone wire; often he bedded down in his office suite at the Hotel Pierre rather than journey twenty blocks to their apartment at 1040 Fifth Avenue. Jackie was not heard to complain. When the press raised the question of this "open marriage," Daddy-O gave out with a public statement: "Jackie is a little bird that needs its freedom as well as its security and she gets them both from me. She can do exactly as she pleases . . . and I, of course, will do exactly as I please."

With $3 million in tax-free government bonds as part of their premarital contract, a $33,000-a-month allowance for personal expenses, and $5,000 a month for each of her children, Caroline and John, Jr., Jackie seemed as assured of freedom as any fluttering "little bird" could be—yet almost daily her secretary, Nancy Tuckerman, called Creon Brown, Onassis's financial manager, demanding more funds.

Events finally came to a head in the autumn of 1973, when

Jackie talked Onassis into accompanying her on a trip to Acapulco, Mexico. It was the tenth anniversary of Jack Kennedy's death, and here she and Jack had spent their honeymoon. But though Onassis went along with this nostalgic journey, he was incensed to find it had a dual purpose: Jackie was out to secure an Acapulco villa. He had, Onassis pointed out, five homes already—apartments on the avenue Foch, in Paris, in Buenos Aires and Monte Carlo, a house in Athens and on Skorpiós Island, to say nothing of the *Christina*. All through their stay the angry argument continued—and was still raging on the private plane that brought them back to New York.

Abruptly Onassis got up, transferring his seat to another part of the aircraft, to scribble on large sheets of yellow paper. He was, he said, "writing letters," and Jackie, of course, accepted this—unaware that he was redrafting his will.

As things then stood, Jackie was to inherit $100 million on Onassis's death, but the devious "Daddy-O" would now use his high-level connections to subvert Greek law. Up to this time, a Grecian widow automatically received a quarter of her husband's estate—until Onassis's lawyer, Stelios Papadimitrou, paid a covert call on one of the ruling junta's most powerful figures, Minister Stelios Triantailou. One month later, unreported by the muzzled Greek press and thus unknown to Jackie's lawyers in New York, the Greek Parliament passed a law stipulating that any marriage contract between a Greek citizen and a foreigner was legally invalid.

Not that Jackie would be left penniless. Asked to accept an amendment that guaranteed her $200,000 a year for life and $25,000 a year for each of her children until they came of age, Jackie readily agreed, confident that this was just an additional increment to those millions she would one day inherit.

Much sooner than either of them knew, this last will and testament became relevant. On November 4, 1974—exactly one week before Maria Callas gave her last, disastrous concert at Sapporo, Japan—a New York hospital diagnosed Onassis as suffering from myasthenia gravis, a debilitating disease that weakens the body muscles. Despite massive cortisone injections, his eyelids began to droop uncontrollably; soon they had to be secured to his forehead with transparent tape to enable him to see. He wore heavy dark glasses to conceal this; he could not hide his slurred and rambling speech. At long last, it seemed, he had lost the Midas touch. On January 15, 1975, he signed over Olympic Airways to the Greek Government. The airline was so close to bankruptcy it was unable to keep its planes in the air.

For all the Rainbows, an era was ending; their time was running out. It had been coming for years, slowly but relentlessly; even those who still chronicled their doings had come to despise them. "These people are a joke, wasteful and unimportant," declared John Fairchild, the boss of *Women's Wear Daily*, in September 1970. "To be living like that in this day and age is unforgivable." Already, technology had changed much of their life-style. The age of the great liners, when it was better to travel in style even than to arrive, died on October 4, 1958, with the first commercial jet flight from New York to London; there was no Rainbow aura surrounding 300 trepidant humans sitting nine-abreast, listening to piped-in music. Other rituals had fallen into desuetude. In that same year the last of 1,441 debutantes to crowd in under the wire made the last curtsy.

In-phrases like Third World, Guilt Complex, Crisis of Conscience, and "the changed molecular structure of society"—to wit, socialism—invoked new worlds and concepts of which the Rainbows knew nothing. The new-rich of the 1970s understood them sufficiently well to keep a low profile at all times; their El Grecos were not on display for gossip columnists to gawk at. They lived, and still live, out their lives discreetly, in Mediterranean villas policed by Dobermans and security guards, behind electrified wire fences. They knew who they were without consulting social arbiters like "Sherm" Billingsley; the Stork Club closed its doors in 1965.

Anti-resorts, like Fishers Island, off New London, Connecticut, or Hobe Sound, Florida, were now more dernier cri than Palm Beach. Hotels were not permitted. Men did not dress for dinner. The approved attire for ladies was a shantung or linen dress, with a cashmere cardigan sweater worn over the shoulders—"A lady putting her arms actually in her cardigan," noted Cleveland Amory, "is socially suspect." At Fishers, the First Citizen, John Nicholas Brown, once the world's richest baby, who passed his youth tied to his governess with a blue silk cord, was typical of this reticent breed. "We have people here worth 20 million dollars," explained Henry L. Ferguson of Fishers, "but you wouldn't know it."

In February 1975, the last of the Rainbows, Ari Onassis, collapsed in Athens. He was flown to the American Hospital at Neuilly, outside Paris, for the speedy removal of his gallbladder; a severe kidney malfunction was also diagnosed. Nor did he ever entirely recover consciousness. For five weeks, in Room 217 of the Eisenhower Wing, he was kept alive by a respirator and fed intravenously. When he died on March 15, 1975, and a way of life died with him, only his daughter, Christina, was at his bedside. It was one day later before Jackie arrived from New York.

It was as if the Rainbows knew their time was done; one by one, like actors taking their last curtain calls, they were departing from the stage. Cole Porter was first to go, in 1963, and perhaps was glad of it; the victim of a riding accident in 1937, when a horse fell on him and crushed both legs, he underwent more than thirty agonizing operations, only to have his right leg amputated. Next went "dahling Tallulah," a victim of emphysema, in the smoggy, flu-ridden December of 1968. On May 28, 1972, the Great Bell of St. Paul's Cathedral in London chimed the news that David had died of throat cancer in Paris—mercifully spared the gibes of his old adversary, Walter Winchell, who had died three months earlier. A year later, at his hilltop retreat in Jamaica, Noel Coward told his house guests, "Good night, my darlings. I'll see you tomorrow," then slept his life away.

It was a hitherto anonymous matron, Mrs. William S. Moore, of Bar Harbor, Maine, who best summed up the ethos of the era. In those golden and far-off days, she recalled, a friend had once called attention to her one marked peculiarity. "You never," she pointed out, "talk money."

Mrs. Moore paused. She pondered awhile. Then at length the realization dawned on her. "Why should I?" she asked with undeniable logic. "I've never even had to think about it."

ACKNOWLEDGMENTS

I should like to thank all those who over a period of more than thirty years have shared with me their memories and *aperçus* of that now fast-fading tribe, the Rainbow People. Without their guidance and generosity, much would have otherwise gone unrecorded. I hope they will accept the bare mention of their names in token of my gratitude:

M. Abel Alban (Savoy, London); Ian J. Adcock (Rolls-Royce Motors, Ltd.); Hardy Amies; Donald Amor (Hawes and Curtis Tailors, Ltd.); Michael Arlen; Armando Armanni (Excelsior, Rome); Mrs. Gay Ball; Tallulah Bankhead; Lt.-Col. Eric Barrass (Rolls-Royce Appreciation Society); Frank Beard (Truefitt and Hill); Pamela Beard (Alfred Dunhill, Ltd.); Denise Beckles; James B. Bell (New-York Historical Society); Mrs. Rae Boxall (Yacht Brokers, Designers and Surveyors Association); Count Brandolino Brandolini D'Adda; Gerald Bright (Geraldo); Douglas Byng; Santos Casani; Leon Cassel-Gerard; Count René de Chambrun; Mrs. Elspeth Champcommunal (House of Worth); Eddie Clarke (United Kingdom Bartenders Guild); Noel Coward; Count Rudi Crespi; George Criticos (Ritz, London); Angus Cundey (Henry Poole, Sullivan Woolley); Judith Dagworthy (Savoy, London); Mrs. Louise E. Davis (Norland Nursery Training College); Sigmund Deanfield; Cosimo de Giorgio (Excelsior, Rome); Gustave Delbanco (Roland Browse and Delbanco); the Marquess of Donegall; Polly Peabody Drysdale; Miss Mary Dunhill (Alfred Dunhill, Ltd.); Cmdr. Alistair Easton; Rosalind Elliott (Savoy, London); Alfred Elvin; Jonathan Falkner (Louis Vuitton); Diane Farris; Charles Feldman; Patrick Forbes (Moët and Chandon [London], Ltd.); Roy Fox; Mario Gallati; Mary Joan Glynn (Bloomingdale's, New York); S. F. Gomershall (Alfred Dunhill, Ltd.); Michael Gonley (Ritz, London); Count Dino Grandi; Capt. Harry Grattidge; Mrs. Sewell Haggard; Nina Hamnett; David Hicks; Tommy Holmes (J. H. Peal, Ltd.); Leslie Jackson; Nancy Jarratt (Moët and Chandon [London], Ltd.); Herbert Johnson (Herbert Johnson [Bond Street], Ltd.); M. Eugene Kaufeler (Dorchester, London); Seymour Kearney (Edward Molyneux, Ltd.); Dr. Patricia Kelvin (Savoy, London); Reginald Kimpton; Leonard Kingston (Mayfair Catering Co.); Charlie Kunz; Marjorie Lee (Dorchester, London); Christine Lortie (Waldorf-Astoria, New York);

Peter Hope Lumley; Fritz Mandl; Stanley Marcus (Neiman-Marcus, Dallas, Texas); Joe Mattli; Rosa Monckton (Asprey & Co., PLC); Ivor Moreton; Mrs. Charlotte Mortimer (House of Worth); Digby Morton; Denisa, Lady Newburgh; Beverley Nichols; Bruce Ogden Smith (Ogden Smith's); Constance-Anne Parker (Royal Academy of Arts); Tom Parr (Colefax and Fowler Designs, Ltd.); J. H. Peal (J. H. Peal, Ltd.); Robert Perkins; James Pile; Janine Pollock (Harrods, Ltd.); the Marchese Emilio Pucci; C. F. Quinn (Kilgour, French, and Stanbury); Edward Rayne (H. and M. Rayne, Ltd.); Quentin Reynolds; George Ronus (Dorchester, London); Sonia Roy; Peter Russell; George Scheuer (Ritz, Paris); Robert Shadforth (Edward Molyneux, Ltd.); Michael Sherrard; Victor Stiebel; Frank Stockman; Joyce Stone (Colefax and Fowler Designs, Ltd.); Billy Tarling (United Kingdom Bartenders Guild); Imogen Taylor (Colefax and Fowler Designs, Ltd.); Rachel Morran Teggin; Aage Thaarup; Edward Trimble (Kilgour, French, and Stanbury); Jennie Turton (Harrods, Ltd.); Brigadier Michael Wardell.

My deepest debt is to those who worked closely alongside me throughout: to my wife, who kept the home fires burning as well as conducting so much of the research, to Margaret Duff, an invaluable amanuensis as always, and to Hildegard Anderson and Amy Forbert, who carried out the bulk of my American research. My agents in London and New York, Anne McDermid and Emilie Jacobson, offered the staunchest of support; my English and American editors, John Curtis and Allen Klots, generously granted an extension of time that made all the difference to the completed draft. Elsie Couch and Ann Walker produced their usual impeccable typescript. In addition, I have to thank the staffs of the British Library, the London Library, and the New York Public Library for their help and courtesy at all times.

BIBLIOGRAPHY

Abels, Jules. *The Rockfeller Millions*. London: Frederick Muller, 1967.
Aberconway, Christabel. *A Wiser Woman?* London: Hutchinson, 1966.
Acton, Harold. *Memoirs of an Aesthete*. London: Methuen, 1948.
———. *More Memoirs of an Aesthete*. London: Methuen, 1970.
———. *Nancy Mitford*. London: Hamish Hamilton, 1975.
Adburgham, Alison. *Shops and Shopping*. London: George Allen & Unwin, 1981.
———, ed. *A Punch History of Manners and Modes*. London: Hutchinson, 1961.
Adburgham, Roland. "Harrods, Past, Present and Future." *Harrods Magazine*, December 1981.
Ager, Stanley, with Fiona St. Aubyn. *The Butler's Guide to Clothes Care, Managing the Table, Running the Home and Other Graces*. London: Papermac, 1982.
Aldrich, Richard S. *Gertrude Lawrence as Mrs. A*. London: Odhams Press, 1955.
Allen, Frederick L. *The Great Pierpont Morgan*. New York: Harper, 1949.
———. *Lords of Creation*. New York: Harper, 1935.
———. *Only Yesterday*. London: Pelican Books, 1938.
———. *Since Yesterday*. London: Hamish Hamilton, 1940.
———, with Agnes Rogers. *I Remember Distinctly*. London: Hamish Hamilton, 1947.
Ambler, Eric. "Maxim's—The Legend of the Rue Royale." *Holiday*, August 1957.
Amies, Hardy. *Just So Far*. London: William Collins, 1954.
Amory, Cleveland. "About Millionaires, Past, Present, Future." *The New York Times Magazine*, May 22, 1959.
———. "The Last Resorts." *Holiday*, August 1952.
———. *The Last Resorts*. New York: Harper Bros., 1952.
———. "The Last Stand of the Rich." *The Saturday Evening Post*, November 1, 1952.
———. "My First Resorts." *Holiday*, July 1959.
———. *The Proper Bostonians*. New York: E. P. Dutton, 1955.
———. *Who Killed Society?* New York: Harper, 1960.

Andrews, Wayne. *The Vanderbilt Legend*. New York: Harcourt Brace, 1941.
Andrieu, Pierre. *Fine Bouche: A History of the Restaurant in France*. Translated by Arthur L. Hayward. London: Cassell, 1956.
Argyll, Margaret, Duchess of. *Forget Not*. London: W. H. Allen, 1975.
Beaton, Cecil. *The Glass of Fashion*. London: Weidenfeld & Nicolson, 1954.
———. *The Parting Years*. London: Weidenfeld & Nicolson, 1978.
———. *Photobiography*. London: Odhams Press, 1951.
———. *The Restless Years*. London: Weidenfeld & Nicolson, 1976.
———. *Self Portrait with Friends*. London: Weidenfeld & Nicolson, 1979.
———. *The Wandering Years*. London: Weidenfeld & Nicolson, 1961.
"Beautiful $7 Billion of Moonbeams, A." *Newsweek*, June 3, 1968.
Beebe, Lucius. *The Big Spenders*. New York: Doubleday, 1966.
———. "Dining on the Cars." *Holiday*, June 1953.
———. "Luxury on Wheels." *Scribner's Magazine*, May 1938.
———. *Mansions On Rails*. Berkeley, Calif.: Howell-North, 1959.
Behrend, George. *Great European Expresses*. London: George Allen & Unwin, 1962.
———. *Pullman in Europe*. London: Ian Allan, 1962.
Behrman, S. N. *Duveen*. London: Hamish Hamilton, 1952.
———. *Tribulations and Laughter*. London: Hamish Hamilton, 1972.
Bemelmans, Ludwig. *For the One I Love the Best*. London: Hamish Hamilton, 1955.
Benchley, Peter. "Five in Spots for the Midnight Chic." *The New York Times Magazine*, November 8, 1970.
Bennett, Helen Christine. "Fr-r-ront!" *The Saturday Evening Post*, June 11, 1927.
Bennett, Richard. *A Picture of the Twenties*. London: Vista Books, 1961.
Bentley, Nicholas. *Edwardian Album*. London: Weidenfeld & Nicolson, 1974.
Bergamini, John D. *The Tragic Dynasty*. London: Constable, 1970.
Bertin, Celia. *Paris à la Mode*. Translated by Marjorie Deans. London: Victor Gollancz, 1956.
Bessie, Simon Michael. *Jazz Journalism*. New York: E. P. Dutton, 1938.
Billingsley, Sherman. "How To Behave in a Night Club." *Good Housekeeping*, July 1947.
Bird, Anthony, and Ian Hallows. *The Rolls-Royce Motor Car*. London: B. T. Batsford, 1964.
Birmingham, Nan Tillson. *Store*. New York: G. P. Putman's Sons, 1978.

Birmingham, Stephen. *Duchess*. London: Hamish Hamilton, 1974.
———. *Jacqueline Bouvier Kennedy Onassis*. London: Victor Gollancz, 1979.
———. *Our Crowd*. London: Longman, 1968.
———. *The Right People*. Boston: Little, Brown, 1968.
Blanche, J. E. *Portraits of a Lifetime*. Translated and edited by Walter Clement. London: J. M. Dent, 1937.
———. *More Portraits of a Lifetime*. Translated and edited by Walter Clement. London: J. M. Dent, 1939.
Bloch, Michael. *The Duke of Windsor's War*. London: Weidenfeld & Nicolson, 1982.
Blow, Simon. *Fields Elysian*. London: J. M. Dent, 1983.
Boal, Sam. "Monte Carlo." *Holiday,* November 1953.
———. "St. Moritz." *Holiday,* December 1953.
Bocca, Geoffrey. *Bikini Beach*. London: W. H. Allen, 1963.
———. "The Shy Genius of French Fashion." *Coronet,* December 1960.
———. *The Woman Who Would be Queen*. New York: Rinehart, 1954.
———. "There'll Always be a British Nabob." *The Saturday Evening Post,* March 29, 1952.
Booth, Mark. *Camp*. London: Quartet Books, 1983.
Bowden, Gregory Houston. *British Gastronomy: The Rise of Great Restaurants*. London: Chatto & Windus, 1975.
Brady, Maxine. *Bloomingdale's*. New York: Harcourt Brace Jovanovich, 1980.
Brandon, Ruth. *The Dollar Princesses*. London: Weidenfeld & Nicolson, 1980.
Brendon, Piers. *The Life and Death of the Press Barons*. London: Secker & Warburg, 1982.
Brian, Dennis. *Tallulah, Darling!* London: Sidgwick and Jackson, 1980.
Briggs, Asa, ed. *They Saw It Happen*. Oxford: Basil Blackwell, 1960.
Brinnin, John Malcolm. *Beau Voyage*. London: Thames & Hudson, 1982.
Broackes, Nigel. *A Growing Concern*. London: Weidenfeld & Nicolson, 1979.
Brody, Iles. *The Colony*. London: Jarrolds, 1946.
———. *Gone With the Windsors*. Philadelphia: The John C. Winston Co., 1953.
———. *On the Tip of My Tongue*. London: Jarrolds, 1946.
Brook-Shepherd, Gordon. *Uncle of Europe*. London: Weidenfeld & Nicolson, 1974.
Brooks, Van Wyck. *Days of the Phoenix*. London: J. M. Dent, 1957.

Brophy, Brigid. *Prancing Novelist*. London: Macmillan, 1973.
Brown, Eve. *Champagne Cholly*. New York: E. P. Dutton, 1947.
Bruccoli, Matthew J. *Some Sort of Epic Grandeur*. London: Hodder & Stoughton, 1981.
Bryan, J. III. *The Windsor Story*. London: Granada, 1979.
———, with Charles Murphy. "Hotel du Cap: 'The Best Hotel in the World'." *Holiday,* May–June 1972.
Buchwald, Art. "Paris! City of Night Life." *Holiday,* April 1953.
Burgess, Anthony. "Temple to the Goddess Chance." *The Radio Times,* May 23–29, 1981.
Burkhart, Charles. *Herman and Ivy and Nancy: Three Lives in Art*. London: Victor Gollancz, 1977.
Burt, Nathaniel. *The Perennial Philadelphians*. Boston: Little, Brown, 1963.
Byng, Douglas. *As You Were*. London: Duckworth, 1970.
———. *Byng Ballads*. London: John Lane, 1932.
———. *More Byng Ballads*. London: John Lane, 1935.
Caffrey, Kate. *Edwardian Lady: Edwardian High Society, 1900–1914*. London: Gordon & Cremonesi, 1980.
Callaghan, Morley. *That Summer in Paris*. London: Macgibbon & Kee, 1963.
Cameron, Roderick. *My Travel's History*. London: Hamish Hamilton, 1950.
Capa, Robert. "The Winter Alps." *Holiday,* January 1951.
Carter, Ernestine. *Magic Names of Fashion*. London: Weidenfeld & Nicolson, 1980.
Cartland, Barbara. *We Danced All Night*. London: Hutchinson, 1970.
Cassini, Oleg. "Paris Gives Women A Break." *The Saturday Evening Post,* January 6, 1962.
Chamberlain, I. and H. *Common Objects of the Riviera*. London: George Routledge, 1913.
Chamberlin, Anne. "Everybody Dance, Dance Wildly—Queen Mary's About To Die." *The Saturday Evening Post,* December 16, 1967.
Channon, Sir Henry. *Chips*. Edited by Robert Rhodes James. London: Weidenfeld & Nicolson, 1967.
Charles-Roux, Edmonde. *Chanel*. Translated by Nancy Amphoux. London: Jonathan Cape, 1976.
Charpentier, Henri, with Boyden Sparkes. *Those Rich and Great Ones*. London: Victor Gollancz, 1935.
Chase, Edna Woolman, with Ilka Chase. *Always in Vogue*. London: Victor Gollancz, 1954.

Chisholm, Anne. *Nancy Cunard*. London: Sidgwick and Jackson, 1979.
Cierplikowski, Antek ("Antoine"). *Antoine: Reminiscences*. London: W. H. Allen, 1946.
———, with Charles Graves. *Devotion to Beauty: The Antoine Story*. London: Jarrolds, 1962.
Clark, Kenneth. *Another Part of the Wood*. London: John Murray, 1974.
Colin, Sid. *And The Bands Played On*. London: Elm Tree Books, 1980.
Collier, Richard. "Beau Brummell's Town." *Holiday,* April 1956.
———. "The Fashion Story." *Housewife,* May–July 1952.
———. "Man Who Mixes Them." *John Bull,* January 2, 1949.
———. "The Poor Little Rich Girl." *The Sunday Chronicle,* January 4–February 1, 1953.
———, with Captain Harry Grattidge. *Captain of the Queens*. New York: E. P. Dutton, 1956.
Collins, James H. "The Beauty Business." *The Saturday Evening Post,* November 22, 1924.
Collins, Larry, and Dominique Lapierre. *Freedom at Midnight*. London: William Collins, 1975.
Colson, Percy. *Close of an Era*. London: Hutchinson, 1946.
———. *I Hope They Don't Mind*. London: Eveleigh Nash & Grayson, 1930.
———. *Melba*. London: Grayson & Grayson, 1932.
———. *Those Uneasy Years*. London: Sampson, Low, 1947.
———. *What If They Do Mind?* London: Jarrolds, 1936.
Contarini, Paolo. *The Savoy Was My Oyster*. London: Robert Hale, 1976.
Cooper, Artemis, ed. *A Durable Fire*. London: William Collins, 1983.
Cooper, Charles W. *Town and County*. London: Lovat Dickson, 1937.
Cornforth, John. "Prince of Humble Elegance: John Fowler." *Country Life,* April 28 and May 19, 1983.
Cornwallis-West, Major George. *Edwardian Hey-Days*. London: Putnam, 1930.
Couling, David. *Steam Yachts*. London: Batsford, 1980.
Coward, Noel. *The Diaries*. Edited by Graham Payn and Sheridan Morley. London: Weidenfeld & Nicolson, 1982.
———. *Future Indefinite*. London: William Heinemann, 1954.
———. *Present Indicative*. London: The Theatre Book Club, 1950.
Cowles, Virginia. *The Astors*. London: Weidenfeld & Nicolson, 1979.
———. *Edward VII and His Circle*. London: Hamish Hamilton, 1950.
———. *The Romanovs*. London: Weidenfeld & Nicolson, 1971.
———. *The Rothschilds*. London: Weidenfeld & Nicolson, 1973.
Cozens-Hardy, Harry. *The Glorious Years*. London: Robert Hale, 1953.

Crabtree, Reginald. *The Luxury Yacht from Steam to Diesel.* Newton Abbot: David & Charles, 1973.
———. *The Royal Yachts of Europe.* Newton Abbot: David & Charles, 1975.
Craddock, Harry, ed. *The Savoy Cocktail Book.* London: Bibliophile Books, 1982.
Crewe, Quentin. *The Frontiers of Privilege.* London: William Collins, 1961.
Criticos, George, with Richard Viner. *The Life Story of George of the Ritz.* London: William Heinemann, 1959.
Crockett, Albert Stevens. *When James Gordon Bennett was Caliph of Baghdad.* New York: Funk & Wagnalls, 1926.
———. *Peacocks on Parade.* New York: Sears Publishing Co., 1931.
Cross, A.G.W. *Scott Fitzgerald.* Edinburgh: Oliver & Boyd, 1964.
Cust, Sir Lionel. *Edward VII and His Court.* London: John Murray, 1930.
Dale, Tim. *Harrods: The Store and the Legend.* London: Pan Books, 1981.
"Dallas in Wonderland." *Fortune,* November 1937.
Dardis, Tom. *Some Time in the Sun.* London: André Deutsch, 1976.
Davenport, Walter. "Bright Girl." *Collier's,* October 26, 1929.
———. "Heat Wave." *Collier's,* March 10, 1934.
Davidoff, Leonore. *The Best Circles.* London: Croom Helm, 1973.
Davies, Marion. *The Times We Had.* London: Angus & Robertson, 1976.
Davis, William. *The Rich: A Study of the Species.* London: Sidgwick and Jackson, 1982.
Dawes, Frank. *Not In Front of the Servants.* London: Wayland Press, 1973.
de Castellane-Novejean, Marie Ernest Paul Boniface. *Confessions of the Marquis de Castellane.* London: Thornton Butterworth, 1924.
De Courtais, Georgine. *Women's Headdress and Hairstyles.* London: Batsford, 1973.
De Courville, Albert. *I Tell You.* London: Chapman and Hall, 1928.
Deghy, Guy. *Paradise in the Strand.* London: The Richards Press, 1958.
Delgado, Alan. *Have You Forgotten Yet?* Newton Abbot: David & Charles, 1973.
De Osma, Guillermo. *Fortuny: Mariano Fortuny, His Life and Work.* London: Aurum Press, 1980.
De Reuty, Germaine. "Bootleg Fashions." *Collier's,* October 5, 1929.

De Ville, Nicholas. *Lenare: The Art of Society Photography, 1924–1977.* London: Allen Lane, 1983.

Dior, Christian. *Dior By Dior.* Translated by Antonia Fraser. London: Weidenfeld & Nicolson, 1957.

Donaldson, Frances. *Edward VIII.* London: Weidenfeld & Nicolson, 1974.

———. *Freddy Lonsdale.* London: William Heinemann, 1957.

Donnelly, Honoria Murphy, with Richard N. Billings. *Sara and Gerald.* New York: Times Books, 1983.

Drawbell, James Wedgwood. *Night and Day.* London: Hutchinson, 1945.

Driberg, Tom. *Beaverbrook.* London: Weidenfeld & Nicolson, 1956.

Drummond, Maldwin. *Salt-Water Palaces.* London: Debrett, 1979.

Duncan, Andrew. "The Cardin Cornucopia." *The Sunday Telegraph Magazine,* June 26, 1983.

Dunn, Vasco B. De. "The Ritz." *Cosmopolitan,* July 1959.

Duveen, James Henry. *Collections and Recollections.* London: Jarrolds, 1935.

———. *The Rise of the House of Duveen.* London: Longman's Green, 1957.

———. *Secrets of an Art Dealer.* London: Robert Hale, 1937.

Easterman, A. L. *King Carol, Hitler and Lupescu.* London: Victor Gollancz, 1942.

Edes, Mary Elizabeth, with Dudley Frasier, ed. *The Age of Extravagance.* London: Weidenfeld & Nicolson, 1955.

Eells, George. *Cole Porter: The Life That Late He Led.* London: W. H. Allen, 1967.

Eliot, Elisabeth. *They All Married Well.* London: Cassell, 1960.

"Elizabeth Arden," *Fortune,* October, 1938.

Elston, D. Roy. *The Travellers' Guide to the French and Italian Riviera.* London: Simpkin, Marshall, Hamilton, Kent, 1927.

Emden, Paul H. *Money Powers of Europe in the Nineteenth and Twentieth Centuries.* London: Sampson Low, Marston & Co., 1937.

Ewen, David, ed. *American Popular Songs From the Revolutionary War to the Present.* New York: Random House, 1966.

Fehl, Fred, with William and Jane Stott. *On Broadway.* London: Thames & Hudson, 1979.

Feinberg, Alexander. "The Why of Night Clubs." *The New York Times Magazine,* May 20, 1945.

Ferguson, Elinor P. R. "Depression Debutantes." *The Saturday Evening Post,* November 12, 1932.

Ferragamo, Salvatore. *Shoemaker of Dreams*. London: George Harrap, 1957.

Ferraro, Filippo. *From Candle Light to Flashlight*. London: The Falcon Press, 1952.

Field, Julian Osgood. *More Uncensored Recollections*. London: Eveleigh Nash & Grayson, 1926.

———. *Things I Shouldn't Tell*. London: Eveleigh Nash & Grayson, 1924.

———. *Uncensored Recollections*. London: Eveleigh Nash & Grayson, 1924.

Field, Leslie. *Bendor, The Golden Duke of Westminster*. London: Weidenfeld & Nicolson, 1983.

Fielding, Daphne. *Before the Sunset Fades*. Warminster, Wilts: The Longleat Estate Co., 1951.

———. *The Duchess of Jermyn Street*. London: Eyre & Spottiswoode, 1964.

———. *Emerald and Nancy*. London: Eyre & Spottiswoode, 1964.

———. *Mercury Presides*. London: Eyre & Spottiswoode, 1954.

Fitzgerald, F. Scott. *Letters*. Edited by Andrew Turnbull. London: The Bodley Head, 1963.

Fitzgerald, Zelda. *Save Me The Waltz*. London: Jonathan Cape, 1968.

Flanner, Janet. *An American in Paris*. London: Hamish Hamilton, 1940.

———. *London Was Yesterday*. Edited by Irving Drutman. London: Michael Joseph, 1975.

———. *Paris Journal, 1965–1971*. New York: Atheneum, 1971.

———. *Paris Was Yesterday*. London: Angus & Robertson, 1973.

Flower, Raymond. *The Palace: A Profile of St. Moritz*. London: Debrett, 1982.

Folsom, Merrill. *Great American Mansions and Their Stories*. New York: Hastings House, 1963.

Forbes, Patrick. *The Story of The Maison Moët & Chandon*. London: Carey and Claridge, 1972.

Forbes-Robertson, Diana. *Maxine Elliott*. London: Hamish Hamilton, 1964.

Fowler, Gene. *Beau James*. New York: Viking Press, 1949.

———. *Skyline*. New York: Viking Press, 1961.

Fowles, Edward. *Memories of Duveen Brothers*. London: Times Books, 1976.

Fox, Roy. *Hollywood, Mayfair And All That Jazz*. London: Leslie Frewin, 1975.

Frazier, Brenda. "My Debut A Horror." *Life,* December 6, 1963.
Frischauer, Willi. *The Aga Khans.* London: The Bodley Head, 1970.
———. *An Hotel is Like a Woman.* London: Leslie Frewin, 1965.
———. *Millionaires' Islands.* London: Michael Joseph, 1973.
———. *Onassis.* London: The Bodley Head, 1968.
Furnas, J. C. *Great Times.* New York: G. P. Putnam's Sons, 1974.
———. *Stormy Weather.* New York: G. P. Putnam's Sons, 1977.
Furness, Thelma, and Gloria Vanderbilt. *Double Exposure.* London: Frederick Muller, 1959.
Gallati, Mario. *Mario of the Caprice.* London: Hutchinson, 1960.
Gathorne-Hardy, Jonathan. *The Rise and Fall of the English Nanny.* London: Hodder & Stoughton, 1972.
Gehman, Richard. "Prince of Hollywood." *Cosmopolitan,* 1954.
Gerhardi, William. *God's Fifth Column.* London: Hodder and Stoughton, 1981.
Gerson, Noel B. *Because I Loved Him.* London: Robert Hale, 1971.
Gifford, James Noble. "The Education of the Million-Dollar Child." *The Saturday Evening Post,* May 24, 1930.
Gill, Brendan. *Cole: A Memoir.* London: Michael Joseph, 1971.
———. *Tallulah.* London: Michael Joseph, 1973.
Girouard, Mark. *Life In The English Country House.* New Haven, Conn.: Yale University Press, 1978.
Goldring, Douglas. *The Nineteen Twenties.* London: Ivor Nicholson & Watson, 1945.
Goldsmith, Barbara. *Little Gloria . . . Happy At Last.* New York: Alfred A. Knopf, 1980.
Gordon, Jane. *Married to Charles.* London: William Heinemann, 1950.
Gorer, Geoffrey. *Hot Strip Tease.* London: The Cresset Press, 1937.
Gorst, Frederick J., with Beth Andrews. *Of Carriages and Kings.* London: W. H. Allen, 1956.
Gottlieb, Bill. "Good-Time Street." *Collier's,* July 3, 1948.
Gough, Barbara Worsley. *Fashions in London.* London: Allan Wingate, 1952.
Graham, Lee H. "The Big Business of Beauty." *The New York Times Magazine,* May 12, 1946.
Graham, Sheila. *College of One.* London: Weidenfeld & Nicholson, 1967.
———. *For Richer, For Poorer.* London: W. H. Allen, 1975.
———. *The Real Scott Fitzgerald.* London: W. H. Allen, 1976.
Graves, Charles. *And the Greeks.* London: Geoffrey Bles, 1930.
———. *The Big Gamble.* London: Hutchinson, 1951.

———. *Champagne and Chandeliers.* London: Odham's Press, 1958.
———. *None But the Rich.* London: Cassell, 1963.
———. *Panorama.* London: Ivor Nicholson & Watson, 1932.
———. *The Rich Man's Guide to Europe.* Englewood Cliffs, N. J.: Prentice-Hall, 1966.
———. *The Riviera Revisited.* London: French Railways National Tourist Office, 1939.
———. *Royal Riviera.* London: William Heinemann, 1957.
Graves, Robert, and Alan Hodge. *The Long Week-End.* London: Four Square Books, 1961.
Gray, Mitchel, with Mary Kennedy. *The Lingerie Book.* London: Quartet Books, 1980.
Green, Stanley. *The World of Musical Comedy.* San Diego, Calif.: A. S. Barnes & Co., 4th ed, 1980.
Guiles, Fred Lawrence. *Marion Davies.* London: W. H. Allen, 1973.
Gulbenkian, Nubar. *Pantoraxia.* London: Hutchinson, 1965.
Gunther, John. *Inside Asia.* London: Hamish Hamilton, 1939.
Hahn, Harry. *The Rape of La Belle.* Kansas City, Mo.: Frank Glenn Publishing Co., 1946.
Hall, Carolyn. *The Twenties in Vogue.* London: Octopus Books, 1983.
Hamilton, Alan. "Monte Carlo and Bust." London *Times,* March 5, 1983.
Hamnett, Nina. *Is She a Lady?* London: Allan Wingate, 1955.
———. *Laughing Torso.* London: Constable, 1932.
Hardy, Alan. *The King's Mistresses.* London: Evan Brothers, 1980.
Harris, Leon. *Merchant Princes.* New York: Harper & Row, 1977.
Harrison, Michael. *Rosa.* London: Peter Davies, 1962.
Harrison, Rosina. *Gentlemen's Gentlemen.* London: Arlington Books, 1970.
———. *Rose: My Life in Service.* London, Cassell, 1975.
Harrity, Richard. "The International Set." *Cosmopolitan,* July 1959.
Hartcup, Adeline. *Below Stairs in Great Country Houses.* London: Sidgwick and Jackson, 1980.
Hartwell, Dickson. "Walter Winchell—An American Phenomenon." *Collier's,* February 28, 1948.
Harvey, George. *Henry Clay Frick: The Man.* New York: Charles Scribner's Sons, 1928.
Hauser, Ernest O. "The Merry Widow Still Waltzes Here." *The Saturday Evening Post,* August 23, 1952.
———. "Mlle. Chanel Comes Back." *The Saturday Evening Post,* June 13, 1959.

Bibliography

———. "Will the Ladies Obey M. Dior?" *The Saturday Evening Post,* October 17, 1953.

Hearnshaw, F. J. C. *Edwardian England.* London: Ernest Benn, 1933.

Heckstall-Smith, Anthony. *Sacred Cowes.* London: Anthony Blond, 1965.

Hendrick, Burton J. *The Age of Big Business.* New Haven, Conn.: Yale University Press, 1930.

Hendrickson, Robert. *The Grand Emporiums.* New York: Stein & Day, 1979.

Henrey, Mrs. Robert. *Madeleine Grown Up.* London: J. M. Dent, 1952.

Herbodeau, Eugene, with Paul Thalamas. *Georges Auguste Escoffier.* London: Practical Press, 1955.

Herd, Harold. *Panorama.* London: George Allen and Unwin, 1942.

Hergesheimer, Joseph. "The Golden Littoral." *The Saturday Evening Post,* July 26, 1930.

———. "The Marble Lily." *The Saturday Evening Post,* November 15, 1930.

Hibbert, Christopher. *Edward: The Uncrowned King.* London: Macdonald, 1972.

———. *Edward VII: A Portrait.* London: Allen Lane, 1976.

Hicks, David: *Living With Design.* London: Weidenfeld & Nicolson, 1979.

———. *On Bathrooms.* Britwell Salome, Oxon: Britwell Books, 1970.

———. *On Decoration.* London: Leslie Frewin, 1966.

———. *On Living—With Good Taste.* London: Leslie Frewin, 1968.

Higham, Charles. *Ziegfeld.* London: W. H. Allen, 1975.

Hillier, Bevis. *Asprey: 1781–1981.* London: Quartet Books, 1981.

Hine, Al. "The Broadmoor." *Holiday,* September 1953.

Hofman, Erik. *The Steam Yachts.* Lymington, Hants: Nautical Publishing Co., 1970.

Holbrook, Stewart. *The Age of the Moguls.* London: Victor Gollancz, 1954.

———. *The Story of American Railroads.* New York: Crown Publishers, 1947.

Holroyd, Michael. *The Life of Augustus John.* 2 vols. London: William Heinemann, 1974–75.

Hood, Dina Wells. *Working With the Windsors.* London: Allan Wingate, 1957.

Hough, Richard. *Edwina.* London: Weidenfeld & Nicolson, 1983.

Howarth, Patrick. *When the Riviera Was Ours.* London: Routledge & Kegan Paul, 1977.

Hoyt, Edwin P. *The House of Morgan*. New York: Dodd, Mead, 1966.
———. *The Vanderbilts and Their Fortunes*. London: Frederick Muller, 1963.
Hungerford, Edward. "The Big-Store Business." *The Saturday Evening Post*, November 26, 1921.
———. *The Story of the Waldorf-Astoria*. New York: G. P. Putnam's Sons, 1925.
Iddon, Don. *Don Iddon's America*. Edited by Charles Sutton. London: Falcon Press, 1951.
Israel, Lee. *Miss Tallulah Bankhead*. London: W. H. Allen, 1972.
Jablonski, Edward, and Lawrence D. Stewart. *The Gershwin Years*. London: Robson Books, 1974.
Jackson, Bee. "Hey! Hey! Charleston!" *Collier's*, December 10, 1927.
Jackson, Stanley. *The Savoy*. London: Frederick Muller, 1979.
Jackson, Stanley. *The House of Sassoon*. London: William Heinemann, 1968.
Jackson, Winifrede. "He Designed for Royalty." *Everybody's*, December 2, 1950.
James, Edward. *Swans Reflecting Elephants*. London: Weidenfeld & Nicolson, 1982.
James, Edward T., ed. *Notable American Women, 1607–1950*, Vol. 2. Cambridge, Mass.: Harvard University Press, 1971.
James, John. *Memoirs of a House Steward*. London: Bury, Holt and Co., 1949.
Jarman, Rufus. "Biggest Things Afloat." *The Saturday Evening Post*, September 5–12, 1949.
Jenkins, Alan. *The Forties*. London: William Heinemann, 1976.
———. *The Rich-Rich*. London: Weidenfeld & Nicolson, 1977.
———. *The Thirties*. London: William Heinemann, 1976.
———. *The Twenties*. London: William Heinemann, 1974.
Johnston, Alva. *The Incredible Mizners*. London: Rupert Hart-Davis, 1953.
Joseph, Richard. "The Three Greatest Hotels in the World." *Esquire*, October 1973.
Josephson, Matthew. *The Robber Barons*. New York: Harcourt Brace, 1934.
Julyan, Herbert E. *Sixty Years of Yachts*. London: Hutchinson, 1950.
Kanin, Garson. *Remembering Mr. Maugham*. London: Hamish Hamilton, 1966.
Kavaler, Lucy. *The Astors*. London: George G. Harrap, 1966.

———. *The Private World of High Society.* New York: David McKay, 1960.
Keats, John. *Howard Hughes.* London: Macgibbon & Kee, 1967.
Keenan, Brigid. *The Women We Wanted To Look Like.* New York: St. Martin's Press, 1977.
Kennedy, John B. "For the Wife and Kiddies." *Collier's,* October 5, 1929.
———. "How the Wasters Play." *Collier's,* October 3, 1925.
Kent, George. "Brotherhood Of The Golden Keys." *The Reader's Digest,* January 1964.
Keppel, Sonia. *Edwardian Daughter.* London: Hamish Hamilton, 1958.
Ketchiva, Paul de. *The Devil's Playground.* London: Sampson Low, Marston, 1934.
Kimball, Robert. *Cole.* New York: Holt, Rinehart & Winston, 1971.
———, with Alfred Simon. *The Gershwins.* London: Jonathan Cape, 1974.
King, Ernest, with Richard Viner. *The Green Baize Door.* London: William Kimber, 1963.
"Klosters: Athletic Elegance." *Holiday,* February 1958.
Kobler, John. "Eden Roc." *Cosmopolitan,* February 1953.
———. "Hotel Excelsior." *Cosmopolitan,* December 1954.
———. "Master of Cookery." *The Saturday Evening Post,* January 21, 1961.
Korda, Michael. *Charmed Lives.* London: Allen Lane, 1980.
Lancaster, Marie-Jacqueline. *Brian Howard: Portrait of a Failure.* London: Anthony Blond, 1968.
Lanceley, William. *From Hall Boy to House Steward.* London: Edward Arnold, 1925.
Lang, Theo. *My Darling Daisy.* London: Michael Joseph, 1966.
Langtry, Emilie Charlotte. *The Days I Knew.* London: Hutchinson, 1925.
Lartigue, Jacques-Henri. *Les Femmes Aux Cigarettes.* New York: The Viking Press, 1980.
Latham, Aaron. *Crazy Sundays.* London: Secker & Warburg, 1972.
Latour, Anny. *Kings of Fashion.* Translated by Mervyn Savill. London: Weidenfeld & Nicolson, 1958.
Laver, James. *The Age of Optimism.* London: Weidenfeld & Nicolson, 1966.
———. *A Concise History of Costume.* London: Thames & Hudson, 1969.
———. *Edwardian Promenade.* London: Edward Hulton, 1958.
Lavery, Sir John. *The Life of a Painter.* London: Cassell, 1940.

Lawrence, Gertrude. *A Star Danced*. London: W. H. Allen, 1945.

Lawton, Mary. *The Queen of Cooks—And Some Kings*. New York: Boni & Liveright, 1925.

Lee, Laurie. "Luxurious Capsule: Venice, Harry's Bar." *The Sunday Telegraph Magazine,* November 13, 1983.

Lees-Milne, James. *Ancestral Voices*. London: Chatto & Windus, 1975.

———. *Harold Nicolson*. London: Chatto & Windus, 1980–81.

———. *Prophesying Peace*. London: Chatto & Windus, 1977.

Leighton, Isabel, ed. *The Aspirin Age, 1919–1941*. London: The Bodley Head, 1950.

Lehmann, John. *I Am My Brother*. London: Longmans, 1960.

Lehr, Elizabeth Drexel. *"King Lehr" and the Gilded Age*. London: Constable, 1935.

———. *Turn of the World*. Philadelphia: J. B. Lippincott, 1937.

Lesley, Cole. *Life of Noel Coward*. London: Jonathan Cape, 1976.

Levin, Phyllis Lee. *The Wheels of Fashion*. Garden City, New York: Doubleday, 1965.

Lewis, Dorothy Rowe. "Fashion Fever." *Collier's,* June 22, 1946.

Lewis, Oscar. *The Big Four*. New York: Alfred A. Knopf, 1940.

———. *Bonanza Inn*. New York: Alfred A. Knopf, 1938.

Liebling, A. J. "The French Line." *Holiday,* July 1949.

Lillie, Beatrice, with John Philip and James Brough. *Every Other Inch A Lady*. London: W. H. Allen, 1973.

Lloyd, Kate. "Charles Revson: The Man From Beauty." *Vogue,* April 1973.

Lloyd, R. W. *The Cult of Old Paintings and The Romney Case*. London: Skeffington, 1917.

Lockhart, Robert Bruce. *The Diaries*. Edited by Kenneth Young. 2 vols. London: Macmillan, 1973–80.

———. *Your England*. London: Putnam, 1955.

Lombardo, Guy, with Booton Herndon. *The Sweetest Music This Side of Heaven*. New York: McGraw-Hill, 1964.

Long, Lois. "Playing the Fashion Game." *The Saturday Evening Post,* October 27, 1962.

Loos, Anita. "Darling Unforgettable Tallulah." *The Reader's Digest,* August 1969.

Lord, John. *The Maharajahs*. London: Hutchinson, 1972.

Lord, Walter. *The Good Years*. London: Longmans, 1960.

———. *A Night to Remember*. London: Longmans Green, 1956.

Lundberg, Ferdinand. *America's 60 Families*. New York: The Vanguard Press, 1937.

———. *Imperial Hearst*. New York: The Modern Library, 1937.
———. *The Rich and the Super-Rich*. London: Nelson, 1969.
Lurie, Alison. *The Language of Clothes*. London: William Heinemann, 1981.
Lynham, Ruth, ed. *Paris Fashion*. London: Michael Joseph, 1972.
Macandrew, Donald. "The Prince of Tailors." *The Saturday Book*, Vol. 18. London: Hutchinson, 1958.
McCarthy, Albert. *The Dance Band Era, 1910–1950*. London: Studio Vista, 1971.
McCarthy, James, with John Rutherford. *Peacock Alley*. New York: Harper, 1931.
Maclean, Evalyn Walsh, with Boyden Sparkes. *Father Struck It Rich*. London: Faber & Faber, 1936.
MacNaghten, Patrick, with Lord Montagu of Beaulieu. *Home, James*. London: Weidenfeld & Nicolson, 1982.
McNulty, Henry. *Vogue Cocktails*. London: Octopus Books, 1982.
Magnus, Sir Philip. *Edward VII*. London: John Murray, 1964.
Maloney, Russell. "Hattie Carnegie." *Life,* September 10, 1945.
Mannin, Ethel. *Young in The Twenties*. London: Hutchinson, 1971.
Marcus, Stanley. *Minding The Store*. London: Elm Tree Books, 1975.
Margetson, Stella. *The Long Party*. Farnborough, Hants: Saxon House, 1974.
Mariano, Nicky. *Forty Years with Berenson*. London: Hamish Hamilton, 1966.
Marlborough, Laura, Duchess of. *Laughter From a Cloud*. London: Weidenfeld & Nicolson, 1980.
Marlowe, Dave. *Coming, Sir!* London: George Harrap, 1937.
Marshall, Michael. *Top Hat and Tails: The Story of Jack Buchanan*. London: Elm Tree Books, 1978.
Martin, Frederick Townsend. *Things I Remember*. London: Eveleigh Nash, 1913.
Martin, Ralph G. *A Hero For Our Time*. New York: Macmillan, 1983.
Masters, Anthony. *Inside Marbled Halls*. London: Sidgwick and Jackson, 1979.
———. *Nancy Astor*. London: Weidenfeld & Nicolson, 1981.
Masters, Brian. *Great Hostesses*. London: Constable, 1982.
Maxwell, Elsa. *The Celebrity Circus*. London: W. H. Allen, 1964.
———. *I Married The World*. London: William Heinemann, 1955.
Meneghini, Giovanni Battista, with Renzo Allegri. *My Wife Maria Callas*. Translated by Henry Wisneki. London: The Bodley Head, 1981.

Meyrick, Kate. *Secrets of the 43.* London: John Long, 1933.
Middlemass, Keith. *The Pursuit of Pleasure.* London: Gordon & Cremonesi, 1977.
Milford, Nancy. *Zelda Fitzgerald.* London: The Bodley Head, 1970.
Mizener, Arthur. *Scott Fitzgerald And His World.* London: Thames & Hudson, 1972.
Moats, Alice-Leone. *Lupescu.* New York: Henry Holt, 1955.
———. *The Million-Dollar Studs.* London: Robert Hale, 1978.
Montgomery, John. *1900: The End of an Era.* London: George Allen & Unwin, 1968.
Montgomery-Massingberd, Hugh, and David Watkin. *The London Ritz.* London: Aurum Press, 1980.
Morehouse, Ward. *Matinee Tomorrow.* New York: Whittlesey House, 1949.
Morel, Julian. *Pullman.* Newton Abbot: David & Charles, 1983.
Morgan, Ted. "Adieu to the Luxury Liner." *The New York Times Magazine,* May 12, 1974.
———. *Somerset Maugham.* London: Jonathan Cape, 1980.
Morison, Samuel E., Henry Steele Commager, and William E. Leuchtenberg. *The Growth of the American Republic,* Vol. 2. London: Oxford University Press, 1969.
Morley, Sheridan. *A Talent To Amuse.* London: Penguin Books, 1974.
Morrell, Parker. *Diamond Jim.* New York: Simon & Schuster, 1934.
Morris, Lloyd. *Incredible New York.* New York: Random House, 1951.
———. *Not So Long Ago.* New York: Random House, 1949.
———. *Postscript to Yesterday.* New York: Random House, 1947.
Morton, Frederick. "El Morocco." *Holiday,* February 1966.
———. "The Palace." *Holiday,* November 1965.
———. *The Rothschilds.* London: Secker & Warburg, 1962.
Mosley, Diana. *A Life of Contrasts.* London: Hamish Hamilton, 1977.
Mosley, Leonard. *Castlerosse.* London: Arthur Barker, 1956.
Mosley, Nicholas. *Rules of the Game.* London: Secker & Warburg, 1982.
Mosley, Sir Oswald. *My Life.* London: Nelson, 1968.
Mount, Charles Merrill. *John Singer Sargent.* London: The Cresset Press, 1957.
Mowry, George E., ed. *The Twenties: Fords, Flappers and Fanatics.* Englewood Cliffs, N. J.: Prentice-Hall, 1963.
Newborough, Denisa, Lady. *Fire In My Blood.* London: Elek Books, 1958.

Newby, Eric. "Harrods—Everything for Everybody Everywhere." *Holiday,* November 1968.

Nichols, Beverley. *Are They the Same at Home?* London: Jonathan Cape, 1940.

———. *A Case of Human Bondage.* London: Secker & Warburg, 1966.

———. *The Sweet and Twenties.* London: Weidenfeld & Nicolson, 1958.

———. *The Unforgiving Minute.* London: W. H. Allen, 1978.

Nicol, Jean. *Meet Me at The Savoy.* London: Museum Press, 1952.

Nicolson, Harold. *Diaries and Letters.* Edited by Nigel Nicolson. 3 vols. London: William Collins, 1966–1968.

O'Connor, Harvey. *The Astors.* New York: Alfred A. Knopf, 1941.

O'Connor, Richard. *Courtroom Warrior.* Boston: Little, Brown, 1963.

———. *Down to Eternity.* Manchester: Fawcett Publications, 1957.

———. *Mellon's Millions.* New York: The John Day Co., 1933.

———. *The Scandalous Mr. Bennett.* New York: Doubleday, 1962.

O'Gara, James V. "The Shop That Sells Dreams." *Coronet,* September 1957.

Orczy, Baroness. *Links In The Chain of Life.* London: Hutchinson, 1947.

Owen, Roderic, with Tristan de Vere Cole. *Beautiful and Beloved.* London: Hutchinson, 1974.

Pakenham, Mary. *Brought Up and Brought Out.* London: Cobden-Sanderson, 1938.

Paoli, Xavier. *My Royal Clients.* Translated by Alexander Teixeria De Mattos. London: Hodder and Stoughton, 1911.

"Park Avenue's Sulka." *Newsweek,* October 14, 1957.

Pearsall, Ronald. *Edwardian Life and Leisure.* Newton Abbott: David & Charles, 1973.

Pearson, John. *Edward The Rake.* London: Weidenfeld & Nicolson, 1975.

Phelan, James. *Howard Hughes: The Hidden Years.* London: William Collins, 1977.

Pless, Daisy, Princess of. *By Herself.* Edited by Desmond Chapman-Huston. London: John Murray, 1928.

———. *From My Private Diary.* London: John Murray, 1931.

———. *What I Left Unsaid.* London: Cassell, 1936.

Poiret, Paul. *My First Fifty Years.* Translated by Stephen Haden Guest. London: Victor Gollancz, 1931.

Polovtsoff, Gen. Petr'. *Monte Carlo Casino.* London: Stanley Paul, 1937.

Portland, Duke of. *Men, Women and Things.* London: Faber & Faber, 1937.

Pound, Reginald. *Arnold Bennett*. London: William Heinemann, 1952.
——. *Selfridge*. London: William Heinemann, 1960.
Powell, Margaret, with Leigh Crutchley. *Below Stairs*. London: Peter Davies, 1968.
Powell, Violet. *A Substantial Ghost*. London: William Heinemann, 1967.
Pringle, Margaret. *Dance Little Ladies*. London: Orbis, 1977.
Pritchett, V. S. "Farewell to the Queens." *Holiday,* February 1968.
Probert, Christina. *Shoes in Vogue Since 1910*. London: Thames & Hudson, 1981.
Pullar, Philippa. *Gilded Butterflies*. London: Hamish Hamilton, 1978.
Purdy, Ken W. *Knights of The Road*. London: Hutchinson, 1955.
Quennell, Peter. *Customs and Characters*. London: Weidenfeld & Nicolson, 1982.
——. *The Marble Foot*. London: William Collins, 1960.
——. *The Wanton Chase*. London: William Collins, 1980.
——. *The Sign of the Fish*. London: William Collins, 1960.
——, editor. *Genius in the Drawing Room*. London: Weidenfeld & Nicolson, 1980.
Quinn, Frank. *Well Britched*. Unpublished manuscript, courtesy C. F. Quinn, Esq., Kilgour, French & Stanbury.
Rees, Goronwy. *The Multi-Millionaires*. London: Chatto and Windus, 1961.
Reitlinger, Gerald. *The Economics of Taste*. London: Barrie & Rockliff, 1960.
Reynolds, Quentin. "Have You a Reservation?" *Collier's,* October 1, 1938.
——. "Prices to Suit." *Collier's,* April 13, 1935.
"Richest U.S. Women." *Fortune,* November 1936.
Ridley, Pauline, ed. *Fashion Illustration*. London: Academy Editions, 1979.
Rigby, Douglas and Elizabeth. *Lock, Stock and Barrel: The Story of Collecting*. Philadelphia: J. B. Lippincott, 1944.
Ridley, Laura Date. "America's Ten Richest Women." *The Ladies' Home Journal,* September 1957.
Ritz, Marie-Louise. *César Ritz—Host To The World*. London: George Harrap, 1938.
Robert, Jacques. *Paris By Night*. Translated by Stephanie and Richard Sutton. London: Charles Skilton, 1959.
Rodgers, Richard. "Star! Unforgettable Gertrude Lawrence." *The Reader's Digest,* January 1969.

Rostron, Captain Sir Arthur, with James R. Crowell. "From The Bridge." *The Saturday Evening Post,* July 23 and October 1, 1927.
Rubenstein, Helena. *My Life For Beauty.* New York: Simon & Schuster, 1964.
Ruffer, Jonathan Garnier. *The Big Shots.* London: Debrett, 1977.
Rushmore, Robert. *The Life of George Gershwin.* New York: The Crowell-Collier Press, 1968.
"Saks Fifth Avenue." *Fortune,* November 1938.
Samuels, Ernest. *Bernard Berenson: The Making of a Connoisseur.* Cambridge, Mass.: Harvard University Press, 1979.
Saunders, Edith. *The Age of Worth.* London: Longmans Green, 1954.
Schiaparelli, Elsa. *Shocking Life.* London: J. M. Dent, 1954.
Schneider, P. E. "Today It's Saint-Tropez—Tomorrow?" *The New York Times Magazine,* August 20, 1961.
———. "What Makes Paris Fashion's Capital?" *The New York Times Magazine,* July 27, 1958.
Schriftgiesser, Karl. *Families.* New York: Howell & Soskin, 1940.
Schwartz, Charles. *Cole Porter.* London: W. H. Allen, 1978.
———. *Gershwin: His Life and Music.* London: Abelard-Schuman, 1973.
Seebohm, Caroline. *The Man Who Was Vogue: The Life and Times of Condé Nast.* London: Weidenfeld & Nicolson, 1982.
Secrest, Meryle. *Being Bernard Berenson.* London: Weidenfeld & Nicolson, 1979.
Selfridge, Harry Gordon. "Selling Selfridge." *The Saturday Evening Post,* July 27, August 10, August 24, and September 7, 1935.
Shaw-Sparrow, Walter. *John Lavery And His Work.* London: Kegan Paul, Trench, Trübner, 1912.
Sheppard, Eugenia. "Voila! Les Girls Return." *The Saturday Evening Post,* March 17, 1963.
Sherwood, Shirley. *Venice Simplon Orient-Express.* London: Weidenfeld & Nicolson, 1983.
Simon, George T. *The Big Bands.* New York: Macmillan, 1971.
Sinclair, Andrew. *Corsair.* London: Weidenfeld & Nicolson, 1981.
Sitwell, Osbert. *Great Morning.* London: Macmillan, 1948.
———. *Laughter in the Next Room.* London: Macmillan, 1949.
Sklar, Robert. *F. Scott Fitzgerald: The Last Laöcoon.* New York: Oxford University Press, 1967.
Slater, Leonard. *Aly.* London: W. H. Allen, 1966.
Slosson, Preston William. *The Great Crusade and After.* New York: Macmillan, 1930.

Small, Collie. "A Millionaire and His Mountain." *The Saturday Evening Post,* January 10, 1948.
Sprigge, Sylvia. *Berenson.* London: George Allen & Unwin, 1960.
Stamper, C. W. *What I Know.* London: Mills & Boon, 1913.
Stanford, Donald. *Ile de France.* London: Cassell, 1960.
Stassinopoulos, Arianna. *Maria: Beyond the Callas Legend.* London: Weidenfeld & Nicolson, 1980.
Stephens, W. P. *American Yachting.* New York: The Macmillan Co., 1904.
Stern, Mike. *Farouk.* New York: Bantam Books, 1965.
Stevens, Mark. *Like No Other Store In The World: The Inside Story of Bloomingdale's.* New York: Thomas Y. Crowell, 1979.
Strachey, Barbara, and Jayne Samuel, eds. *Mary Berenson: A Self Portrait from Her Letters and Diaries.* London: Victor Gollancz, 1983.
Strakosch, Avery. "Not Another Stitch." *Collier's,* October 8, 1938.
Sullivan, Mark. *Our Times.* 6 vols. New York: Charles Scribner's Sons, 1926–1933.
Swaebe, Albert V. *Photographer Royal.* London: Leslie Frewin, 1967.
Swanberg, W. A. *Citizen Hearst.* London: Longman's, 1962.
Swanson, Gloria. *Swanson on Swanson.* London: Michael Joseph, 1981.
Sykes, Christopher. *Evelyn Waugh.* London: William Collins, 1975.
Tabori, Paul. *Alexander Korda.* London: Oldbourne, 1959.
Taylor, A. J. P. *Beaverbrook.* London: Hamish Hamilton, 1972.
Taylor, Derek. *Fortune, Fame and Folly: British Hotels and Catering from 1878 to 1978.* London: Caterer & Hotelkeeper, 1977.
Terkel, Studs. *Hard Times: An Oral History of the Great Depression.* London: Allen Lane, 1970.
Thomas, Bob. *Winchell.* New York: Doubleday, 1971.
Thomas, Gordon, and Max Morgan-Witts. *The Day the Bubble Burst.* London: Hamish Hamilton, 1979.
Thomson, George Malcolm. *Lord Castlerosse: His Life and Times.* London: Weidenfeld & Nicolson, 1973.
Thorndike, Joseph J., Jr. *The Magnificent Builders and Their Dream Homes.* London: Paul Elek, 1978.
Tolbert, Frank X. *Neiman-Marcus.* New York: Henry Holt, 1953.
Tomkins, Calvin. *Living Well is the Best Revenge.* London: André Deutsch, 1972.
Trefusis, Violet. *Don't Look Round.* London: Hutchinson, 1952.
Trodd, Kenith. *Lew Stone: A Career in Music.* London: Inchbrook Printers, 1971.

Tschumi, Gabriel. *Royal Chef.* London: William Kimber, 1954.
Tully, Andrew. *Era of Elegance.* New York: Funk & Wagnalls, 1947.
Tunney, Kieran. *Tallulah—Darling of the Gods.* London: Secker & Warburg, 1972.
Turnbull, Andrew. *Scott Fitzgerald.* London: The Bodley Head, 1962.
Tweedie, Mrs. Alec. *Thirteen Years of a Busy Woman's Life.* London: John Lane, 1912.
Vanderbilt, Cornelius, Jr. *Farewell to Fifth Avenue.* London: Victor Gollancz, 1935.
———. *Man of the World.* London: Hutchinson, 1961.
———. *Queen of the Golden Age.* New York: McGraw-Hill, 1956.
Van Rensselaer, Philip. *Million Dollar Baby.* London: Hodder and Stoughton, 1980.
Vickers, Hugo. *Gladys, Duchess of Marlborough.* London: Weidenfeld & Nicolson, 1979.
Walker, Stanley. *Mrs. Astor's Horse.* London: The Bodley Head, 1936.
Warshow, Robert Irving. *The Story of Wall Street.* New York: Greenberg, 1929.
Watts, Stephen. *The Paris Ritz.* London: The Bodley Head, 1963.
Waugh, Alec. *The Lipton Story.* London: Cassell, 1951.
Waugh, Auberon. "The Fixer—Roman Style." *Holiday,* August 1969.
Waugh, Evelyn. *Diaries.* Edited by Michael Davie. London: Weidenfeld & Nicolson, 1976.
Wechsberg, Joseph. "Creating an Atmosphere." *The New Yorker,* August 17, 1957.
———. *Dining at the Pavilion.* London: Weidenfeld & Nicolson, 1963.
———. *Red Plush and Black Velvet.* London: Weidenfeld & Nicolson, 1962.
Wector, Dixon. *The Age of the Great Depression.* New York: Macmillan, 1949.
———. *The Saga of American Society.* New York: Charles Scribner's Sons, 1932.
Wendt, Lloyd, and Herman Kogan. *Bet A Million!* Indianapolis: Bobbs-Merrill, 1948.
Westminster, Loelia, Duchess of. *Grace and Favour.* London: Weidenfeld & Nicolson, 1961.
Wharton, Edith. *A Backward Glance.* New York: D. Appleton-Century, 1934.
Whipple, A. B. C. "The Winning Loser of the America's Cup." *The Smithsonian,* August 1980.

Whitbourn, Frank. *Mr. Lock of St. James's Street*. London: William Heinemann, 1971.
Whitcomb, Ian. *After the Ball*. London: Allan Lane, 1973.
Wigs [pseud.]. *The Work of Ambrose McEvoy*. London: The Morland Press, 1923.
Wilding, Dorothy. *In Pursuit of Perfection*. London: Robert Hale, 1958.
Williams, A. H. *No Name on the Door*. London: W. H. Allen, 1956.
Williams, Mrs. Hwfa. *It Was Such Fun*. London: Hutchinson, 1935.
Wilson, Earl. "Fabulous Jacques Fath." *Collier's,* October 1, 1949.
Wilson, Sandy. *The Roaring Twenties*. London: Eyre Methuen, 1976.
Windsor, Duchess of. *The Heart Has Its Reasons*. London: Michael Joseph, 1956.
Windsor, H. R. H. The Duke of. *A King's Story*. London: Cassell, 1960.
Winkler, John. *Five and Ten*. London: Robert Hale, 1941.
―――. *John D.: A Portrait in Oils*. New York: Blue Ribbon Books, 1929.
―――. *The Life of J. Pierpont Morgan*. New York: Alfred A. Knopf, 1931.
―――. *Tobacco Tycoon*. New York: Random House, 1942.
―――. *W. R. Hearst: An American Phenomenon*. London: Jonathan Cape, 1928.
Winslow, Thyra Santer. "To Eat, Drink and Be Mentioned." *The New York Times Magazine,* February 24, 1946.
Wishart, Michael. *High Diver*. London: Blond & Briggs, 1977.
Wolfe, Elsie de (Lady Mendl). *After All*. London: William Heinemann, 1935.
―――. *The House in Good Taste*. New York: The Century Co., 1913.
Woolf, Leonard. *Downhill All the Way*. London: Hogarth Press, 1967.
Woolf, Virginia. *The Diaries*. Edited by Ann Oliver Bell and Andrew McMeillie. London: The Hogarth Press, 1977–82.
―――. *Letters*. London: The Hogarth Press, 1982.
Worth, Jean Philippe. *A Century of Fashion*. Translated by Ruth Scott Miller. Boston: Little, Brown, 1928.
Wraight, Robert. *The Art Game*. London: Leslie Frewin, 1965.
Wright, William. *Heiress*. Washington, D.C.: New Republic Press, 1978.
Ziegler, Philip. *Diana Cooper*. London: Hamish Hamilton, 1981.
Zolotow, Maurice. "Fine Jewels Are His Business." *The Saturday Evening Post,* May 1–8, 1948.
Zwerin, Michael. "Flash! Winchell Is A Reluctant Anachronism." *Esquire,* August 1968.

INDEX

Aaron's Rod (D. H. Lawrence), 149
Aberconway, Christabel, Lady, 200
Ackroyd, Bill, 79
Abercrombie and Fitch, 224-25
Acosta, Rita de (Mrs. Philip Lydig), 91
Acton, Harold, 54
Adelphi Theatre, 146, 168
Aga Khan, 82, 88, 135, 151, 185, 203, 219, 222
Agnelli, Gianni, 234
Agnew, Lady, 122
Aird, Sir John, 174, 176
Alexander III, Tsar, 28-29
Alexandra, Queen, 2, 6, 7, 16, 29, 64, 72, 75, 85
Alexandra, Tsarina, 26
Alfonso XIII of Spain, King, 9, 25, 74, 107, 151, 157, 161, 212-13
Alington of Crichel, Lord, 3, 85, 89, 127, 149
Allen, F. L., 99
Allom, Sir Charles, 58
d'Alte, Viscomte, 90
Altman, Benjamin, 57
Alwar, Maharajah of, 31
Aly Khan, Prince, 107, 191, 212, 221, 232
Ambassador Hotel, New York, 52, 143
Ambrose, Bert, 108, 136, 151, 181
America's Cup, 3
American in Paris, An (George Gershwin), 88
Amies, Hardy, 79, 115
Amon, Luisa (later Marchesa Casati), 81

Amory, Cleveland, 241
Anglesey, Marquis of, 63
Antic Hay (Aldous Huxley), 149
Antoine (Antek Cierplikowski), 113
Anything Goes (Cole Porter), 182
Apraxine, Count, 83
Arden, Elizabeth (Florence Nightingale Graham), 90, 111, 112, 122, 160
Arlen, Michael (Dikran Kouyoumdjian), 79, 89, 91, 144-49, 178, 200
Ascot Races, 5, 106; "Black Ascot," 75
Ashridge, 22
Asprey, New Bond Street, 12, 93
Asquith, Lady Cynthia, 106
Asquith, Margot, 114
Astaire, Adele, 125, 128
Astaire, Fred, 125, 128
Astor, Alice (Princess Obolensky), 85
Astor, Caroline (Mrs. William Backhouse Astor), 41-43, 45-46, 49, 50, 52, 114
Astor Hotel, New York, 104
Astor, John Jacob, 42, 80
Astor, Mary (Mrs. William Waldorf Astor), 41
Astor, Nancy Langhorne, 23, 88, 212
Astor, Waldorf, 19, 23
Automobile Club, 37
Ava, Earl of, 63

BadischerHof Hotel, Baden-Baden, 229
Bagnold, Enid, 149
Bailey's Beach, Newport, 48

267

Baker, Josephine, 184
Baldwin, Stanley, 204-6
Balenciaga, Cristobal, 93, 228
Balfour, Arthur James, 7
Balfour, Patrick, 86
Balmain, Pierre, 115, 223
Balmoral Castle, 5, 62
Balsan, Chasseur Etienna, 116
Bankhead, Tallulah, 86, 89, 100, 105, 122, 126-27, 131, 146, 148, 180, 242
Bar Harbor Club, 165
Baring, Poppy, 97, 150
Barnato, Barney, 86, 177
Baroda, Maharajah of, 223
Barry, Philip, 149
Barrymore, Blanche, 91
Barrymore, John, 91
Bartenders' Guild, UK, 178
Barton, Alfred Ilko, 218
Barucci, Giulia, 15
Bassano Studio, 123
Bath, Marquis of, 18, 22
Bathe, Sir Hugo de, 139
Battling Butler (musical), 126
Beaton, Cecil, 26, 75, 87, 91, 105, 116, 124-25, 175, 177, 199, 234
Beautiful and Damned, The (F. Scott Fitzgerald), 141
Beaudouin, Edgar, 138
Beaux Arts Ball, New York, 104
Beaverbrook, Lord, 87, 90, 157-58, 202
Beavor-Webb, James, 10
Bedaux, Charles, 209, 212
Beecham, Sir Thomas, 199
Beerbohm, Max, 26
"Begin the Beguine" (Cole Porter), 183
Behrman, S. N., 149
Belmont, Alva Smith Vanderbilt, 46, 51, 64, 120, 164
Belmont, August, 43, 85, 105
Belmont, Oliver Hazard Perry, 46
Bennett, Arnold, 83, 149
Bennett, James Gordon, 10
Bennett, James Gordon Jr., 78, 83, 89, 154
Berners, Lord, 38
Berenson, Bernhard, 58-61, 88, 140
Berenson, Mary, 58-60, 88
Berkeley Hotel, London, 26, 35, 87
Bernhardt, Sarah, 1, 33-34, 113, 121
Best People, The (Avery Hopwood), 149
Bestigui, Charlie de, 229
Beverly Wilshire Hotel, 181, 231

Billings, C. K. G., 82, 162
Billingsley, Sherman, 179-80, 241
Biltmore Hotel, New York, 140
Blenheim Palace, 14, 17, 19, 21, 65
Bloomingdale, Samuel, 37, 226, 238
Blue Train (Mediterranean Express), 135, 226
Bocher, Main Rousseau, 208, 228
Bodossakis, "Bodo", 232
Boldt, George, 44, 49
Borden, M. C., 78
Bordoni, Irene, 182
Boris of Russia, Grand Duke, 46, 50
Boussac, Marcel, 222
Boyds, Ernest, 141
Boyd-Rochfort, Captain Cecil, 23
Brady, James Buchanan ("Diamond Jim"), 44-45, 79, 80, 81, 157
Bridgwater, Duke of, 22
Broadhurst Theatre, New York, 146
Bromfield, Louis, 147
Brooks, Van Wyck, 141
Brougham, Lady, 8, 20
Brown, John Nicholas, 242
Browne, Valentine Charles. *See* Castlerosse.
Brownlow, Perry, 176, 203, 205
Bryant, James McKinley, 76
Buchanan, Jack, 126, 131
Buckingham Palace, 2, 4, 7, 16, 21, 44, 169, 206
Buist, Colin, 176
Burton, George, 155
Byng, Douglas, 184
Byrne, St. Clare, 10

Café de Paris, London, 17, 98, 109, 176, 181, 183-85, 194, 218
Café de Paris, New York, 136
Café Marguery, 79
Café Society Register, 76
Callaghan, Morley, 143
Callas, Maria (Maria Kalogeropuolos), 233-37, 240
Cameron, Roderick, 200
Campbell, Mrs. Patrick, 121, 200
Canaries Sometimes Sing (Frederick Lonsdale), 149
Capel, Arthur ("Boy"), 116, 119
Capon, Alphonse ("Al"), 128
Caprice Restaurant, London, 88, 224
Caraman-Chimay, Princesse de, 143

Index

Cardin, Pierre, 223
Carlos of Portugal, King, 69
Carlton Hotel, Cannes, 90, 125, 136
Carlton Hotel, London, 34-35, 185
Carnegie, Andrew, 56
Carnegie, Hattie, 218, 228
Carol of Rumania, Prince, 218-219
Cartier, Pierre, 77, 216
Cartier's London, 146, 227-28
Cartier's New York, 125, 164
Caruso, Enrico, 9, 28, 178
Casani, Santos, 98
Casati, Marchesa, 81, 122, 152
Casino, Deauville, 151, 178
Casino Theater, 74
Cassatt, Alexander, 165
Cassel, Sir Ernest, 3, 72, 75, 97, 108, 216
Castellane-Novejean, Count Maric, 65-71
Castlerosse, Lord, 87, 89, 90, 149, 157-58, 194
Cecil, Hugh, 123
Central Park Casino, 184
Cercle Nautique, Cannes, 4
Chamberlain family, 101
Chamberlain, Samuel, 154
Champassak, Prince Doan Vinh Na, 231
Chanel, Gabrielle Bonheur ("Coco"), 116-19, 125, 135, 172, 219, 222
Channon, Henry ("Chips"), 175, 199, 200, 205
Chantecler (Rostand), 72
Charleston, the, 98
Charlot, André, 148
Charpentier, Henri, 17
Chatsworth, 10, 11, 24
Cherkassy, Prince, 81
Chichester family, 19
Children of the Ritz (Noël Coward), 168-69
"Cholly Knickerbocker" (Maury Henry Biddle Paul), 94, 119, 154-56, 180, 194, 220
Cholmondelely, Lord, 137
Christopher of Greece, Prince, 7
Churchill, Winston (later Sir), 65, 102, 199, 202, 205, 217, 232, 234
Ciro's Restaurant, 78, 79, 93, 153
Citroën, Andre, 151, 153
Clair, Ina, 117
Clancarty, Lady, 169
Claremout, A. E., 36
Claridge's, 27, 88, 187, 195, 211, 219

Clark, Kenneth (later Lord), 56
Clarkson, Willie, 112
Clifton, Henry de Vere, 77
Cliveden, 19-20, 22-23
Club Richman, New York, 98
Club Sportiva, 179
Coats, Audrey Dudley, 97, 110
Cochrane, Alexander Smith, 57
Cochran, Charles B., 148
Cole, Horace de Vere, 101
Cole, James Omar, 182
Colefax, Lady (Sibyl), 200
Collier, Constance, 150
Colonial Theater, New York, 98
Colony Restaurant, New York, 85, 154
Connaught, Duke of, 22
Connolly, Cyril, 144
Considine, Mrs. Robert, 236
Coolidge, Calvin, 160, 166
Cooper, Duff, 229
Cooper, Lady Diana, 87, 91, 99, 100, 103, 121, 126, 129, 149, 160, 175, 199, 203-4, 232
Cornell, Katherine, 146-47
Cornell University, 79
Cornwallis-West, Daisy, 71
Corrigan, Laura, 120, 202, 219
Cosden, Joshua, 161-62
Courville, Albert de, 108
Covent Garden, Royal Opera House, 5, 8, 9, 33, 191, 234
Coward, Noël, 81, 91, 126, 139, 148-49, 152, 168, 173, 181-82, 205, 207, 242
Coyne, Joe, 62
Cramm, Baron Gottfried von, 230-31
Criterion Theater, 74
Cromwell, Mrs. Jimmy (formerly Doris Duke), 195
Crowninshield, Frank, 105
Cunard, Lady (Emerald), 86, 89, 90, 91, 121, 145, 175, 191, 199, 200, 202-3, 205, 212, 215, 217
Cunard, Nancy, 89, 100, 149, 202
Curzon, Cynthia, 91
Curzon, Grace, 91
Cutting, James de Wolfe, 50
Cyclax, House of, 112

Dabescat, Olivier, 86
Daché, Lilly, 218
Dahlgren, Elizabeth (formerly Drexel), 49-50

Daily Chronicle, 73
Daily Express, 148
Daily Mail, 154, 157
Daily Sketch, 86
Daily Telegraph, 63
Daimler cars, 38
Daly's (Empire Music Hall), 62
Davies, Marion, 85-86, 104, 213
Davis, Arthur J., 35
Dawson of Penn, Lord, 192
Dean, Charles, 85
Décazes, Duc Elie, 64
Delmonico's restaurant, New York, 27
Demarest, Charlotte, 155
Derby, Lord, 11, 20, 95, 137
Deslys, Gaby, 16, 100
Dessès, Jean, 103
Devonshire family, 10
Devonshire, Duchess of, 17
Diaghilev, Sergei, 139
"Diamond Horseshoe", 41, 53
Diamond, Jack ("Legs"), 128
Dierk, Barry, 136-37, 160
Dillingham, Louise, 89
Dior, Christian, 222, 228
Ditchley Park, 20
Dodge, Harold, 152
Doherty, Helen Lee Eames, 146
Dollar Princess, The, 62
Dolly Sisters (Rosie and Jennie), 152-53, 182, 221
Donahue, Jimmy Woolworth, 197, 228-30
Donegall, Marquess of, 157
Don't Tell Alfred (Nancy Mitford), 149
Doran, George, 221
Dorchester Hotel, London, 77, 190, 213, 215, 217-18, 234
Dorn family, 82
Doucet, 114
Douglas, James, 148, 231
Drayton, Alfred, 150
Drexel, A. J., 9, 10
Drexel, Elizabeth, 41
Dudley Ward, Freda, 106-7, 110-12, 150, 165, 174, 191
Duff-Gordon, Lady (Lucy), 110, 115
Duke, Doris, 195, 222, 230
Duncan, Isadora, 143
Dunhill, Alfred, 30-31, 36, 38, 106
Dunhill, Mary, 30
Dupont, Liz, 89

Dupuch, Etienne, 220
Duveen, Joseph (later Lord), 54-62, 86, 131, 166, 182

Edward VII, King, coronation of, 1; social life, 2-6; motor cars, 6-7; clothes, 7-8; entertainment, 8-9; weekend house parties, 10-14; mistresses, 15-16; meals, 16-17; 24, 25-27, 29, 33-35, 42, 44-45, 52, 54, 57, 62-63, 67-68; last illness and death, 72-74; funeral, 74-75; 80-81, 95, 97, 100, 106, 114, 119-20, 122-23, 144, 225
El Fay Club, 129
El Morocco, Club, 180, 220, 229
Elliott, Maxine (Jessica Dermot), 91, 137, 222
Elsie, Lily, 62
Embassy Club, London, 107, 108, 125, 136, 146, 151, 158, 176, 199, 218
Empire Music Hall, 8
Ena, Queen of Spain, 26
English National Opera, 81
Escoffier, Georges Auguste, 31-33
Esher, Lord, 1, 75
Evanloff, Prince Michael, 113
Evening Graphic, 156
Evening News, 90
Everglades Club, 162
Excelsior Hotel, Rome, 186
Expressen, Stockholm, 238

Fabergé, Peter Carl, 28-29, 38, 82, 197
Fairbanks, Douglas, Sr., 30, 178
Faisel of Iraq, King, 202
Falaise, Marquis de la, 188
Fallen Angels (Noël Coward), 148
Farouk of Egypt, King, 77, 83, 224
Farquhar, Lord, 4
Faucigny-Lucinge, Princesse de (formerly Baba d'Erlanger), 113, 151
Fawzia, Princess, 224
Fay, Larry, 129
Fellowes, Hon. Mrs. Reginald (formerly Daisy Decazes), 113, 152
Ferber, Edna, 89
Ferdinand of Austria, Archduke Franz, 74
Ferraro, Filippo, 35, 87
Festetics, Count Andor, 92
Filippo, Eduardo de, 186
Finney, Ben, 139

Index

Fish, Mamie Stuyvesant, 46-47, 49, 50, 52, 80, 120, 129, 154, 223
Fitzgerald, F. Scott, 99, 139-44, 147, 149
Fitzgerald, Zelda, 84, 139-44
FitzJames, Comtesse Robert, 70
Flagler, Henry Morrison, 159--60
Floors Castle, 20
Folies Bergères, 131
Follow the Sun, 134
Ford, Henry, 37, 229
Fortune, 92
Fortuny, Mariano, 12
Forty-Three Club, 131
Foy, Mrs. Byron, 218
Frick, Henry Clay, 54-56, 58
Faud I of Egypt, King, 202
Furness, Marmaduke, Viscount, 176
Furness, Lady (Thelma), 165, 174, 176-77, 190-91, 199

Gaiety Theatre, London, 9, 16, 28, 32, 73
Gallati, Mario, 88, 224
Gallier, Humbert de, 31
Garbo, Greta, 232
Gardner, Mrs. Isabella Stewart, 59
Gates, John Warne, 27, 44
George V, as Prince of Wales, 73; as King, 74, 95, 123, 168, 174, 191-92; death of, 192
George White's Scandals, 140
Gershwin, George, 88, 126, 181-82
Gibbs, Philip, 73
Gilda Gray's Rendezvous, 98
Gimpel, René, 59, 60
Givenchy, 239
Globe Theatre, London, 150
Gloucester, Prince Henry, Duke of, 106
Glyn, Elinor, 115
Goelet family, 42, 120
Goelet, May (later Duchess of Roxburgh), 64
Goelet, Mrs. Ogden, 50
Golden Arrow (train), 135
Golden Keys (concierges), 185-86
Gomershall, S. F., 31
Goodwood races, 5, 8, 27
Gould, Anna, 65-71, 170
Gould, Frank Jay, 138
Gould, George, 43, 121
Gould, Jay, 42, 65
Gourielli-Tchkonia, Prince Artchil, 113
Graham, Virginia, 127

Grand Central Hotel, Manchester, 37
Grand Hotel, Monaco, 31
Grand Hotel, Monte Carlo, 32
Grandi, Count Dino, 212
Grant, Cary, 219
Graves, Charles, 157
Graves, Lord, 110
Great Gatsby, The (F. Scott Fitzgerald), 142
Green, Leonard, 123
Green Hat, The (Michael Arlen), 145-47, 178
Greenwich Village Follies of 1924, 182
Greville, Margaret, 202-3, 205, 212, 215-16
Greville, Ronald, 202
Grey, Lady de, 14, 33-35
Grosvenor House, 62, 217
Groult, Camille, 67
Guinan, Texas (Mary Louise Cecilia), 129-31, 133, 162
Gulbenkian, Calouste, 57, 149
Gulbenkian, Nubar, 24, 88, 107, 224
Gump's, 55
Gwalior, Maharajah of, 223
Gwynne, Alfred, 52

Hale, George, 93
Halsey, Admiral Sir Lionel, 198
Halton Manor, 14, 20
Happy Days Are Here Again!, 167
Hapsburg, Archduke Otto of, 216
Hardinge, Sir Charles, 4
Harewood, George, 7th Earl of. 81
Harmsworth, Esmond, 205
Harper's Bazaar, 124, 222
Harris, Jack, 80, 195
Harris, Marion, 183
Harrods, London, 77, 112, 225
Harry's Bar, Venice, 231
Hart, Moss, 93
Hartington, Lord, 3, 10
Hartmann, Mrs., 1
Hastings, Sir Patrick, 210
Hatchard's bookshop, 81
Haugwitz-Reventlow, Count Kurt, 195, 210-11
Havemeyer, Henry O., 59
Hawes & Curtis, 106, 126, 146, 184
Hearst, William Randolph, 57-58, 78, 89, 94, 104, 154, 202, 220
Hecht, Ben, 156
Heinemann, William, 144

Hemingway, Ernest, 138, 141, 143
Henry of Prussia, Prince, 53
Herald, New York, 89
Herbert, Victor, 77
Hergesheimer, Joseph, 28, 47, 87, 162-63
Hertford, 6th Marquess of, 63
Hi Diddle Diddle (musical), 183
Hicks, David, 93
Hill, Derek, 60
Hirsch auf Gereuth, Baron Maurice von, 3
Hoffman House, New York, 177
Hoover, President Herbert, 102, 166, 224
Hopwood, Avery, 149
Horder, Lord, 197, 206
Hotel Ambassador, New York, 181
Hotel Bristol, Paris, 4, 71
Hôtel du Cap d'Antibes, 83, 139
Hôtel Lutetia, Juans-les-Pins, 138
Hôtel du Palais, Biarritz, 211
Hôtel du Palais, Paris, 72
Hôtel de Paris, Monte Carlo, 83, 136, 152, 157
Hotel Pierre, New York, 211, 239
Hôtel Provençal, 138
Hôtel de Provence, Cannes, 32
Hôtel Ritz, Paris, 34
Hôtel Splendide, Paris, 32
Hotel Universe (Philip Barry), 149
Howard, Brian, 105, 121
Howard, Leslie, 147
Howe, Lord and Lady, 12
Howard, Roy, 220
Hoyningen-Heune, Baron George, 125
Hubbard, Elizabeth, 111
Huntington, Collis P., 55
Huntington, Henry E., 55, 57, 121, 182
Hutton, Barbara Woolworth, 80, 168-73, 179-80, 184, 186-87, 194-99, 210, 219, 228, 230
Hutton, Edna, 170
Hutton, Franklyn Laws, 169, 172
Hutton, Irene, 169-70, 172
Hutton, Marjorie (formerly Mrs. Post), 163, 165
Huxley, Aldous, 149

International Sportsmen's Club, 158
Ironside, Janey, 222
Ismay, Thomas, 55
"It's De-Lovely" (Cole Porter), 183
Iveagh, Lady, 12

Jackson, Bee, 98
Jackson, Jack (bandleader), 216
James, Henry, 15, 122
James, Mrs. Willy, 15, 29, 119
Jauze, Mme. Leon de, 70
Joel, Solly, 83
John, Augustus, 121-22, 131
John, Dorelia, 122
Joyce, Peggy Hopkins, 129
Julyan, Herbert E., 10
Junagadh, Maharajah of, 223

Kahn, Otto, 131, 151
Keller, Louis, 43
Kennedy, Jacqueline Bouvier, 236-42
Kennedy, President John F., 237, 240
Kent, A. Atwater, 83
Kent, Prince George, Duke of, 99, 192, 196, 202, 203
Kent, Marina, Duchess of, 192, 196, 203
Keppel, Alice, 2, 15, 29, 33, 65, 73, 97, 106, 119, 198, 202, 203, 207, 216
Keppel, Hon. George, 74
Keppel, Sonia, 3, 74
Keppel, Violet, 65
Kern, Jerome, 62
Kerr, Archibald Clark, 73
Kerr-Smiley, Maud, 174
Kessler, George A., 27-28, 49
Kilmorey, Lady, 2
Kipling, Rudyard, 15
Kit Kat Club, 108, 185
Kitchener, Field Marshal Lord, 96
Knowsley, 10, 11, 20, 24
Kress, Rush, 61

Lady Chatterley's Lover (D. H. Lawrence), 149
Lamaze, George, 92
Langtry, Emilie Charlotte (Lillie), 15-16, 32-33, 35, 88, 112, 114, 121, 139
Lascelles, Sir Alan, 191
Last of Mrs. Cheyney, The (Frederick Lonsdale), 149
Lavery, Hazel, 120-21
Lavery, Sir John, 120-21
Lawrence, D. H., 145, 149
Lawrence, Gertrude, 90, 125-26, 180
Lawson, Sir Edward, 3
Leeds, Nonnie May, 100, 110, 160, 163
Lehar, Franz, 9
Lehman, Robert, 186

Index

Lehr, Elizabeth (formerly Dahlgren), 50
Lehr, Harry Symes, 45, 48-50, 90, 101, 120
Lenare Studio, 123
"Let's Do It, Let's Fall In Love" (Cole Porter), 182
Levant, Oscar, 88
Lewis & Simmons, 57
Lewis, Wyndham, 149
Lilian (Arnold Bennett), 149
Lillie, Beatrice, 89, 126, 128, 183
Lily Christine (Michael Arlen), 147
Lipton, Sir Thomas, 44, 48
Little Club, The, 131
"Little White Lies," 180
Livanos, Stavros, 232
Lock, James, 107
Lockhart, Robert Bruce, 131
Loder, Major Eric, 214
Loft, George, 162
Lombardo, Guy (bandleader), 180-81
Londesborough, Lord and Lady, 95
London Calling (revue), 125-26
London Hippodrome Theatre, 99
London Venture, The (Michael Arlen), 144
Londonderry House, 19
Longleat, 20-21, 40
Lonsdale, 5th Earl of, 10, 25
Lonsdale, Frederick, 85-86, 88, 149
Louis of Monaco, Prince, 134
Loved and Envied, The (Enid Bagnold), 149
Lowther Castle, 10, 25
Luce, Claire, 134
Lunt, Alfred, 201
Lupescu, Helena, 218-19
Luxembourg, Grand Duchess Charlotte of, 216
Lydig, Rita, 91, 124
Lynn, Olga, 100
Lyric Theatre, London, 35

McAllister, Ward, 41-45, 49, 94
McAuley, Edna, 45, 80
McEachern, Captain Neil, 105
McEvoy, Ambrose, 121
Mackay, Clarence, 49, 61, 105
MacLeish, Archibald, 138
MacMullan, Mrs. Edward J., 164
Mlle. Modiste (Victor Herbert), 77
Manchester, Duke of, 8, 64
Manners, Lady Diana (later Lady Diana Cooper), 87

Manuel of Portugal, King, 74
Mantacheff, Dmitri, 77
Maple, Sir John Blundell, 3
Margetson, Arthur, 182
Mariano, Nicky, 58-59
Marie of Rumania, Queen, 26, 152
Marienbad, Hotel Weimar, 5
Marina of Greece, Princess, 192
Marlborough family, 17
Marlborough, Consuelo, Duchess of (formerly Vanderbilt), 64, 114, 121
Marlborough, Dowager Duchess of, 65
Marlborough, Duchess of, 8
Marlborough, 9th Duke of, 64
"Marlborough House Set," 2, 5, 32, 103, 144
Mary, Queen, 73, 168, 191-92, 202, 205
Maugham, Syrie, 201
Maugham, W. Somerset, 30, 88, 134, 136, 150, 199, 200, 216-17, 219, 221
Maxim's, Paris, 16, 103
Maxwell, Elsa, 115, 134-35, 137, 139, 152, 169, 171, 179, 183, 195, 211, 214, 219-20, 222, 226, 232, 234, 236
May, Edna, 28
Mayfair (Michael Arlen), 147
Mayfair and Montmartre (Cole Porter), 182
Mayfair Hotel, London, 181, 218
Mdivani family, 171-72, 196
Mdivani, Prince Alexis, 80, 171-73, 194-96
Melba, Nelly (Helen Porter Mitchell), 9, 33, 34, 71, 90, 112, 114
Mellon, Andrew W., 86
Mencken, H. L., 157
Meneghini, Giovanni Battista, 234-35
Menken, Mrs. S. Stanwood, 104
Mercati, Atlanta (Mrs. Michael Arlen), 147
Mérode, Cléo de, 16
Merry Widow, The (Franz Lehar), 9
Merryman, Bessie, 175, 191, 204, 210
Messager *(Veronique)*, 35
Messel, Oliver, 103-5
Metcalfe, Lady Alexandra, 174, 176, 209
Metcalfe, Major Edward Dudley, 107, 130, 174, 176, 209
Metropolitan Opera, New York, 41, 227, 234
Mewès, Charles, 34-35
Meyer, Adolphe, Baron de, 123-24
Meyer, Olga de, 123-24

Meyrick, Mrs. Kate Evelyn, 131-33
Michelham, Lady Geraldine, 113, 150
Mills, Mrs. Darius Ogden, 53
Mirror, New York, 156
"Miss Otis Regrets" (Cole Porter), 183
Mistinguett, 113
Mitford, Diana, 91
Mitford, Nancy, 149
Mizner, Addison, 160-61, 164-65
Mizner, Wilson, 92, 161-62
Molyneux, Captain Edward, 115, 118, 125, 139, 172, 195, 198, 208, 219
Monckton, Walter, 205
Mondl, Fritz, 80
Monseigneur Club, 181, 184, 229
Monte Carlo Casino, 83, 92, 153
Moore, George, 145
Moore, Grace, 139
Morgan, J. Pierpont, 1, 9, 10, 27, 32, 37, 53, 54, 56, 57, 59, 74, 91, 164, 218
Morton, Frederic, 179
Mosley, Sir Oswald, 91
Moulin Rouge, 16
Mountbatten, Lady (Edwina), 108, 130, 156, 176
Mountbatten, Lord Louis, 99, 107, 108, 130, 156, 161, 176, 192, 205
Murphy, Gerald, 138-39, 142-43, 149
Murphy, Patrick Francis, 114-115
Murphy, Sara, 138-39, 142-43, 149
Murray, Mae, 171
Mysore, Maharajah of, 39, 223

Naintre, Luigi, 108, 151
Nash, Ogden, 62
Nast, Alfred Condé, 124-25
National Theatre, New York, 207
Negri, Pola, 171, 196
Neiman-Marcus, 226
New Age, The, 145
New Yorker, The, 147, 207
Niarchos, Stavros, 222
Nicholas II, Tsar, 9, 29, 50, 78
Nichols, Beverley, 100, 168
Nicolson, Harold, 26, 73, 86, 122, 175, 198
"Night and Day" (Cole Porter), 183
Nine O'Clock Revue, The, 126
Noblemen's Club, New York, 171
Norland Nursing School (later Nursery Training College), 23
Northcliffe, Lord, 154

Oberon, Merle (Estelle O'Brien Thompson), 109
Obolensky, Alice Astor, 85, 110, 199
Obolensky, Prince Sergé, 85
O'Brien, Jay, 103
Odescalchi, Princess, 113
Oelrichs, Tessie Fair, 46, 120, 154
"Oh, Johnny, how you can love!," 218
On Approval (Frederick Lonsdale), 149
On With the Dance (Nöel Coward), 173
Onassis, Aristotle, 76, 77, 93, 231-42
Onassis, Christina, 232, 242
Onassis, Tina, 232, 234-35
Orage, Alfred R., 145
Orczy, Baroness, 135, 159
Osgood-Field, Julian, 8
Otero, Caroline, 16
Our Betters (W. Somerset Maugham), 150
Oursler, Fulton, 156
D'Oyly Carte, Richard, 32

Paget, Arthur, 2, 63
Pakenham, Mary, 170
Palace Car Company, 43
Palace Hotel, Biarritz, 4
Palace Hotel, St. Moritz, 89, 152, 186, 194, 219, 224
Palace Hotel, San Francisco, 32
Palm Beach, 84, 92, 218, 241
Panhard cars, 38
Paquin, 53, 208
Paris, 182
Paris Bound (Philip Barry), 149
Parsons, Schuyler, 55, 125
Patiala, Maharajah of, 31, 39
Patou, Jean, 104, 172
Patti, Adelina, 33
Paul, Mary Astor, 82
Paul, Maury Henry Biddle. *See* "Cholly Knickerbocker."
Peña, Florence de, 145
Pennsylvania Hotel, 167
Perkins, Maxwell, 140
Petit Moulin Rouge, Le, 31
Picasso, Pablo, 102, 138
Piccadilly Theatre, 217
Piracy (Michael Arlen), 145
Plaza Hotel, New York, 155, 187
Pless, Princess Daisy of, 69, 71, 72
Point Counterpoint (Aldous Huxley), 149
Poiret, Paul, 103, 104, 114-16, 118
Polignac, Prince Pierre de, 134

Index

Ponce de León Hotel, 159
Ponsonby, Frederick, 4, 75
Poole, Henry, 7, 107, 125
Portarlington, Countess of, 107, 150
Porte-Saint-Martin, Theatre de, 72
Porter, Cole, 80, 83, 84, 93, 102, 178, 180, 242
Portland, Duchess of, 122
Portland, Duke of, 10, 17, 19, 21, 22, 75, 122
Post, Emily, 120
Post, Marjory Merriweather, 92, 163
Pougy, Liane de, 16
Poulsen, Martin, 109-10, 218
Pratt, Mrs. Ruthven, 136
Pretty Lady, The (Arnold Bennett), 149
Private Lives (Nöel Coward), 149
Prohibition (Eighteenth Amendment), 128-31
Pullman, George Mortimer, 43
Punch, 27, 29, 100

Quaglino's, 108, 136, 176, 185, 190, 199
Queen, The, 15, 97
Queensborough family, 21
Quennell, Peter, 199
Question Mark, The, 98

Radziwill, Princess Lee Caroline, 236
Rainier, Prince, 232
Rayne, Edward, 110
Reagan, Ronald, 225-26
Reboux (milliner), 113
Rector, Charles, 27, 45, 79, 185-86
Redesdale, Lord, 91
Reeves-Smith, Sir George, 215
Reichenbach, Harry, 160
Reith, Sir John, 206
Renselaer, Philip van, 219
Rhapsody in Blue (George Gershwin), 88, 126
Rhodes, Cecil, 3
Ribbentrop, Joachim von, 212
Ribuffi, Luigi, 133
Richelieu, Duc de, 160
Rickatson-Hatt, Bernard, 198
Richmond, Duke of, 5
Ripon, Marquis of, 14
Ritz, César, 31-35, 38, 67, 108, 187
Ritz, Charles, 79, 187
Ritz Hotel, London, 35, 73, 74, 77, 82, 97, 148, 168, 177, 185, 195, 207, 215-17

Ritz Hotel, New York, 119, 169
Ritz Hotel, Paris, 34, 86, 93, 142, 178, 184, 195, 210, 219
Ritz-Carlton Hotel, New York, 147
Ritz, Marie-Louise, 32-35
Roaring Queen, The (Wyndham Lewis), 149
Rochefoucauld, Duchesse de la, 69
Rockefeller family, 159
Rocksavage, Lord, 67
Rogers, Herman and Kathleen, 203, 205, 210
Rogers, Millicent, 171
Rolls, Hon. Charles Stewart, 137-39
Rolls-Royce cars, 37-39, 90, 146, 172, 181, 196, 224
Romano, Alfonso Nicolino, 32, 108
Roosevelt Hotel, New York, 180
Roosevelt, President Franklin D., 156, 194, 220
Rosebery, Earl of, 9, 17
Ross, Harold, 207
Rossi, Count Theo, 222
Rostand, Edmond, 72
Rothermere, Lady, 137
Rothermere, Lord, 202, 205
Rothschild, Alfred de, 12-14, 77, 79
Rothschild, Aline de, 79
Rothschild, Baron Eric de, 219
Rothschild, Baron Eugene de, 208, 216
Rothschild family, 34, 43, 88
Rothschild, Ferdy de, 13
Rothschild, Baron Henri de, 10, 70
Rothschild, Baroness Kitty, 208, 216
Rothschild, Leonora, 80
Rothschild, Mrs. Leopold de, 29
Rothschild, Baron Maurice de, 152
Rothschild, Nathan de, 3
Rothschild, Baron and Baroness Robert de, 216
Roxburgh, Duke of, 20
Roy, Harry (bandleader), 181
Royal Naval College, Dartmouth, 96
Royal Opera House. *See* Covent Garden.
Royal Poinciana Hotel, Florida, 159
Royce, Henry, 36-39
Rubinstein, Artur, 81
Rubinstein, Helena, 93, 112, 166
Rubirosa, Porfirio, 230
Rue Royale Club, 70
Rufford Abbey, 10, 24

Running Wild (Lida Webb), 98
Ryan, Thomas Fortune, 84

Sackville, Lady (Anne), 175
Sagan, Princesse de, 15, 71
St. Helier, Lady, 26
St. John of Bletso, Lady, 169
St. Johns, Adela Rogers, 202, 220
Saint-Laurent, Yves, 223
Sandars, Rosemary, 102
Sandringham, 4, 9, 13, 14, 26, 63, 72, 81, 95, 192
Sargent, John Singer, 122-23
Sassoon family, 3
Sassoon, Sir Philip, 79, 122
Saturday Evening Post, 58, 140
Saud of Arabia, King, 232
Savile family, 10
Savoy Hotel, 27-28, 32-33, 43, 82, 88, 89, 108, 136, 146, 158, 177, 185, 187, 199, 215, 218
Savoy Plaza, New York, 172
Savoy Theatre, London, 32, 73
Sawyer, Colonel Eric, 136-37
Scala, La, 234-36
Schiaparelli, Elsa, 90, 208
Schneider, Hortense, 4
Schwab, "Smiling Charlie," 44, 166
Scoop (Evelyn Waugh), 149
Second Man, The (S. N. Behrman), 149
Sedelmeyer's art gallery, 66
Selby, Sir Walford, 209
Selfridge's, London, 101
Selfridge, Gordon, 150, 152
Seligman, Jacques, 67
Sella, André, 139
Shaftesbury Theatre, London, 125
Sharland, Reginald, 99
Shaw, Charlotte, 200
Sherry, Louis, 82, 189
Silver Slipper, The, 98, 131-32
Simpson, Bessie Wallis Warfield Spencer, 174-77, 190-92, 198-99, 201-10, 212-14, 216, 227-29, 238
Simpson, Ernest, 174, 190-92, 198, 204
Singer, Isabelle, 64
Sitwell, Osbert, 104, 201
Sitwell, Sacheverell, 104
Social Register, The, 43
Spencer, Earl Winfield, 175
Spry, Constance, 104, 189
Steichen, Edward, 54, 124-25

Stettiner's, 67
Stevens, Minnie (later Mrs. Paget), 63
Stewart, Irene, 103
Stiebel, Victor, 217
Stop Flirting!, 125
Stork Club, New York, 179, 220, 229
Stotesbury, Edward Townsend, 54, 163-66, 241
Stotesbury, Eva, 80, 97, 100, 150, 160, 163-66, 195
Strader, Mona, 92
Strauss, Johann, 33
Stravinsky, Igor, 102, 138
Strong, L. A. G., 122
Suggia, Guilhermina, 122
Sunday Dispatch, 157
Sunday Express, 87, 148, 157-58
Sunday News, 157
Sutherland, Duke of, 62, 84
Sutherland, Duchess of, 160, 180
Sutton nightclub, 128
Suvretta House, St. Moritz, 224
Swaebe, Albert, 194
Swanson, Gloria (Marquise de la Falaise), 152, 224
Sweeny, Charles, 150, 183
Swift, Mabelle, 63, 85
Sykes, Charles, 38

Telegraph and Argus, Bradford, 207
Tender Is The Night (F. Scott Fitzgerald), 149
Thaw, Alice Cornelia, 63
These Charming People (Michael Arlen), 147
This Side of Paradise (F. Scott Fitzgerald), 139
Thomas, Linda Lee (Mrs. Cole Porter), 83, 182
Tiffany's, 81
Times, The, London, 3, 24, 25
Times, The New York, 165-66, 197
Titled Americans, 62-63
Tonight at 8:30 (Coward), 207
Town Topics, 15
Toye, Francis, 89
Trees, Ronald, 103
Tribune, New York, 5, 41, 64
Trocadero, New York, 128
Trotter, Brigadier Gerald, 107, 110, 198
Troubetzkoy, Prince Igor, 230
Truefitt & Hill, 78

Index

Tschirky, Oscar, 44, 86
Turner, Nora (later Lady Docker), 109
"21" Club, 179
"Two Little Babes In The Wood" (Cole Porter), 182
Twombley, Mrs. Hamilton K., 43

Uncle's Club, London, 133
Urban, Joseph, 163
d'Uzès, Duc, 63, 69

Vacani, Betty, 170
Vallee, Rudy, 169, 187
Van Alen, Louise, 171-72, 196
Vanderbilt, Alice (Mrs. Cornelius), 51-52
Vanderbilt, Alva, 46, 64
Vanderbilt, Consuelo (later Duchess of Marlborough), 64, 114, 121, 170
Vanderbilt, ("Commodore") Cornelius, 42, 43, 50
Vanderbilt, Cornelius, II, 42, 51
Vanderbilt, Cornelius, III, 78, 180
Vanderbilt, Cornelius, IV, 24, 40, 53
Vanderbilt, George, 42
Vanderbilt, Grace Wilson, 52-53, 81, 97, 164, 202
Vanderbilt, Reggie, 52
Vanderbilt, William H., 42
Vanderbilt, William Kissam, 9, 42, 46, 51, 64
Vane Tempest, Lady Susan, 15
Vanity Fair, 105
Veblen, Thorstein, 51, 82
Véronique (Messager), 35
Victoria, Queen, 1, 2, 15, 95-96, 123
Vionnet, Madeleine, 115-16
Vivian, Daphne, 146, 170
Vivian, Mona, 99
Vogue, 124
Voisin (restaurant), 143
Vortex, The (Coward), 148

Waddesdon, 13
Waldorf-Astoria Hotel, New York, 43, 86, 103, 104, 125, 154, 181, 186, 220
Wales, Edward David, Prince of, 30, 81, 95-101, 105-10, 116, 119, 121-22, 125-26, 130, 134-37, 139, 144, 150, 152, 157-58, 161, 165, 169, 173-77, 190-93; King Edward VIII, 197-99, 201-7; abdication, 206-7; as Duke of Windsor, 207-10, 213, 216, 219-21, 227-30, 242
Walker, Mayor Jimmy, 127
Walker, John, 61
Walter, Lionel, 13
Walters, Henry, 60
Ward, Mrs. Emilie, 23
Ward, Fanny, 100
Warfield, Mrs. Henry Mactier, 175
Warren, Whitney C., Jr., 120
Warwick, Countess of, 4, 62, 81, 92
Warwick, Earl of, 62
Watson, G. L., 10
Waugh, Evelyn, 102, 149
Wavell, Archibald (later Field Marshal), 172
Webb, Lida, 98
Wector, Dixon, 82
Welbeck Abbey, 10, 11, 18, 21, 40, 122
Wellman, Mrs. Gouverneur, 119
Wertheimer, Betty, 122
Wertheimer, Charles, 66
Wertheimer, Ena, 122
West, Rebecca, 147
Westminster, Loelia, Duchess of, 77, 84
Westminster, 2nd Duke of, 57, 77, 84, 93, 107, 119, 153, 195
Westmoreland, 14th Earl of, 107, 174
Wetzel, Charles, 43, 49, 125
Wharton, Edith, 26, 42
Whigham, Margaret (later Duchess of Argyll), 24, 174, 183
Whistler, James McNeill, 122
White, Jimmy, 131
Wiborg, Sara Sherman (later Mrs. Gerald Murphy), 138
Wichfeld, Count Axel de, 63, 85
Wichfeld, Mabelle Swift de, 136
Widener, "Fifi", 63
Widener, Joe, 55, 57, 63, 120, 122
Widener, Peter Arrell Brown, 54-57
Wilde, Oscar, 9, 66, 87, 90
Wildenstein, Felix, 59, 60
Wilding, Dorothy, 124
Wilhelm of Germany, Kaiser, 26, 53, 74
Williams, Mrs. Florence Hwfa, 29, 103
Williams, Mrs. Harrison, 100, 100, 160, 163
Willis, Frederick, 119
Winchell, Walter, 156-57, 170, 179, 218, 220, 242
Windsor Castle, 5, 7, 41, 74, 205-6

Wine of Choice (S. N. Behrman), 149
Winter Garden Theatre, New York, 74
Wolfe, Elsie de (later Lady Mendl), 56, 69, 88, 113, 124, 137, 197, 219
Wolfe, Tom, 24
Women's Wear Daily, 6, 231, 238, 241
Woods, Al, 146-47
Woolf, Leonard, 101
Woolf, Virginia, 101, 200
Woollcott, Alexander, 139
Woolley, Monty, 81
Woolton, Lord, 217
Woolworth, Frank Winfield, 170, 197, 228
Words and Music (Coward), 168
Worth, Charles Frederick, 114
Worth, Gaston, 114
Worth, Jacques, 115
Worth, Jean-Philippe, 12, 16, 41, 53, 114

Yarmouth, Earl of, 63
Yerkes, Henry, 84
York, Prince Albert, Duke of, 106, 202, 205, 209
"You're Driving Me Crazy", 180
"You're The Top" (Cole Porter), 183
Young, Mr. and Mrs. Robert R., 227
Yule, Lady, 203
Young Men in Love (Michael Arlen), 149

Zerbe, Jerome, 180, 229, 236
Zernsdorff, Count von, 83
Zichy, Count Ed., 155
Ziegfeld, Florenz, 37, 163
Zimmerman, Eugene, 64
Zimmerman, Helen, 64
Zog of Albania, King, 216, 219, 225